a beginner's guide to

a beginner's guide to

Shaun Best

Sage Publications

London • Thousand Oaks • New Delhi

First published 2003

 SAGE Publications Ltd
6 Bonhill Street
London EC2A 4PU

SAGE Publications Inc
2455 Teller Road
Thousand Oaks, California 91320

SAGE Publications India Pvt Ltd
32, M-Block Market
Greater Kailash – I
New Delhi 110 048

British Library Cataloguing in Publication data
A catalogue record for this book is available from the British Library

ISBN 0 7619 6532 7
ISBN 0 7619 6533 5 (pbk)

Library of Congress control number available

Typeset by Mayhew Typesetting, Rhayader, Powys
Printed and bound in Great Britain by TJ International Ltd, Padstow, Cornwall

To Jane, Jessica and Jonathan

Contents

Chapter contents

Introduction:
The Theoretical Self

Many people will look at this book because they need to have a knowledge of social theory so they can successfully complete assignments or attempt exams. I hope to change the perception that many such readers have of social theories as mere obstacles that they have to overcome in an effort to get better marks. I want this book to assist the reader in finding their *theoretical consciousness*. We are *theoretical beings*: we theorise about everything most of the time. Very often because the assumptions we make about the world are so closely tied to the events that surround us and our role within such events, we tend not to view this activity as theorising; but it is.

Activity

This is the first of many activities in the book. The purpose of each activity is to give you an opportunity to reflect upon the theory under discussion. You may be asked to draw upon your personal experience to find examples that support or refute some aspect of a theory, or perhaps to consider strengths and weaknesses of a given theory in an effort to enhance your evaluative skills.

Ask yourself the following questions: What is a 'theory'? Are theories ever of any value in helping you to understand your everyday life? Share your answers with fellow students.

You might want to return to this activity at the end of the chapter and again at the end of the book and reflect upon any change in your answers.

As individuals we seem to be unable to experience the world directly; our experience of what goes on around us is mediated by theory. Most of us do not regard our personal explanations of how and why things happen to us as *theory*, but it is. Whenever we have cause to reflect on how or why things happen in the way that they do, we are theorising. Most of us do not write down our reflections on how and why things happen as they do around us. However, many people *do* write down such reflections, and this book is a beginner's guide to such writing.

At some time or another every teacher, whilst outlining their favourite social theory, will have been faced by students who, with a glazed look on their face have said, 'It's boring, it's boring, this.' As a teacher how do you react? One approach is to justify the choice of theory by referring to future assignments or exams where the theory can be used to good effect. In essence, this approach is one of agreeing with the students. In effect you are saying: 'I know this is a boring theory, I find it boring myself, and what is more I found it boring when I came across it as a student, but we have to do it because you may fail without a knowledge of it.'

An alternative approach is to attempt to identify why some people find some theories 'boring'. This book is built upon the assumption that we find only tedium in some theories and 'turn off' from them because they have little to say about the things that are relevant to our everyday lives. Everybody has a theory that fascinates him or her. Reflect for one moment on your favourite social theory and why you like it. People are thinking beings and our thought is related to society, politics, economics and history although this may not be expressed in terms of the universal categories or formal structures that one finds in textbooks. We theorise about our relationships at work, our personal relationships, the soaps we watch, the sports we enjoy, and the future. We constantly reproduce the world inside our heads and play out imaginary situations over and over again, introducing various factors in an effort to explore possible consequences. Such predictions are built upon theoretical assumptions that we make about the world and how it works. The vast majority of people make use of this theorising to manage practical situations that they find themselves in and then discard the theory, or adapt it for future guidance. A tiny minority of us write down our theories and publish them for other people's consumption. As individuals we can make use of published theories to make sense of our lives, and I am sure that many readers already do this. The application of labels to people, for example, provides ample evidence of people drawing upon a theoretical consciousness in an effort to make sense of the world. Some examples are obvious: people who describe others as 'sexist' draw upon notions of patriarchy. Other examples are less obvious; when an adult asks a child, 'What do you want to do when you grow up?' is the adult drawing upon Alfred Schutz's notion of the *life project*?

Activity

In this activity you are asked to suggest a possible explanation as to why some people choose to stay in their homes on Friday evening and watch gardening programmes, while other people go out drinking and clubbing for the evening.

Once you have thought of a possible explanation ask a fellow student to suggest assumptions that you are making about the people involved in these activities. You might consider if older people are more likely to be involved in one activity rather than another; are people without gardens more likely to be involved in one activity rather than another; are affluent people more likely to be involved in one activity rather than another?

What is the purpose of this activity? To show you that you are a theorist who makes assumptions about the world, which are always open to question.

Whenever you read a theory ask yourself, what does this theory say about me and how I choose to lead my life? Attempt to identify what it is about the theory that makes it inadequate as an explanation of your life. What assumptions does the theory make about the circumstances you find yourself in? What assumptions does the theory make about how people interact with others, about intersubjectivity? What assumptions does the theory make about the abilities you have or may not have as a person? Do forces outside your control push you about or do you have complete control? Perhaps like the character Neo in the film *Matrix*, all you need to keep in mind is that there is no spoon! If you attempt to identify the assumptions upon which theories are built and apply these assumptions to your own experiences, evaluating the adequacy of the theory to your experience of the world, then you are well on the way to evaluating social theory. The starting point for a thorough evaluation of any social theory has to be our own personal knowledge.

Personal knowledge: from *knowing that* to *knowing how*

A human being cannot make sense of information without it becoming personal, without having feelings about the information. We have to know how the things we are interested in work in order to function as a person. We may have the knowledge that 'things' work in a particular way, but we may not have a complete knowledge of the underlying theoretical principles of how 'things' work in the way that they do. This personal knowledge has no obvious form of measurement, because it is based upon feelings and an understanding of oneself as a person: likes, dislikes, prejudices and the underlying motivation for these choices. This knowledge may be ambiguous and/or partially based upon intuition and be gained without formal reasoning, but all of us have a perception of why things happen to us in the way that they do. This perception may not be based upon systematically gathered research findings, but it is based upon the personal observation of causes and consequences that are real to us. We all have a need to know on a need to know basis and it is this which provides us with the personal motivation to discover a reality beyond our safe subjectivity. This process of moving from our personal knowledge *that* to a more objective knowledge of *how* may bring us into conflict with widely shared conceptual frameworks – such as sociological perspectives or political ideologies. When we construct knowledge of a situation or event and can justify the validity of our perceptions we can escape the pressure to conform and as learners escape the mere memorization of concepts that hold no personal value for us as learners. We have to relate personal knowledge from our own interactions to theories. This book is intended to help you inform your prejudices and justify your personal knowledge.

Social theory and its recent history

What makes social theory distinctive? The purpose of social theory is not simply to describe the social world – this has already been done by individual people themselves. Social theory is concerned with going beyond uncomplicated description and attempting to answer the humble question: 'How is society possible?' It is one of the most interesting questions that can be asked. Some social theorists attempt to answer the question in a scientific fashion, suggesting that research should be built upon forms of measurement and logic that one would expect to find within the natural sciences. For these people, who are commonly lumped together as 'the positivists', social research is about gathering facts and figures to test explanations. In contrast, other social theorists suggest we answer the question by making use of the techniques developed by poets and novelists, or by becoming like an investigative reporter, searching for meaning and understanding of what people do, why and how they do it.

Social theory is directly linked to the practice of research: the two should be inseparable. Social theory is about developing and understanding the 'social', which is the foundation of contemporary society. This is suggested by some of the key concepts used by theorists whom we shall look at in this book, for example:

o   Durkheim – 'social facts'
o   Marx – 'social relations'
o   Weber – 'social action'

Individual people are unique and have both the skills and the ability, in most cases, to do whatever they wish. However, you will have heard phrases such as 'Man is born free yet everywhere he is in chains' and 'Men make history but not in circumstances of their own choosing'. In other words, as people we seem to spend most of the time doing things that we may not want to do; behaving in ways that are 'appropriate'. As individuals, we experience the world as a place that contains a great many rules and other forms of constraint. If you walk down any crowded city street you will come into contact with a great many people you have never met before, and yet there are 'appropriate' ways of behaving with these strangers: avoiding eye contact and avoiding any physical contact such as bumping into each other. In addition, there are 'appropriate' statements such as 'I'm sorry' if you do break such 'rules'. The constraint we are talking about is part of what sociologists refer to as 'the social'. Sociology was invented in the nineteenth century to make sense of the modern industrial society that contained ways of behaving and ways of relating to others that did not exist in pre-industrial societies. Sociology was born then in the transition from the traditional to the modern society. People wanted to make sense of the emerging 'new world' after:

o   the Enlightenment
o   the Great Reform Bill of 1832
o   the French Revolution of 1789
o   Chartism
o   the Industrial Revolution
o   Urbanisation
o   the 1848 revolutionary movements

As Anthony Giddens explains:

> Sociology is concerned with the comparative study of social institutions, giving particular emphasis to those forms of society brought into being by the advent of modern industrialism. There might be differences of opinion as to how modern societies should best be studied, but to suggest that such societies are not worthy of systematic enquiry seems more than faintly absurd. (Giddens, 1987: 1)

In the nineteenth century the social was believed to shape our lives and our individual experience of the world. It was said to affect our life chances, help us to shape and form our individual identity and for many sociologists it is still the source of our thoughts, culture and ideas. The social mediates our relationships with others and at the same time we as individuals produce it. However, there is much discussion and much disagreement as to the nature of 'the social' and its origins. Whatever theories sociologists invent, and whatever methods they use to find out about the world and how it works, they are concerned with attempting to make sense of the nature of constraint. In most sociology texts, this issue of the nature of constraint in society is referred to as 'The problem of order'.

What is a social theory?

Although the following points are a crude generalisation that you might want to take issue with, my view is that all social theories are made up of four elements. If you want to evaluate any theory it is a good starting point to identify the assumptions that the theorists make about these four elements and state if you agree with the assumptions or not, giving the reasons you have for why you agree or disagree.

All social theories contain:

o an epistemology – this is a theory of knowledge and it attempts to answer the question 'How do we know what we know?' All social theories make assumptions about how we know what we know.

o an ontology – this is a theory of what reality consists of. All social theories make assumptions about the nature of reality.

o a historical location – all social theories were written at a particular point in time, and reflect something of the historical period in which they were produced.

o a set of prescriptions – all social theories give the reader some advice on how to behave in everyday life. Again you may want to take issue with the advice that is suggested.

What do social theorists do?

Social theorists are people who step back and attempt to identify, outline and explain what 'the social' is and how it works. To do this, they invent theories about the nature of 'the social' and attempt to discover how people endeavour to recreate the social in their everyday lives. As an activity, doing social theory can give people an opportunity to invent concepts, as well as analyse and clarify the concepts and theories of other people. However, as the sociologist C. Wright Mills suggested in the 1950s, more importantly than the analysis and clarification of theories and concepts, doing sociology allows a person to discover if what were previously considered to be 'personal problems' might in fact be 'public issues'. Consider the following example. During the winter a person cannot afford to buy a warm coat or a pair of winter shoes, or cannot afford to buy a birthday card for a friend. We can say that such a person is inhibited from participating fully in society because they have little money. Moreover, that person experiences the exclusion from doing things that the rest of us take for granted, as a personal problem. However, what we are also looking at here is the 'public issue' of poverty, which may be caused by factors that are outside the control of the individual. For some social theorists the causes of many personal problems are to be found within the social, outside of the control of the individual person experiencing them.

How do social theorists view the nature of constraint? Social theory appears to be both chaotic and incoherent, but some of the most common theories do deal with this:

- **Marxism** sees constraint as emerging from class relationships, and the issue here is how people can overthrow those who impose the constraint.
- **Feminism** views constraint as 'patriarchal': in nature constraint was invented by men to control the behaviour of women, and again the issue here is how people can remove the constraint.
- **Structuralists** believe that there is a structure within society which is external to the individual, outside of the control of the individual and which shapes the life experience of the individual.
- Those social theorists who take their lead from Anthony **Giddens** view structures as the product of a process of 'structuration' in which people actively create structures within society. Here constraint is both a 'medium' and an 'outcome' of the activities of individual people. If we take the example of the social class structure, parents make every effort to give their children the skills and abilities to get 'good' jobs in later life. Parents endeavour to secure advantages for their children because they love their children, but the unforeseen consequence of this parental love is to reproduce the class structure. Parents from middle-class backgrounds secure places for their children within the middle class of the future.
- In contrast to all the above approaches, **postmodernists** argue that the social, and the constraint associated with it, are dissolving.

In course of this book we shall show why social theorists have such very different theories of the 'social'.

Doing social theory is not like solving crossword puzzles; it is about learning to think about a range of issues and problems from a number of different perspectives. All social theory is about your relationships with others. It is about the nature and meaning of our existence as human beings; it is about understanding the organising principles of the society that you live in. I know it sounds pompous but I would argue that by refusing to engage with social theory you impoverish your own life.

Over the course of this book we examine how social theorists have engaged with issues of:

- compliance–resistance
- difference–togetherness
- agency–structure
- individual–totality
- the person–the people
- gay–straight
- public–private
- male–female
- equality–inequality
- change–stability
- whole–part
- within–without
- involvement–detachment

o   modernity–postmodernity
o   macro–micro
o   inside–outside

The limits of what social theory can do

Social theorists tend to look for and find general patterns within social life. Doing social theory is about discovering *how 'the social' operates*. In addition, social theorists spend a great deal of time inventing theories that attempt to explain how 'the social' operates. This book gives you an opportunity to become acquainted with such theories, and shows you how to interpret and evaluate them. It cannot explain why you have no friends, why nobody wants to fall in love with you. In other words, it is important to make a distinction between 'doing theory' and 'needing therapy'. This is not to say that social theorists avoid issues such as love; Anthony Giddens, for example, has written a very full account of why people fall in love, seeing it as part of our need to feel secure in an increasingly uncertain world. The approach to issues is not simply to base everything upon our own personal experience, but to show how our personal experience also has a general quality to it. Many people may experience what we may have experienced as a personal problem, in the same way and for very similar reasons. It is the role of social theorists to identify and describe that general quality of so-called unique personal experiences, which make up social life.

What makes this activity of 'doing social theory' doubly difficult is that why people behave in the way that they do may not be fully understood by them, and in addition, the nature of the social is not static. The social is constantly changing, and the actions and reactions of the individual people, who shape the social, are themselves to be found within a social framework.

One of the assumptions I make is that all social theorists are concerned with understanding the nature of power relationships. The exercise of power is concerned with the ability of people to make others do things they may not want to do. For me, one of the central issues within social theory is to identify the resources that individuals and groups can draw upon to make others do what they want them to do. All social action – all actions carried out by people with intentions – involves drawing upon resources of power. All social actions involve making changes in the world, even if the changes are small. When you bring about a change in the world, you have to combat other people's vested interests. If you wish to turn on the television set, you have to combat the vested interests of the people who do not want to watch it. If you want to live in one place rather than another you will have to combat the vested interests of the people who live there.

In summary, what is social theory all about?

o   It is concerned with the problem of order, it is searching for an answer to the question 'How is society possible?'

o   It is about understanding the nature of 'social action', attempting to identify the social nature of the reasons people have for why they behave in the way that they do.

o   It is concerned with the relationship between the individual and the society, attempting to explain whether people are pushed about by forces outside of their control or whether they construct the constraints within society.

o   It is concerned with describing and explaining the nature of power relationships.

o   It is concerned with attempting to describe and explain the changing nature of 'the social'.

Social theory and the search for truth

You may ask yourself, is social theory simply the search for 'truth'? The problem here is that many social theorists have questioned what we mean by 'truth'. Each social theory has its own notion of truth, and its favoured methods of finding that 'truth'.

Activity

How do people know if something is 'true'? Given that news pro-grammes on radio and television often ask for expert opinion from scientists, it is reasonable to assume that many people will accept that a statement is true if it is supported by 'scientific' evidence. Apart from science what other possible sources of truth can you identify? Religion? Information from political leaders? Information from parents?

'Truth' is difficult to achieve in the social sciences. The following discussion is complex, but what you should draw from it is the idea that we cannot take it for granted that the assumptions you and I make about the world and how it works are true. We should question all assumptions, including our own, about the world and how it works.

There are at least two distinct theories of truth which the social sciences can make use of: the *coherence theory*, which looks at theorising about the world as a 'holistic' activity in which theorists/researchers make theoretical assumptions which are assumed to be both internally consistent, and consistent with the theorists'/researchers' own assumptions about the world and how it works; and the *correspondence theory* of truth, in which the theorist/researcher assumes that there is an objective reality out there beyond their personal impressions, and the task of research is to devise a set of categories that fully and completely reflect the contours of this external reality in an objective fashion. According to Donald Davidson (1969), these reflective links are built upon a set of principles or rules of inference that he terms 'Convention T'. The significance of 'Convention T' is that it allows us to deduce the truth content of any statement against a finite benchmark that we know to be true. 'Convention T' is based upon first order logic, hence we know that 'Convention T' is true because what links the statements we make about the world ('T-Statements') with the external reality of the world are the words we use, which by convention explicitly and fully describe the factual order that is the external world.

Davidson's theory of truth is then a theory of translation. We know that if a person says: 'The rain is wet' that this is true, because we know that rain is wet. Moreover, because the statement corresponds to the first order logic of 'Convention T', we also know the *meaning* of the statement. There must be such an automatic triggering of meaning from statements that conform to 'Convention T', otherwise such a statement would not appear to us to be so obvious. 'Convention T' assumes that we share the same assumptions about the world as the people who speak to us; because we take to be true what we interpret the statement to be saying is true, then it is true. However, we have to assume or guess that the person we are speaking to shares our assumptions about the world, shares our underlying logic about the world, and assume that we share the same meaning of the words we use to describe that world. In other words, correspondence theories of truth assume that we have the ability to know what goes on inside the head of another person, to the degree that we can make a judgement about the logic of their thought processes and make a factually correct assessment of the 'T content' of such thoughts and the logic of how such thoughts were arrived at. Even if we assume that such a procedure is possible, such a theory assumes a superiority of our own 'Convention T' and our own 'T-Statements' that I believe to be without justification.

As Davidson explains:

> I suggest that it may be enough to require that the T-sentences be true. Clearly this suffices uniquely and correctly to determine the extension of the truth predicate. If we consider any one T-sentence, this proposal requires only that if a true sentence is described as true, then its truth conditions are given by some true sentence. But when we consider the constraining need to match truth with truth throughout the language, we realize that any theory acceptable by this standard may yield, in effect, a usable translation manual running from object language to metalanguage. The desired effect is standard theory building: to extract a rich concept (here something reasonably close to translation) from little bits of evidence (here the truth values of sentences) by imposing a formal structure on enough bits. If we characterize T-sentences by their form alone, as Tarski did, it is possible, using Tarski's methods, to define truth using no semantical concepts. If we treat T-sentences as verifiable, then a theory of truth shows how we can go from truth to something like meaning – enough like

meaning so that if someone had a theory for a language verified only in the way I propose, he would be able to use that language in communication. (Davidson, 1969: 85)

Conclusion

We are all involved in the process of making theory: we are theoretical beings, and you should be actively involved in theorising and evaluating the theorising of others. All sociological theories, for example, make assumptions about the nature of the self and its relationship with the social structure. Interactionists, and other theorists who place a great deal of emphasis on social action, argue that the self has the ability to make a difference in the world. Interactionists argue that the person is a human agent and, as such, the author of their own actions. Marxists, feminists and functionalists, in contrast, believe that people are pushed about by forces outside of the control of the self. For Marxists, feminists and functionalists the self has very little 'agency' – people are unable to control their own thoughts and have little or no ability to make a difference in the world. When evaluating any theory, outline the assumptions that the researcher is making about the human agent, and state if you agree or disagree with those assumptions, giving your reasons. In this book we shall look at a range of published theories. Rather than giving you a bland and superficial outline of theory from a distance, I have attempted to give an insight into how the chosen theorists think, what concepts they use and how they make use of them. I have tried to give a feel for the detail of each theory and to provide the opportunity for you to reflect upon what the theorist has to say, in order for you to have some ownership of your evaluation.

References

Davidson, D. (1969) 'In defense of convention-T', *Journal of Philosophy*, 66: 76–86.

Chapter contents

1 Functionalist Perspectives: Theorising Systems and Structures

By the end of this chapter you should have:

- o a critical awareness of the contribution of Emile Durkheim to modern social theory;
- o an awareness of the way in which Durkheim's contribution to social theory is treated in textbooks;
- o a familiarity with the work of Ferdinand Tönnies;
- o a critical understanding of the work of Talcott Parsons, Neil Smelser and Alex Inkeles;
- o a critical understanding of Niklas Luhmann's systems theory.

Emile Durkheim (1858–1917)

Durkheim introduced a number of ideas and arguments that are still of importance to social theorists today. Durkheim argued that we should treat social facts as things. In other words that we should study the factors that influence social behaviour as if they were concrete objects and external to the individual.

Like all sociologists, Durkheim was interested in the question 'How is society possible?' One of the central themes of his work was to identify the relationship between the individual personality and the wider society. For Durkheim, human consciousness without categories of thought is 'fragmentary' – a constant flow of representations which have no relationship to each other. Moreover, Durkheim was no stranger to uncertainty, his sociology was written against the background of Nietzsche's philosophy; the Franco-Prussian War; the Industrial Revolution, with its urbanisation, social movements, etc., and the First World War. But Durkheim believed that classification does exist and that it extends to all areas of social life. It forms the basis of pre-cognition, and as such allows us to organise our ideas. Categories exercise constraint upon us so that the world appears to be arranged according to a set of rigid principles, which allow us to read acts and signs.

Activity: Durkheim

Look at Durkheim's book *The Rules of the Sociological Method* and read the first chapter: 'What is a social fact?' Then read the following passage and say if you agree with it. Give three reasons for your answer.

Durkheim is very good at explaining the common ways of behaving within a society. However, his understanding of the human agent – what it means to be a person – is very limited. Durkheim assumes that individual people are pushed about by forces outside of their control. That ways of behaving are determined by forces outside of the individual's command so that people are powerless and have limited choice in terms of ways of behaving, what to do and how to do it. For Durkheim, the individual human agent is a 'cultural dope', doing what it is told, following the rules, with question.

All sociology textbooks assume that Durkheim's argument on classification is Kantian in nature. However, adopting a distinctly anti-Kantian stance was one of the positions that Durkheim took in an effort to distance sociology from philosophy. For Durkheim, an empirical analysis of morality is always necessary. In contrast, for Kant all moral concepts are *a priori*, in that what we perceive depends upon our subjective apparatus, which is given and not dependent upon our experiences. Any objective principle which we find compelling Kant termed an *imperative*. There are two forms of imperative for Kant:

o the **hypothetical imperative** – you must do X if you wish to achieve end Y;

o the **categorical imperative** – which states that a certain type of action is objectively necessary without any regard to an end.

As Russell explains: 'Kant holds that the mind orders the raw material of sensation, but never thinks it necessary to say why it orders it as it does and not otherwise' (Russell, 1946: 687). In Durkheim's analysis, however: 'There is no rule, no social prescription that is recognized or gains its sanction from Kant's moral imperative or from the law of utility as formulated by Bentham, Mill, or Spencer' (Durkheim, 1973: 25).

Our faculties such as definition, deduction and induction form part of the mechanism we use to 'construct, project, and localize in space our representations of the tangible world' (Durkheim and Mauss, 1963: 3). We have no reason to suppose that the human mind contains within it a framework for classification. No such framework was given by nature: these mechanisms had to be formed from a combination of elements drawn from a range of sources. In addition, people have to be educated in the nature of the categories, and how to use them: 'humanity in the beginning lacks the most indispensable conditions for a classificatory function' (Durkheim and Mauss, 1963: 7).

Any system of classification, Durkheim argues, is 'extra-logical'. There is no given or preconceived logic for classification. Classification is hierarchical and involves looking for arrangements between categories, but this is not a spontaneous process based upon abstract reasoning, it is the product of a human process. The reasons why we developed such a system of classification may have been forgotten, but the categories remain and new ideas are assimilated into existing categories. However, it is perfectly legitimate to ask why we have classified the world in this way. As Durkheim made clear: 'We have no justification for supposing that our mind bears within it at birth, completely formed, the prototype of this elementary framework of all classification' (Durkheim and Mauss, 1963: 8).

Ideas are organised on a model which is contained within the *conscience collective*. What is the 'conscience collective'? For Durkheim, whenever individuals interact with each other they make expectations of each others' behaviour. These expectations come together to form a 'normative order' which is over and above the individual. Once the *conscience collective* is established, it exercises a constraint upon people, which can inhibit future change within or between the categories. Hence, Durkheim argues that there is a close link 'between the social system and this logical system' (Durkheim and Mauss, 1963: 41). However, the system of classification can change. In *Primitive Classification*, Durkheim and Mauss give the example of the decline of 'totemism' on the islands of the Torres Straits.

Durkheim is often presented as a naive precursor of a caricature of Parsonian Functionalism found in sociology textbooks. This view ignores the ontological status of Durkheim's key ideas. He was primarily interested in social facts, which are not 'absolute' facts and have a very different ontological status rooted in the practical ideas and perceptions of human agents.

As we have seen, for Durkheim, classification is simply about the concepts that we use to describe the relations between things. Everything is labelled and given a place within an integrated system: 'such classifications are thus intended, above all, to connect ideas, to unify knowledge' (Durkheim and Mauss, 1963: 81). The classes and the relationship between the classes are social in origin. Concepts are collective representations, they are ideas about the shared ways of doing things in practice. The relationship between the idea and the activity is like the relationship between the rules of a game of football and the activity of playing a game. The rules were clearly made by people, and people can change them if they so wish. However, in order to avoid an extreme relativist position, Durkheim argued that the collective representation was a social fact which exercised a constraint upon people. It is important to note that the external constraint of the social fact is totally dependent upon the internal constraint of the human agent upon itself. We both possess agency and are aware of this shared perception. We can then choose to behave in the way that others do in similar circumstances – classifying this as the 'right' way. Or we can choose to behave in some other fashion. Excessive individualism, as the root of egoistic suicide, would not be possible otherwise. For Durkheim, if a person becomes separated from the influence of the 'conscience collective' and is no longer subject to its moral constraint they are much more likely to commit suicide. Durkheim refers to this form of suicide as egoistic suicide. One cannot have the Durkheimian conception of 'egoistic suicide' without the ability of the human agent to place itself outside of the expectations of others.

Many commentators assume that if the human agent chooses to reproduce an existing collective representation, behaving in the same way as others, then the person is not exercising their agency. This 'reciprocal imitation' is a psychological factor which is highly social in nature: 'since it is co-operative elaboration of a common sentiment' (Durkheim, 1952: 130). He further explains:

> In following a manner or observing a custom one does what others have done and do, daily. But the definition itself implies that this repetition is not owing to the so-called instinct of imitation, but on the one hand, to the sympathy constraining us not to wound the feelings of our fellows, lest we forfeit their intercourse, and on the other, to the respect we feel for collective ways of acting and thinking and the direct or indirect pressure exerted on us by this collectivity to avoid dissension and maintain in us this sense of respect. (Durkheim, 1952: 127)

The question then becomes: why do people want to conform? Here Durkheim assumes that people have a psychological need for attachment, because this increases their chances of survival: 'since morality determines, fixes, regularizes man's conduct, it presupposes a certain disposition in the individual for a regular existence – a preference for regularity' (Durkheim, 1973: 34). The more active people are in their interactions with each other, the more intense will be the collective life of the society. However, according to Durkheim 'whatever is social in us is deprived of all objective foundation' (Durkheim, 1952: 213). People participate in the social because of the direct benefits that such reciprocity can give them.

What is Durkheim's theory of agency?

For Durkheim the human being as a biological entity has biological needs and security needs. For Durkheim, every person has a choice in every area of their lives: they can choose to do what others do or they can choose to do something which is independent of others. In addition, the human being has a need to survive and does not have the skill to survive without the cooperation of others. Hence, the human agent has a practical consciousness. Durkheim's practical consciousness appears to have three elements to it:

o   A **collective expression**: the person may choose to carry out an action which is of benefit to others, in order to enhance a communal response in others: 'behaviour . . . directed exclusively toward the personal ends of the actor does not have moral value' (Durkheim, 1973: 57).

o A **reflective expression**: the person may choose to behave in a way which is acceptable within the community; this will reduce feelings of 'otherness' and enhance feelings of solidarity: 'To act morally is to act in terms of the collective interest' (Durkheim, 1973: 59) and: 'If a man is to be a moral being, he must be devoted to something other than himself' (Durkheim, 1973: 79).

o A **reasoning expression**: the person may choose to limit their own independence as to follow a collective representation. A central element of morality for Durkheim is self-mastery.

But as Durkheim so clearly outlined in his study of suicide, we have a need for independence and a need for the security of regulation; these must be kept in balance. Hence the human being is an agent for Durkheim, it makes decisions in every situation that it finds itself in.

What is Durkheim's theory of morality?

For Durkheim, for any aspect of human behaviour to be called 'moral' it must be common in the sense that it involves a relationship between the consciousness of sentient beings and conforms to pre-established rules. This means that morality has an element of 'duty' about it. The function of morality is then to limit the behaviour of the individual to the expectations of the wider society. However, such rules as do exist are general prescriptions: 'It is up to the person to see how it applies in a given situation' (Durkheim, 1973: 23). In addition, the person has to have an understanding that moral authority is *sui generis* and not simply another name for our own personal habits.

Durkheim presupposes that people have the capacity to choose how to behave and that individuals are capable of behaving in a similar fashion in similar circumstances. The purpose of morality then, is to:

o determine conduct
o fix conduct
o eliminate individual arbitrariness

Morality is characterized by its 'regularity'. It is internalized by the person as 'accumulated experience' but expressed externally; 'irregular behaviour is morally incomplete' (Durkheim, 1973: 31). Beyond regularity we have rules that prescribe ways of behaving: we behave according to the rules not because some innate force is at work, or because we like to behave in that particular way but because we are subject to a regulating moral authority. In what Durkheim termed 'simple' societies, morality tended to be religious in nature. However, as things change, human duties and the roles people adopt whilst performing their duties become more clearly defined and placed in a human context of moral transgression rather than sin. We start to experience the moral order as an autonomous order independent of the people: 'morality is a totality of definite rules; it is like so many molds with limiting boundaries, into which we must pour our behavior' (Durkheim, 1973: 26).

In a nutshell, morality has several aims in Durkheim's analysis. It helps us:

o to respect discipline/to accept the rules;
o to be committed to a social group;
o to have knowledge of why people behave in the way that they do and to have mastery over our own behaviour.

What is Durkheim's theory of structure?

Social solidarity is the cohesion that people have within a group. For Durkheim, modern society has a cohesion because of the differences between people. He used the term 'organic solidarity' because he saw society as very much like the human body. In a similar fashion to organs in the body, each of which has a different shape, function and purpose, all making a contribution to the effective functioning of the body; so various groups and individuals with their different skills and abilities all contributed to the smooth running of the society. Moreover, just like the human body, the whole was more than the sum of its parts: there was something additional to the social body which was lacking in each of its individual parts. This was very different from earlier forms of solidarity which Durkheim termed 'mechanical solidarity'. This form of solidarity was held together by the similarities between people. There was a rigid *conscience collective* which was used to impose harsh punishments upon people for even a minor breaking of the rules. There was a minimal division of labour: most people did the same type of job or were divided into a narrow range of roles, such as hunters and gatherers.

Organic solidarity with its citizenship rights, emerged from a highly specialised division of labour. As a form of solidarity it was strong because of the differences between people. However, within organic solidarity there was a need to develop some common states of consciousness, such as morality, otherwise there was the risk that there would be no solidarity at all. It was for this reason that Durkheim wrote at some length about institutions such as the education system which would help to generate common states of consciousness amongst the population.

Durkheim was not the only writer at the time to make such a distinction. Ferdinand Tönnies (1855–1936) argued that the process of modernisation could diminish the strength of social solidarity; it may weaken people's sense of community and generate feelings of isolation. Tönnies argued that there was a movement from *Gemeinschaft* (community) to *Gesellschaft* (association) as modernisation progresses.

In pre-industrial societies people lived within 'unions of *Gemeinschaft*', where individuals have close links with both family and friends within village life. From this we move on to 'associations of *Gemeinschaft*', which are small but increasingly more impersonal communities. This leads on to 'associations of *Gesellschaft*', which are large impersonal societies.

Mechanical and organic solidarity

Trait	Mechanical solidarity	Organic solidarity
Character of activities/Main social bond	Similar, uniform moral and religious consensus	Highly differentiated Complementarity and mutual dependence
The position of an individual	Collectivism, focus on a group, community	Individualism, focus on autonomous individuals
Economic structure	Isolated, autarkic, self-sufficient groups	Division of labour, mutual dependence of groups, exchange
Social control	Repressive laws punishing offences (criminal law)	Restitutive law, safeguarding contracts (civil law)

Source: Sztompka (1993: 105)

Durkheim rejected the sharp distinction between *Gemeinschaft* and *Gesellschaft*, in favour of a more evolutionary transition. There are still many aspects of mechanical solidarity within modern societies. Moreover, it is not a totally pessimistic picture which Tönnies presents: he argues that the final stage of the evolutionary path is when 'unions of *Gesellschaft*' emerge. These unions are large, bureaucratic societies, but they contain welfare programmes which both benefit less fortunate members of the community and establish bonds of community.

What is the relationship between the agency and structure?

For Durkheim 'structures' are the situated activities of human agents, they are formed from practice and are not outside time or space: 'Collective representations are the result of an immense co-operation, which stretches out not only into space but into time as well' (Durkheim, 1915: 16). In *The Rules of Sociological Method*, Durkheim states in his discussion of social facts that: 'It [a social fact] results from their being together, a product of the actions and reactions which take place between individual consciousnesses' (Durkheim, 1966: 9).

In *Suicide*, at several points Durkheim states the relationship between agency and structure, as he did in each of his works. Replying to a critique from Tarde, he explained:

> We clearly did not imply . . . that society can exist without individuals, an obvious absurdity we might have been spared having attributed to us. But we did mean: 1. that the group formed by associated individuals has a reality of a different sort from each individual considered singly; 2. that collective states

exist in the group from whose nature they spring, before they affect the individual as such and establish in him a new form a purely inner existence. (Durkheim, 1952: 320)

This theme is perhaps more clearly stated in *Moral Education*, where Durkheim states that:

because men live together rather than separately, individual minds act upon one another; and as a result of the relationship thus established, there appear ideas and feelings that never characterized these minds in isolation. (Durkheim, 1973: 62)

The social fact then, for Durkheim, has all the essential principles that you would expect to find in a set of *a priori* conceptions, but is empirical in nature.

Society for Durkheim is expressed in and through the individual. Society is outside of us and is experienced as a 'constraint', but at the same time society is within us: we experience sociality as part of our nature. Mentally we make use of ideas and sentiments from the wider society which allow us to carry out our practices as people with a degree of confidence. Society is then both constraining and enabling. There is nothing 'metaphysical' in the nature of this relationship between the individual and society; this can be seen in the fact that 'morality' as a set of collective representations varies from society to society, as it is a social product.

Durkheim's critics have classed his sociology as conservative in nature. For Durkheim, socialism was built upon the assumption that the person was a worker/producer. In contrast, for Durkheim people participated in an intellectual and moral life that went beyond 'the economic'. In addition, they existed within a society, and socialism could not predict what would happen if there was a destruction of capitalist society. To destroy capitalist society is to run the risk of destroying civilisation.

Durkheim did want people to live in better societies. There was a need to provide welfare services to improve the position of the poor in society, but he could not accept the view that the destruction of capitalist society was the way forward. Rather, Durkheim argued that the moral, legal and political institutions could transform our economic life for the better. As he states in the final part of *The Division of Labour* on 'abnormal forms', there was a need for a more stable society. Lukes quotes Durkheim as saying that the bourgeoisie and the proletariat 'inhale the same moral atmosphere, they are, though they deny it, members of a single society, and as a result, cannot but be impregnated with the same ideas' (Durkheim cited in Lukes, 1992: 545).

As Steven Lukes explains, for Durkheim, socialism should be reformist, optimistic and built upon cooperation. Socialism should draw upon social science data in an effort to be both critical and constructive.

Most socialists misunderstand the nature of discipline and their actions may seriously damage the nature of our collective life. This is not to suggest that Durkheim did not take socialism seriously: he recognised that it was often a collective expression of the oppression felt by some people in the poorer sections of society.

Durkheim on methodology

Durkheim's 'rules of the sociological method' are not simply a set of methodological rules but are part of his wider theoretical position. For Durkheim society is an entity which is over and above the individual. In other words, Durkheim sees society as a 'thing'. Society is treated as a concrete object which we can study in an objective fashion. The subject matter of sociology is the *social fact*, and Durkheim's first rule of the sociological method is to treat social facts as things.

The characteristics of a social fact are that it:

o   is external to the individual;
o   exercises a constraint upon the individual.

The social fact can consist of ways of acting and/or ways of thinking which have a degree of power or coercion over the individual. Even within unorganised crowds there are collective sentiments which put pressure upon individuals to conform to the crowd behaviour. If the constraint is no longer felt by people then this is because new habits have become internalised and new collective representations are at work.

What are we to understand by Durkheim's concept of 'thing'? To treat something as a 'thing' is according to Durkheim to have an objective opinion about whatever it is that we are looking at; to have no preconceived ideas about what it is or how it works. According to Emile Benoit-Smullyan the notion of 'thing' has four characteristics in Durkheim's work. It is:

o   an entity possessing certain characteristics which are independent of people's observations;
o   an entity which can be known only *a posteriori*. The social fact is known through experience not in an *a priori* fashion as described by Kant;
o   an entity which is independent of human volition;
o   an entity which can only be known through 'external' observation, rather than by introspection.

Durkheim on suicide

In his classic study of suicide, Durkheim followed his own rules of the sociological method. The first part of the study (Book I) is a 60-page attempt to outline the inadequacies of non-sociological approaches to the study of suicide. Causes such as insanity, race, heredity, climate and imitation are discussed and then dismissed. But why did Durkheim study suicide? On a personal level, while Durkheim was a student a close friend committed suicide and this deeply affected Durkhiem. On a sociological level, Durkheim wanted to show that wider social forces were at work, and that the causes of suicide were not only of a personal nature. However, at the outset we have to say that Durkheim had a rather odd definition of suicide:

> the term suicide is applied to all cases of death resulting directly or indirectly from a positive or negative act of the victim himself, which he knows will produce this result. An attempt is an act thus defined but falling short of actual death. (Durkheim, 1952: 44)

Durkheim's four types of suicide Following his own rules of the sociological method, Durkheim attempted to classify suicides and came up with four logical possibilities. However, combined types of suicide are possible and Durkheim discussed them at some length.

First, **egoistic suicide** is caused by lack of integration into the *conscience collective*. Such subjects are described as having 'excessive individualism'. As Durkheim explains, egoistic suicide:

> results from the fact that society is not sufficiently integrated at all points to keep all its members under control. If it increases inordinately, therefore, it is because the state on which it depends has itself excessively expanded; it is because society, weak and disturbed, lets too many persons escape too completely from its influence. (Durkheim, 1952: 373)

The second type of suicide that Durkheim looks at is the opposite of egoistic suicide, and he named this type **altruistic suicide**. This is brought about by people having become over-integrated into the *conscience collective*. Even minor infractions of the collective representations can bring about feelings of great shame; people feel they have to kill themselves out of a sense of duty. Durkheim subdivided altruistic into three sub-types: obligatory, optional and acute. These sub-types reflect differences in the degree of altruism experienced by the person. With acute altruism for example, the individual is so fully integrated into the *conscience collective* that they lose their individual personality and identity, they no longer exist as individuals in their own right.

The third type of suicide that Durkheim discussed was **anomic suicide**, which resulted from the lack of regulation in people's lives. The concept of anomie is a central one in Durkheimian sociology, and this anomic condition is experienced as a feeling of 'normlessness'. The loss of norms, or normal ways of behaving, can have one of two origins: either a person is unaware of the existence of a set of norms, or alternatively, a person may be faced with two or more competing sets of norms. Durkheim gives the following example: if the Romans were to invade Jerusalem this might lead the Jews to commit suicide *en masse* at the prospect of having to lead a life on the basis of Roman Law but also wanting to lead their lives according to their own Hebrew Law (Durkheim, 1952: 288). In either case the result will be the same: a greater risk of suicide.

Durkheim's fourth type is **fatalistic suicide**: 'It is the suicide deriving from excessive regulation, that of persons with futures pitilessly blocked and passions violently choked by oppressive discipline' (Durkheim, 1952: footnote, p. 276). Durkheim gives a very limited outline of this type of suicide, because he claims that it is of little contemporary importance and examples are difficult to find. They included the husbands of young married women who were childless, the suicide of slaves and others who experience 'excessive physical or moral despotism'.

Durkheim's treatment in textbooks

Durkheim gets a terrible press. In a recent article I argued that A-level sociology textbooks currently on the UK market read as if they were written by people who have never read Durkheim's book on suicide. Such textbooks have a self-referential nature: later textbooks are written from previous textbooks. The descriptions of sociologists' work become further and further removed from what the original authors said. Such textbooks cannot be authoritative sources on Durkheim.

Most textbooks attempt to force Durkheim's analysis into the rigid caricature of 'structural-consensus' functionalism that bears no relationship to the subtlety and persuasiveness of the original Durkheim. All the textbooks invite the reader to assume that Durkheim had a very poor grasp of human agency, that he believed people were pushed about by forces outside of their control and made assumptions about the validity of official statistics which was beyond belief in its naive acceptance. Also it is assumed that the critiques of Douglas (1967) and Atkinson (1978) are valid.

One textbook informs readers that the social fact is 'a product of social construction: it does not create or mould the individual, but rather, individual action creates the social reality' (Kirby et al., 1997: 462). In contrast, Durkheim in his *The Rules of Sociological Method* clearly states in his discussion of social facts that: 'It results from their being together, a product of the actions and reactions which take place between individual consciousness' (Durkheim, 1966: 9).

The Kirby et al. text goes on to express the view that Durkheim made an uncritical use of official statistics to justify his deterministic view of suicide, failing to take into account that suicide statistics were put together by officials who may have their own point of view concerning the causes of sudden death.

Most sociology textbooks such as Jorgensen et al. (1997) assume that Durkheim's study of suicide is seriously flawed and accept without question the critique of Douglas, Atkinson and other interactionists who:

suggest that such statistics are only a reflection of the officials working in the organizations which produce such statistics. These do not reflect the truth or reality of such events. For sociologists, the proper study of suicide must involve an examination of the work on the part of officials in arriving at definitions of what is or is not a suicide. (Jorgensen et al., 1997: 310)

Even a more informed text such as Fulcher and Scott (1999) maintains that 'The main problem was that the suicide rates on which he [Durkheim] based his study were calculated from official statistics' (1999: 9). This is followed by a 27-word evaluation of the Douglas and Atkinson position.

In their discussion of Durkheim's study of suicide, Barnard and Burgess similarly argue that:

> Durkheim's (1897) analysis of the official statistics is regarded by positivists as a masterpiece of sociological enquiry. Durkheim argues that rigorous analysis and comparison of the official suicide statistics provide 'social facts'. But according to interactionism they are social facts compiled by humans – doctors, coroners, the police and the families and friends of the dead person – who all have an axe to grind. Taking these official statistics at face value, they argue, is to ignore the interactive processes which contribute to their creation. (Barnard and Burgess, 1996: 32–3)

In the preceding discussion of Durkheim's analysis on page four, Barnard and Burgess (like most textbook authors) use the term 'collective conscience' which is not an adequate translation of *conscience collective*. This is always left untranslated in Durkheim's work because it might be misunderstood as 'collective conscience'! In English, the word 'conscience' is used to denote a measure of 'rightness' and 'wrongness' that we have inside our minds. However in French the term 'conscience' is used to denote a concept more like 'perception'. Therefore when Durkheim uses the term 'conscience collective', he means something along the lines of common or widely shared perspective, whereas Barnard and Burgess suggest that Durkheim means some form of group mind underpinning the concept of 'conscience collective'.

In summary, the sociology textbook version of Durkheim is of a positivistic/functionalist/structuralist – these terms are used interchangeably in many such textbooks – who was naive in his staunch belief that official statistics were absolute facts. He had no understanding of the process by which statistics were created. He was deterministic, believing that people were pushed about by a collective conscience made up of social facts, over which individual people had no control. Individuals were incapable of exercising control over their lives to the extent that their individual psyche was of no use to them whatsoever, and could not even prevent them from killing themselves if the collective conscience so demanded it. The role of the sociologist was simply to identify which of the four rigid types of suicide (three for some textbooks!) a sudden death should be placed into.

Perhaps textbook writers should ask why we should accept without question the 'interactionist' view. After all, by what criteria can 'interactionists' say that coroners' definitions and interpretations of suicide are wrong? Kirby et al. conclude their view of the interactionist critique of

Durkheim by saying: 'Viewed in this way, suicide statistics are created and shaped through strong social and cultural forces.' Yes, but this is not a critique of Durkheim, it is Durkheim's own view!

Durkheim did look at individual forms of suicide, in a chapter on the subject. In addition, he did not rely solely upon official statistics; he looked at some length at the work of Brierre de Boismont, who in *De Suicide et de la folie-suicide* (1865) analysed the personal papers of 1,507 people who had committed suicide. Durkheim was also conscious of the problems involved in the 'social construction' of official statistics:

> But as Wagner long ago remarked, what are called statistics of the motives of suicides are actually statistics of the opinions concerning such motives of officials, often of lower officials, in charge of this information service. Unfortunately, official establishments of fact are known to be often defective even when applied to obvious material facts comprehensible to any conscientious observer and leaving no room for evaluation. (Durkheim, 1952: 148)

The Wagner referred to in the above quote did start something of a debate about the validity of a whole range of official statistics in the 1860s following the publication of part two of his *Die Gesetzmassigkeit in der scheinbar willkurlichen menschlichen Handlungen* (1864). Some of the contributions to this debate are to be found in *Année sociologique*. Durkheim was fully aware of issues of validity and reliability in relation to official statistics.

Apart from one line in Fulcher and Scott (1999: 9) there is no discussion in the textbooks of 'combined types' of suicide, in which say anomie and egoism are evident in the same sudden death. Hence, the textbooks give a neat and tidy but rather simplistic caricature of Durkheim's four types of suicide. In contrast, Durkheim's 'four types' of suicide should be viewed as four contradictory forces, any one of which could lead to suicide. Too much 'egoism' can lead to suicide, but similarly too much 'altruism' can also lead to suicide. Too much 'anomic' can lead to suicide but similarly too much 'fatalism' can lead to suicide. The individual has to keep the four forces of egoism, altruism, anomic and fatalism in balance in order to lead a healthy and suicide-free life.

There are, however, some flaws in Durkheim's analysis. Durkheim claims: 'This pressure which is the distinctive property of social facts is the pressure which the totality exerts on the individual' (1966: 102). As an example, he claims: 'the social reaction that we call "punishment" is due to the intensity of the collective sentiments which crime offends; but, from another angle it has the useful function of maintaining these sentiments at the same degree of intensity, for they would soon diminish if offences against them were not punished' (Durkheim, 1966: 96): 'Hence, sociological laws can be only a corollary of the more general laws of psychology; the ultimate explanation of collective life will consist in showing how it emanates from human nature in general' (1966: 95). I have assumed, above, that human nature is built out of the *conscience collective*. However, Anthony Giddens (1978) argues that Durkheim's attempt to 'sociologize' Kant is deficient. Giddens gives the example of the category of time. In contradistinction to Kant, for Durkheim all time is 'social time' and as such is a social fact. Both time and space are collective representations, which express a collective reality and 'correspond to the most universal properties of things' (Durkheim, 1915: 9). Time reflects the rhythms of social life or collective activities, for example feasts and public ceremonies. The function of time 'is to assure their regularity' (1915: 11). However, a key element in Durkheim's thinking is that when it comes to regular events or our conception of time itself 'by right we are free to conceive them otherwise . . . or to represent them to ourselves as occurring in a different order' (1915: 14).[1] For Giddens, the argument that the categories of thought which Durkheim called 'social time' presuppose the discrimination which it purports to explain. In other words, a person could not grasp concepts such as space or time without having the intellectual faculty to organise their experience in terms of space and time.

Durkheim never considers the possibility that categories of thought may be based upon ideology; that powerful groups within society may manipulate the ideas of others.

There is also in Durkheim's analysis the assumption that there is only one mode of interpretation, notably of moral obligation and discipline. Also Durkheim only discusses education as a mechanism that people can make use of to share the *conscience collective*. What other mechanisms exist to allow people to share values, attitudes and beliefs which make up the *conscience collective*? Durkheim is unclear about this.

In terms of the scope of the *conscience collective*, there are some areas which are not under its control, which Durkheim terms 'circles of physical necessities'. This sphere of human activity is usually the private sphere of our lives.

Finally, Durkheim's sociology tends to ignore conflict – except for the conflict between the individual and the collective.

In conclusion, for Durkheim, to live in society means to live under the domination of the commonly held ideas or beliefs which form the *conscience collective*. It is often the case that even though people formulate the collective representations that help to create the *conscience collective*, they are unaware that they are following common ways of behaving. However, the categories that make up collective representations are said by Durkheim to be *functional* to society. Many of the arguments and assumptions that Durkheim made about the world and the practice of sociology were carried forward into the sociological theory that we call functionalism. And it is to functionalism that we now turn our attention.

Talcott Parsons: the functionalist approach

For Talcott Parsons there are two essential reference points for his analysis of social systems:

- o   categorisation of the functional requirements of a social system;
- o   categorisation of the cybernetic hierarchy within a social system: an analysis of the processes of control within the social system.

The starting point for this analysis is the *action frame of reference* – the social actions and interactions of individual people which make up the social system. Parsons argued that action was not simply an *ad hoc* reply or response to a stimulus. Individual people developed a strategy of responses based upon a range of possible expectations about a given situation. This range was often based upon the needs of the person and a prediction of the possible gains and losses to the person from various responses to action. This form of interaction is possible because there is a system of shared cultural symbols which are understood within a community. Parsons's definition of a social system is as follows:

> a social system consists in a plurality of individual actors interacting with each other in a situation which has at least a physical or environmental aspect, actors who are motivated in terms of a tendency to the 'optimization of gratification' and whose relation to their situations, including each other is defined and mediated in terms of a system of culturally structured and shared symbols.
> (Parsons, 1951: 6)

Moreover, it is because we are not in a position, claims Parsons, to develop a complete dynamic theory of action that he opted for a developing a theory of the social system in 'structural-functional' terms.

Parsons attempted to describe the 'parts' and 'processes' which he believed were to be found within real social systems. The categories he used were applicable, he argued, to all social systems.

As a functionalist Parsons believed that the social system had to overcome four basic problems:

- o   adaptation – which was dealt with by the economy;
- o   goal attainment – which was dealt with by the political system;
- o   pattern maintenance/tension management – which was dealt with by the family;
- o   integration – which was dealt with by a range of cultural organisations such as schools and the media.

The social system was made up of individual people interacting with each other within institutions and those institutions performed functions both for the individuals and for the social system itself. Underpinning the social system was a 'common value system'. In a simple society Parsons describes the common value system as characterised by pattern variables A, whilst in a complex society the common value system was characterised by pattern variables B. The concept of pattern variables is used by Parsons as a form of classifying the norms and values of different types of society. The modern industrial society is seen by Parsons to be underpinned by pattern variables

A, while rural, non-industrial societies are underpinned by pattern variables B. Eddie Cuff and colleagues have classified pattern variables as follows: (p. 43 E.C. Cuff, C. Payne, D. Francis, D. Hustler and W.W. Sharrock). The process of modernisation was the transition from pattern variables A to pattern variables B: from the simple/traditional society to the complex industrial society. In the eyes of many people Parsons had 'oversolved the problem of order' within the social system. This means that Parsons found it difficult to explain why a social system should change when everyone had a function and every function had a purpose, and all the people were socialised into a common value system.

In 1951, when Parsons published *The Social System*, he stated clearly that he had no theory of social change:

> a general theory of the processes of change of social systems is not possible in the present state of knowledge . . . We do not have a complete theory of the processes of change in social systems . . . when such a theory is available the millennium of social science will have arrived. This will not come in our time and most probably never. (Parsons, 1951: 486)

Similar themes were taken up by Martin Lipset (1960) with his notion of 'political man' and Daniel Bell (1960) with his 'end of ideology thesis'. The assumption was that the United States had solved all the major problems of any social system, hence no social change was needed. However, by the 1960s a whole range of groups were demanding change, not just in the United States but across the world: feminists, black civil rights activists, gay liberation activists, peace movements and many more. This change had to be explained by sociologists.

Parsons makes his most clear and straightforward analysis of social change in his book, *Societies: Evolutionary and Comparative Perspectives* (1971). For Parsons there were two overlapping types of social change:

o   **Structural differentiation** – institutional change within the social system, usually involving institutions swapping functions, for example the family losing its economic functions to the economy or its educational functions to the education system;
o   **Long-term evolution** – movement of the social system along a long-term evolutionary path.

Structural differentiation was brought about by growing dissatisfaction with the outcomes of the social system and, at the same time, by a growing realisation by some individuals that things could be done differently. As Parsons explains, this pressure to bring about change from within the social system had two principal sources: *cultural* and *motivational* sources of change.

These two factors generated 'strains' within the social system. Neil Smelser carried out a case study of the emergence of the cotton industry in Lancashire making use of the Parsonian notion of structural differentiation. According to Smelser (1959), after the initial dissatisfaction with some aspects of the social system, the 'mechanisms of change and adjustment to change' proceeded through the following stages:

o symptoms of disturbance, such as negative emotional reaction;
o covert attempts to handle the tensions;
o tolerance of the new ideas in certain important groups;
o positive attempts to translate the new ideas into concrete efforts at making profit;
o implementation of the innovations;
o routinising of the innovation into society.

As suggested above, for Parsons all social systems are on a long-term evolutionary path. Three basic assumptions underpin the movement of the social system along this path: differentiation, reintegration and adaptation. Differentiation is the motor of social change for Parsons. It involves the establishment of more specialised and more independent units in social life. Neil Smelser (1959) defines differentiation as a process whereby one or more roles or organisations replace less well functioning roles or organisations. The new social units are structurally distinct, but taken together are functionally equivalent to the original unit.

More generally, Smelser describes the process of modernisation as multidimensional in nature. At the economic level modernisation:

o is built upon scientific knowledge;
o involves the change from subsistence farming to commercial farming;
o replaces animal and human power with machines;
o entails the spread of urbanisation;
o involves the concentration of the industrial workforce in towns and cities.

At the non-economic levels modernisation involves:

o the passing from tribal systems to democratic systems;
o the development of education systems to provide training;
o a diminished role for religion;
o a shift from the extended family to the nuclear family;
o greater social mobility, with class position based upon achievement.

Modernisation: a definition

Probably the clearest definition comes from Jürgen Habermas, who argues that modernisation refers to a bundle of processes that are cumulative and mutually reinforcing:

To the formation of capital
The mobilisation of resources

> To the development of the forces of production
> To the increase in the productivity of labour
> To the establishment of centralised political power
> The formation of national identities
> The proliferation of rights of political participation
> The emergence of urban forms of life
> The emergence of formal schooling
> The secularisation of values and norms
>
> *Source:* adapted from Habermas (1987).

Neil Smelser: *Social Paralysis and Social Change*

In the 1990s Neil Smelser returned to the functionalist account of modernisation, which he defines in relation to the education system as 'a universal, compulsory, secular, and free system' (Smelser, 1991: 3). In his *Social Paralysis and Social Change: British Working-Class Education in the Nineteenth Century* (1991) Smelser argues that every society can be regarded as 'in transition' along a number of basic cultural and institutional lines. In the case of Britain these lines were:

o   change from an agricultural to an advanced urban industrial society;
o   change from oligarchy to democracy;
o   change from state established religion to denominational competition;
o   change from allocating social positions by patronage to allocation by merit.

Traditional functionalist accounts of modernisation, in Smelser's opinion, did not always assume that knowledge was preferable to ignorance in social systems. However, functionalists did assume that education fulfils several important functions such as inculcating society's cultural values, socialisation into roles and the generation and transmission of knowledge. With the emergence of modernity, there was a breakdown of shared cultural traditions and a greater need for skills amongst the workforce. The education system provided these. Nevertheless, Smelser is critical of functionalist accounts. To view change in the education system as a process of structural differentiation alone, seeing educational change as adaptation to industrial development, underestimates the role of social movements in various conflicts and compromises. As Smelser points out, how would a simple functionalist account explain that nineteenth-century Ireland had a more 'advanced' educational system than England for several decades? Educational history should be seen as 'a series of sequences of realignment of forces, group dissatisfaction, mobilization and conflict, resolution and the establishment of a new balance' (Smelser, 1991: 26).

Smelser's account of educational change is 'synthetic' in nature; based upon a framework which is described as 'social-structural' and 'social-psychological' and which emphasises functional adaptation and conflict and takes into account the role of class and status groups. The account of education that Smelser puts forward is similar to that of Emile Durkheim. Education is concerned with the process of socialisation at three different levels:

o the individual level – acquisition of values, cognitive skills and information;
o the social level – the allocation of resources and provision of institutional structures;
o the cultural level – socialisation is a mechanism for transmitting values and meanings from one generation to the next.

Forces external to the education system, or 'structural conditions', do not make the first move in the process of social change. These moves take place only when 'meaningful actors' in society perceive a state of affairs to be unsatisfactory in some way because of some aspects of the social context. Social change then presupposes that the 'meaningful actors' have some criteria to evaluate given situations. Social change is not an objective historical process that takes place beyond the perception and control of people within societies; social change must be viewed in relation to the social significance that people place on issues and events within a social context.

For Smelser, any account of social change will involve looking at a developmental sequence in which different combinations of factors are identified and no one explanatory factor or set of factors can be singled out as *the* most important factor in determining the process.

The account that Smelser gives in his 1991 book is still 'functionalist' in nature, in that he gives a full and clear outline of the functional integration and interdependence of institutions. Where Smelser differs from traditional functionalists is that he regards functional integration and interdependence 'as looser, more sporadic, and not necessarily either stable or unstable' (Smelser, 1991: 355). His analysis places much greater emphasis on the 'meaningful actor'. However, what is the 'meaningful actor' for Smelser? The reader might want to assume that *agency* lies with the individual human person, but at no point does Smelser say this.

However, a number of theorists, for example Alex Inkeles (1976), have suggested that modernisation involves changes at a psychological level, with the emergence of a distinctly 'modern' personality which:

o refuses to accept dogmatic thinking
o considers public issues
o is open to new experiences
o has a conviction that science and reason are superior to emotion

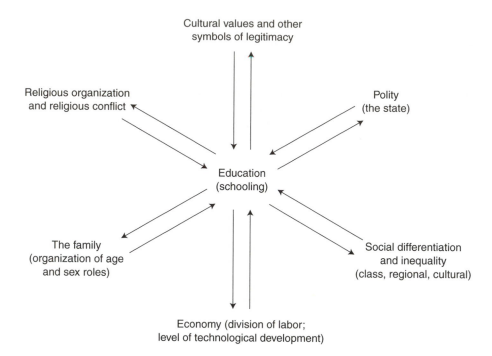

Figure 1.1 *External Forces Impinging on Education (Smelser, 1991: 32)*

o   recognises the value of saving up for a rainy day (deferred gratifi-
     cation)
o   has high aspirations

This conception of the modern self, with its distinct personality traits, is
very different from the self in pre-modern societies.

Niklas Luhmann: 'autopoietic systems theory'

A very different form of systems theory was put forward by Niklas
Luhmann in the latter half of the twentieth century. Luhmann begins his
analysis with the assumption that there are social systems. His intention is
to present a 'general theory' of social systems. The social system includes
all the things that sociologists are interested in; and in this sense
Luhmann's systems theory is a *universal sociological theory*. A social system
is **autopoietic**, in other words it has a self-referential quality. This means
that the social system has the ability to establish 'order' within itself and to
differentiate itself from the environment. Social systems have an abstract
functional nature and are non-psychic in character. They are made up of a
unified or referential bond of communication, whilst psychic systems are
made up of a unified bond between conscious states.

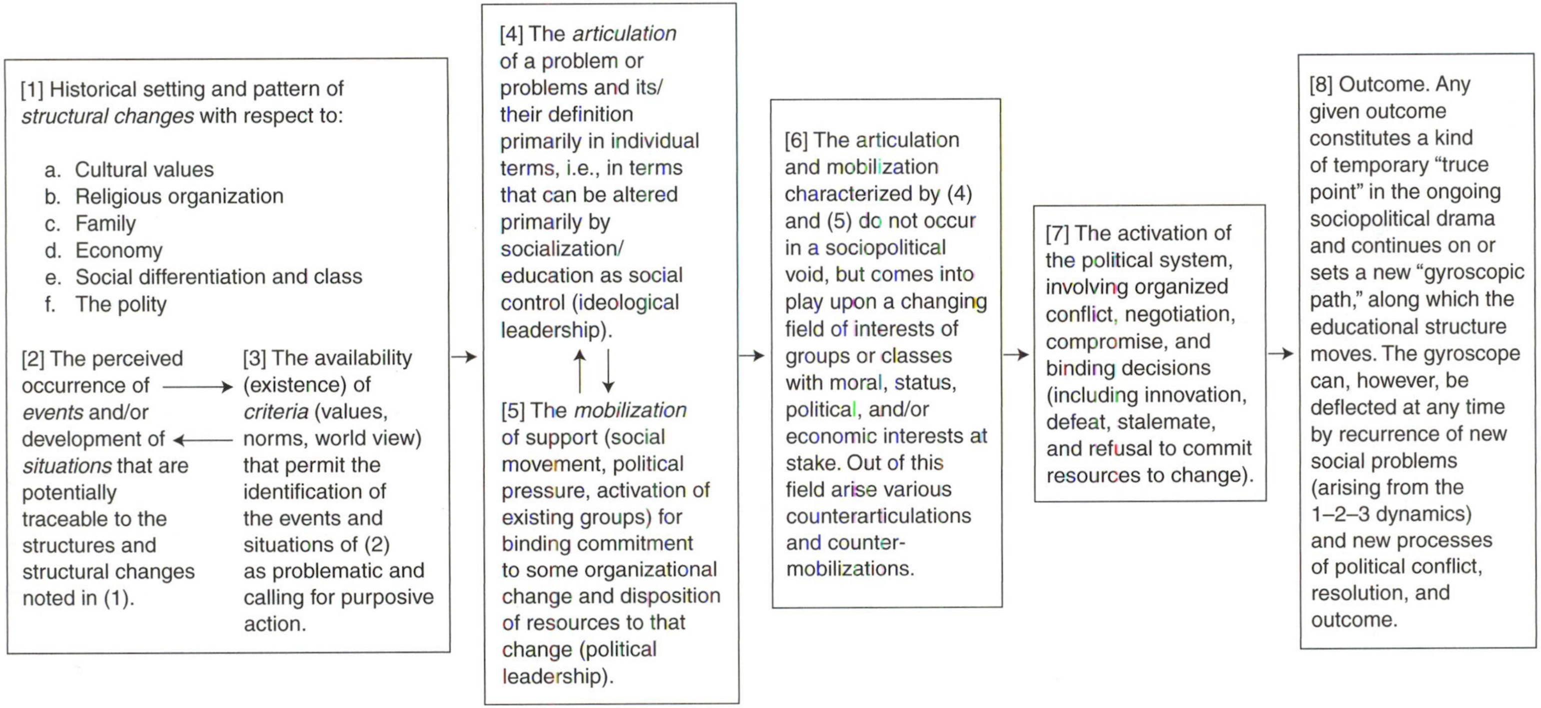

[1] Historical setting and pattern of *structural changes* with respect to:

a. Cultural values
b. Religious organization
c. Family
d. Economy
e. Social differentiation and class
f. The polity

[2] The perceived occurrence of → *events* and/or development of → *situations* that are potentially traceable to the structures and structural changes noted in (1).

[3] The availability (existence) of *criteria* (values, norms, world view) that permit the identification of the events and situations of (2) as problematic and calling for purposive action.

[4] The *articulation* of a problem or problems and its/their definition primarily in individual terms, i.e., in terms that can be altered primarily by socialization/ education as social control (ideological leadership).

[5] The *mobilization* of support (social movement, political pressure, activation of existing groups) for binding commitment to some organizational change and disposition of resources to that change (political leadership).

[6] The articulation and mobilization characterized by (4) and (5) do not occur in a sociopolitical void, but comes into play upon a changing field of interests of groups or classes with moral, status, political, and/or economic interests at stake. Out of this field arise various counterarticulations and counter-mobilizations.

[7] The activation of the political system, involving organized conflict, negotiation, compromise, and binding decisions (including innovation, defeat, stalemate, and refusal to commit resources to change).

[8] Outcome. Any given outcome constitutes a kind of temporary "truce point" in the ongoing sociopolitical drama and continues on or sets a new "gyroscopic path," along which the educational structure moves. The gyroscope can, however, be deflected at any time by recurrence of new social problems (arising from the 1–2–3 dynamics) and new processes of political conflict, resolution, and outcome.

Figure 1.2   A Model of Educational Change (Smelser, 1991: 34)

The function of the social system is to reduce uncertainties, by

o   combining the viewpoints of different social actors;
o   imposing a time horizon upon events (past, present, future);
o   placing occurrences and events in a shared context;
o   providing an epistemic base in the form of a binary code: payment/
    non-payment; power/opposition; truth/falseness.

Meaning within social systems is generated by internal autopoietic self-referencing processes. The social system makes information meaningful by setting all information in an arrangement of binary oppositions, which provides social actors with an epistemic foundation for their everyday lives. Within Luhmann's social system nothing is left 'context-free'.

In Luhmann's analysis social systems are not composed of individual people. Rather than individuals creating social systems by their bodily or psychic processes, an individual psychic system has *expectations* of its environment. The psychic system makes use of shared language to comprehend the complexity of the social system. After a time our expectations take on a social nature and completely random expectations disappear. Our consciousness becomes socially directed. For Luhmann, psychic systems and social systems have a co-evolution.

In many respects Luhmann takes his starting point from the 'General Statement' in Parsons and Shils's *Towards a General Theory of Action* (1951). There is a double contingency inherent in interaction. Person A's (Ego) gratifications are contingent on their selection from the available alternatives. In turn Person B's (Alter) reaction will be contingent on Person A's selection – and is itself based upon a 'complementary selection'. This, we shall see below, is the 'double contingency'.

There are 'conventions' observed by both Ego and Alter:

o   Each actor is both an agent and an object of action orientation.
o   Both Person A and Person B have meaning to themselves and others.
o   From these assumptions the concept of double contingency is built.
    The achievement of our goals as social actors is contingent upon our
    successful cognition and manipulation of the environment.

For Luhmann a differentiated system is not simply a relationship between a number of parts. Systems are made up of a large number of system/environmental oppositions, which are in their own way engaged in different processes of reconstituting a social system as a synthesis of subsystems and environment. Everything which is part of the system is involved in these processes of self-production. The elements which make up the system have no given period of life; everything must be continually reproduced. Without the capacity to generate its own independence from the environment, the social system would cease to exist. As Luhmann explains: 'System differentiation is nothing more than the repetition of system formation within systems' (Luhmann, 1995: 18).

Differentiation is a principle which makes the system harmonious, it provides the system with its *systematicity*. Luhmann's concept of 'differentiation' contains a notion of 'hierarchy' which conditions subsystems in such a way that it only allows subsystems to differentiate into further subsystems.

The environment of a system and systems in the environment

The point of departure of Luhmann is the difference between the system and the environment. The system is involved in a continual process of maintaining its independence from the environment, but cannot exist without an environment. The maintenance of a boundary between the system and the environment is in essence system maintenance. The environment itself is not a system as it has no capacity for self-reflection or action.

Luhmann assumes that the environment is more puzzling than the system. Because of this puzzlement, systems have an element of *complexity*. Luhmann's concept of 'complexity' is about reflecting on experiences and selecting between various approaches to avoid risk. In other words, systems have the capacity for contingency and, it logically follows, the capacity for evolution. The most important evolutionary achievement is the establishment of a boundary. Boundaries define what is within the system and what is beyond the system, they separate the system from the environment and at the same time connect the system to the environment. In addition, complex systems have to adapt both to the environment and to their own complexity. So system self-referencing involves multiple constitution or what Luhmann terms 'double contingency'. A social system exists in the form of its components, and a stable system is made up of unstable components which it uses to construct a stable foundation for itself. Both double contingency and communication are linked to systems theory and the system's constitution. Double contingency is a selective process which reduces the complexity of what is achievable by a social system (which Luhmann terms the *horizon of possibilities*). Communication allows the formation of self-referential systems, because communication has the capacity to self-reference as well as to thematise itself to something else (which Luhmann terms *hetero-reference*). Complexity takes place in Luhmann's analysis when a component of a system is unable to establish connections to every other component within that system and therefore is forced to select which components it is going to establish a relation with.

Luhmann's functional analysis

Luhmann describes his functional analysis as 'holistic' in nature and as a 'kind of theoretical technique' in which a perspective of the lifeworld is established for the purpose of gathering information. This type of analysis allows systems to develop the capacity to specify problems. It is, Luhmann argues, the construction of problems that makes functional analysis an essential element of systems theory.

Systems are firmly attached to meaning and can never be free from meaning. Meaning is used to constitute the boundary between the system and the environment. Moreover, it is meaning that we use to define and analyse *complexity*, *system* and the *self-reference* of the system. Meaning has to be absorbed and processed to generate stability; this is done by what Luhmann refers to as the *'use of differences for connective information processing'* (Luhmann, 1995: 65, italics added). Meaning is distinguished from information, but all reproduction of meaning occurs by the use of information. Meaning is the coming together of actualisation with virtualisation and re-actualisation with re-virtualisation in a self-driving process of giving substance to the system. Systems that operate self-referentially cannot escape from the meaningfulness of their own processes. In addition, when a system comes into contact with another system the meaning processes become *understanding*.

Humans are a special type of animal with the ability to place events in a chronological order and the ability to define social properties. Individuals reflect upon themselves in relation to the social system which they use, which they call 'the other'. Every social relation brings about an attempt to understand that relation. Such understanding makes the behaviour of others easier to foresee. The prediction of behaviour of 'the other' is referred to as *symbolic generalisation*: 'symbolic generalizations stamp identities onto the flux of experience' (Luhmann, 1995: 94).

Double contingency: the problem of behavioural agreement

Luhmann starts his discussion of double contingency with a description of how Talcott Parsons outlines and resolves the same problem:

> Parsons begins with the fact that action cannot take place if alter makes his action dependent on how ego acts, and ego wants to connect his action to alter's. A pure circle of self-referential determination, lacking any further elaboration, leaves action indeterminate, makes it indeterminable. This is not a matter of mere behavioral agreement, nor of coordinating the interests and intentions of different actors. Instead, it concerns a basic condition of possibility for social action as such. (Luhmann, 1995: 101)

No action can take place without first solving the problem of double contingency. This problem is described by Luhmann as follows: 'The basic situation of double contingency is . . . simple: two black boxes, by whatever accident, come to have dealings with one another. Each determines its own behavior by complex self-referential operations within its own boundaries . . . Each assumes the same about the other' (Luhmann, 1995: 109). In other words, participants in a social system have to understand each other in order to communicate. Parsons's solution to this was the socialisation of individuals into a common value system, which underpinned the social system.

Unlike Parsons, Luhmann argues that ego and alter need not be actual human beings.

People can attempt to influence what they observe by their own action. Luhmann makes a distinction between power (*Macht*) and influence (*Einfluss*). Power is defined as a wholly political concept. However, the power/influence distinction is not so clear cut. If we compare power and money, we can see that money allows for a very exact form of measurement: it allows us to measure clearly relationships between people and makes relations quantified and countable. Power is not that exact, so it has to be quantified in different forms: legitimate/illegitimate power, formal/empirical and explicit/implicit. However, (political) power and influence are 'power'.

A social system emerges from the action, feedback to that action and consequent further action taken in response to the feedback. The complexity of the system brings about both action and feedback. Structure is seen by Luhmann as interdependence and constraint. Expectations of how people will or should behave in a given situation have a structural value. The process of system formation constrains the options open to people to safeguard their own behaviour in any situation. As Luhmann explains:

> Persons never meet without some assumption, without some expectations about each other, and they can experience contingency in the sense of 'always being otherwise possible' only by means of behavioral types and expectations. But this objection only confirms that society is an autopoietic system, which must presuppose itself in its own reproduction. (Luhmann, 1995: 133)

The experience of double contingency gives our actions sequences, boundaries and discipline, in which each act has an end. There is then a relationship between 'structure' and 'expectation'. 'Selection domains' for action are 'reductive perspectives' or 'ordering perspectives' on the connection between the system and the environment. In this sense 'the environment' is the theme or reason for our actions. One of the most important repercussions of this is the appearance of concepts of *trust* and *distrust*. However, Luhmann does make it clear that:

> social systems are not built up of actions, as if these actions were produced on the basis of the organico-psychic constitution of human beings and could exist in themselves; instead social systems are broken down into actions, and by this reduction acquire the basis for connections that serve to continue the course of communication. (Luhmann, 1995: 139)

What is 'the environment'?

In Luhmann's analysis the environment is 'a negative correlate' of the system; it is everything else other than the social system. We can view the environment either as a:

o **resource** – in which the social system experiences contingency as 'dependency' upon the environment; or as

o **information** – in this sense the social system experiences contingency as 'uncertainty'.

All social systems have machinery for regulating problems and this often takes the form of rituals. The function of the ritual is to render more intelligible uncertainty from outside the social system by redefining the uncertainty according to an internal set of categories that we feel comfortable with and believe that we understand.

Luhmann argues that collective action is also individual action. The interpretation of individual action through collective action is one essential constituent component of any social system. Individual action needs to be specifically directed towards collective symbols that make it apparent to those people involved in the action that the entire system is bound by the relationship between individual and collective action. In addition, specific conditions must exist for action to be set in motion and reproduced – such as adequate space, means of communication, objects to be 'handled', and a willingness to be motivated. All this must be secured in advance. Only when meaning-constituting boundaries divide from environment can there be a world.

Internal system formation

Internal system formation takes place 'autocatalytically', in other words by self-selection. The development of new subsystems generates a process of adaptation as new forms of environment appear with the new subsystems. The social system of a modern society has the following characteristics:

o the **political function system** and its environment;
o the **economic function system** and its environment;
o the **scientific function system** and its environment;
o the **religious function system** and its environment.

– and so it continues for each subsystem that exists within the social system. This form of differentiation increases the complexity of the social system, and at the same time initiates new arrangements for dealing with that increased complexity.

Interpenetration

For Luhmann, human beings form part of the social system's environment, and the relationship between the human beings and the social system is one of interpenetration. Interpenetration is said to exist when the various components within the environment, which contribute to the formation of social systems, complement each other in their system-forming activity. The boundaries of social systems are found within the psychic systems. It is within our consciousness that boundaries between the social system and the environment are found. Reproduction of the social system must involve the reproduction of consciousness.

Relations of interpenetration and binding also exist between human beings, and Luhmann refers to inter-human interpenetration as *intimacy*. The relationships between humans are not random; ethical theories emerge which establish principles of correct action. Morality represents a convergence of social and interpersonal interpenetration.

What *is* structure *in Luhmann's analysis?*

The relationship between expectation and action is also the relationship between structure and action; this relationship is reciprocally enabling. The distinguishing feature of structure is **constraint**. Other related elements include:

o   **interdependence** – which comes about through selection;
o   **invariance** – the operative requirement for constraints;
o   **self-reproduction** – in which we have the observation and description of the structure.

In the last analysis, structure is a constraint upon constraints. It is the structure upon which rest the choices from which selections are made in the processes of double contingency. Structure regulates the reproduction of systems, in an effort to avoid or minimise uncertainty.

A difference is found in all social systems; this is the distinction between societal systems and interaction systems. Society has an influence upon the selection of interaction and at the same time is a product of those selections. Society can make use of interaction systems to try out innovative forms of action which can bring it to an end if the result is considered to be a failure, from the perspective of the social system. In these circumstances the interaction rather than society comes to an end. Social systems are not simply the sum of interactions; interaction systems always presuppose society.

This distinction between society and interaction is found in all social relationships. The relationship between society and interaction is referred to as an *episode*: 'Interactions are episodes of societal process' (Luhmann, 1995: 406). Such episodes are possible only if there is a high degree of certainty that communication has a societal basis to it. Society acts upon what happens within interaction: 'The beginning and end of an interaction are merely caesuras in society's autopoiesis' (Luhmann, 1995: 407). In summary, every interaction has a relationship to society. Social systems are not interaction systems.

For Luhmann, 'structure' operates at the level of memory. It is structure that is used to solve the problem of getting from one event to the next.

Summary

Functionalism is a perspective within the social sciences which argues that individual people perform roles within a social system. These social roles interact to form social systems. Within social systems there are institutions which perform functions for both individuals and for the social system as a whole. Finally, the social system is underpinned by a set of common values. The common criticism of functionalist analysis is that it under-values the human agent, in other words it is assumed that individual people are pushed about by forces outside their control. Secondly, it is assumed that functionalists have difficulty explaining how social systems change over time. Finally, functionalism is often assumed to be a per-spective which is politically conservative in nature.

Note

1. Adam (1992) is critical of Durkheim's notion of time on a number of grounds, including that his assumption that all time is exclusively human and, secondly, that Durkheim pays no attention to how the meaning of time differs with the change of context.

References

Barnard, A. and Burgess, T. (1996) *Sociology Explained*. Cambridge University Press: Cambridge.

Bell, D. (1960) *The End of Ideology*. Free Press of Glencoe: New York.

De Boismont, Brierre (1865) *De Suicide et de la folie-suicide*. Germer Baillier: Paris.

Durkheim, E. (1915) *The Elementary Forms of the Religious Life*, trans. J. Ward Swain. Allen & Unwin: London.

Durkheim, E. (1933) *The Division of Labour in Society*, trans. G. Simpson. The Free Press: New York.

Durkheim, E. (1952) *Suicide: A Study in Sociology*, trans. J.A. Spaulding and G. Simpson. Routledge & Kegan Paul: London.

Durkheim, E. (1966) *The Rules of Sociological Method*, trans. S.A. Solovay and J.H. Mueller. The Free Press: New York.

Durkheim, E. (1973) *Moral Education: A Study in the Theory and Application of the Sociology of Education*, trans. E.K. Wilson and H. Schnurer. Free Press of Glencoe: New York.

Durkheim, E. and Mauss, M. (1963) *Primitive Classification*, trans. R. Needham. Cohen & West: London.

Fulcher, J. and Scott, J. (1999) *Sociology*. Oxford University Press: Oxford.

Habermas, J. (1987) *The Philosophical Discourse of Modernity*. Polity: Cambridge.

Harris, S. (1996) *Sociology*. Letts: London.

Jorgensen, N. (1997) *Sociology: An Interactive Approach*. Collins Educational: London.

Kirby, M., Kidd, W., Koubel, F., Barter, J., Hope, T., Kirton, A., Madry, N., Manning, N. and Triggs, A. (1997) *Sociology in Perspective*. Heinemann: Oxford.

Lipset, S.M. (1960) *Political Man*. Doubleday: New York.

Luhmann, N. (1995) *Social Systems*, trans. J. Bednarz, Jr., with D. Baecker. Stanford University Press: Stanford, CA.

Lukes, S. (1992) *Émile Durkheim, His Life and Work: A Historical and Critical Study*. Penguin: Harmondsworth.

Parsons, T. (1951) *The Social System*. Routledge & Kegan Paul: London.

Parsons, T. (1968) *The Structure of Social Action: A Study in Social Theory with Special Reference to a Group of Recent European Writers*. The Free Press: New York.

Parsons, T. (1971) *Societies: Evolutionary and Comparative Perspectives*. Prentice-Hall: Englewood Cliffs, NJ.

Parsons, T. and Shils, E. (1951) *Towards a General Theory of Action*. Harper & Row: New York.

Parsons, T. and Smelser, N. (1973) *Economy and Society*. Routledge & Kegan Paul: London.

Smelser, N. (1959) *Social Change in the Industrial Revolution: An Application of Theory to the Lancashire Cotton Industry 1770–1840*. Routledge & Kegan Paul: London.

Smelser, N. (1991) *Social Paralysis and Social Change: British Working-Class Education in the Nineteenth Century*. University of California Press: Oxford.

Chapter contents

2 Marxism: Theorising Capitalism – Debates and Developments

By the end of this chapter you should:

- be aware of the central assumptions that the Marxian contribution to social theory is built upon;
- have a critical understanding of the strengths and weaknesses of the Marxian approach;
- understand why the Critical Theory of the Frankfurt School is viewed as one of the most significant twentieth-century developments within Marxian theorising;
- be aware of Karl Mannheim's critique of the Marxian conception of ideology;
- be aware of the contribution of British cultural studies to the development of Marxian theorising;
- have an understanding of Jean Baudrillard's critique of Marxism;
- have an understanding of the post-Marxist approaches of Ernesto Laclau and Chantal Mouffe, Fredric Jameson and Manuel Castells's 'network society';
- have an understanding of Anthony Giddens's critique of Marxism;
- be aware of Alex Callinicos's arguments on the continued relevance of Marxism today.

lassical Marxism is based upon the nineteenth-century writings of Karl Marx (1818–83) and Friedrich Engels (1820–95). Marx and Engels constructed a philosophy of history which singled out class divisions as the motor of history – this was what pushed history forwards. This is commonly known as dialectical material-ism. For Marx, the type of society in which we live, including its politics, culture, art and literature, is determined by the 'mode of production'. Within capitalism, the mode of production is divided into two parts: the **economic base**, made up of the 'relations of production', in other words class relations and the 'forces of production' – all the things from nature that we need to produce commodities. The mode of production also shapes the **superstructure**, the area of culture, politics and ideas (see Figure 2.1). In the Marxian analysis, people's ideas and beliefs are deter-mined above all by economic factors.

From the Marxian perspective if a group owns the means of production, it not only has economic power; it also has political power. The state is viewed as an institution that helps to organise capitalist society in the best interests of the bourgeoisie. The legitimacy of the capitalist system is maintained by the bourgeoisie, making working-class people victims of a false consciousness. Working-class people are said to hold values, ideas and beliefs about the nature of inequality which it is not in their own econ-omic interests to hold. Their ideas are manipulated by the media, schools and religion, for example, institutions which regard economic inequality as fair and just.

The opening chapter of Marx's most influential book *Capital* (1867) is about 'The Commodity', a concept that plays a key role in Marxian analysis. Any human creation can be a 'commodity' and the commodity contains

The mode of production

Superstructure:
the realm of culture, politics and ideas

the **superstructure** is determined by the **economic base**

The **Economic Base** is made up of two parts

1 the **Relations of Production** – this means **class relations**
2 the **Forces of Production** – made up of all the things from nature
that we need to produce commodities

Figure 2.1 *The key assumptions of the Marxian analysis*

'value' – both **use value**, which is the personal value someone gains from consuming the commodity, and **exchange value**, which is the value in monetary terms: the amount that another person will give to own the commodity. Workers are the people who put the value into any commodity. Marx builds his theory of class exploitation upon these simple ideas.

What does Marx understand by the term 'class relations'? For Marx, capitalist society is a form of society in which factories, shops and offices are privately owned, rather than owned by the government. Within capitalism there are a number of economic classes, but Marx investigates just two: the bourgeoisie, who own the means of production and the proletariat, who do not. These two groups have a structural conflict of interest: to make profits the bourgeoisie must exploit the proletariat, while to improve their own living standards the proletariat must reduce the profits of the bourgeoisie by transferring more profit to the workers as wages.

The labour theory of value

Marx sees the relationship between the bourgeoisie and the proletariat as an exploitative one. The bourgeoisie exploit the proletariat. The theory that Marx develops to explain class exploitation is called 'the labour theory of value'.

Activity

Translate the text below into a flow chart, putting the following points into a logical order:

1   The capitalist starts with an amount of
↓

2   commodity inputs, these are the
↓

---

3   *commodities, which are sold in the market place for*
⟶
4   *materials of production and*
⟶
5   *money, which is put into the purchase of*
⟶
6   *labour power, these come together in the*
⟶
7   *production process, to form*
⟶
8   *money*

Write a short paragraph explaining why Marx started *Capital* with a discussion of 'the commodity'. You might want to begin by considering that the commodity contains 'value' – but where does the 'value' come from? Compare your answer to the paragraph below.

According to Marx, because the bourgeoisie buy the materials of production from other capitalists, who have a rational perception of their situation, these materials are bought at their true market value, so the source of profit for Marx can only come from exploiting labour power. It is extracting **surplus value** from the labour force that provides the difference between the amount of money it takes to set up the production process and the amount of money made at the end of the production process. But surplus value is not simply profit: it also includes the cost of setting up the production process again for the next production run.

In summary, the value of any commodity reflects the amount of labour power needed to make that commodity. In addition, workers are not paid the 'true' value of their labour power and this is what Marx means by 'exploitation'; workers are adding value to a commodity, but are only paid a fraction of the value that they have added.

The perceptive reader will have noticed that for Marx, if the capitalist replaces workers with machines, profits should fall. For the individual capitalist, this is clearly not the case. However, if large numbers of capitalists replace workers with machines, this will result in a fall in profits, because individuals will not have sufficient spending power to buy the commodities produced; this is referred to by Marxists as a **realisation crisis**. In these circumstances, capitalists have to find new markets or sources of cheap raw materials from overseas.

Activity

Below are a number of evaluative statements about the Marxist theory of class. Identify which comments are strengths and which are weaknesses and give a justification for your answer:

1 Marx provided a clever description of capitalism and class.
2 The Marxian conception of class cannot deal with automation, suggesting a fall in profits which does not happen.
3 Marx's labour theory of value is both sex-blind and race-blind. He does not take into account the race or gender of the bourgeoisie or proletariat.
4 In late capitalism 'ownership' of the means of production has become divorced from 'control' of the means of production – the bourgeoisie and proletariat no longer exist.
5 Marx has an informed theory of inequality, and its persistence.
6 Marx predicted that there would be a long-term tendency for the rate of profit to fall.
7 The labour theory of value has generated a great deal of research.
8 Marx has provided the motivation for working-class people to join together and improve their position in society.
9 Marx provided a justification for socialism.

Compare your answers to the points given below.

Strengths of the Marxian approach

o Marx provided a clever description of capitalism and class.
o Marx has an informed theory of inequality, and its persistence.
o Marx predicted that there would be a long-term tendency for the rate of profit to fall.
o The labour theory of value has generated a great deal of research.
o Marx has provided the motivation for working-class people to join together and improve their position in society.
o Marx provided a justification for socialism.

Weaknesses of the Marxian approach

o The Marxian conception of class cannot deal with automation, suggesting a fall in profits which does not happen.
o Marx's labour theory of value is both sex-blind and race-blind. He does not take into account the race or gender of the bourgeoisie or proletariat.
o In late capitalism 'ownership' of the means of production has become divorced from 'control' of the means of production – the bourgeoisie and proletariat no longer exist.

The dominant ideology

For Marxists the dominant ideas of any historical period are the ideas of the ruling class, the bourgeoisie. A 'dominant ideology' is a system of thought which is imposed upon the proletariat in support of capitalism. The Marxian conception of ideology is based upon a humanistic notion that consent should be based upon an authentic consciousness free from distortion. For Marxists, the term 'ideology' suggests that the bourgeoisie manipulate the way in which working-class people think about the world. The bourgeoisie create a 'worldview' for the proletariat; this is shaped via the mass media, the education system and organised religion, together with other institutions which are concerned with ideas. So the bourgeoisie distort the ideas of the proletariat by imposing 'false consciousness' upon them. Television's manipulation of the ideas of individual people is an often-considered example. Working-class people make use of this false consciousness to justify their own subordination within the capitalist system.

However, the Marxian analysis undervalues the role of the human agent. All Marxists assume that forces that are outside their control push people about. This deterministic assumption may not be correct. Marxists also have a very simplistic notion of 'representation' contained within the notion of ideology. As I have suggested, in the Marxian analysis, working-class people have their ideas and worldview manipulated. The bourgeoisie are said to be capable of taking any object or idea and giving it a new representation or meaning in the minds of the working class. This new representation is supportive of capitalism, justifies the position of the bourgeoisie and legitimises the exploitation of the working class. The problem here is that Marxists do not explain how this happens. What goes on, at a cognitive level, inside the mind of a working-class person for them to reject their own economic interests so fully and totally? How can the 'agency' – the ability to make decisions in our own interests for our own reasons – of working-class people be so completely destroyed without their revolutionary potential not also being destroyed?

The term 'dominant ideology' could mean at least two very different things. On the one hand, the term suggests that there is one ideology that all people accept because it is imposed upon everybody. In contrast, the term could equally mean that there is one dominant ideology and any number of non-dominant ideologies. The suggestion here is that any group of like-minded people could construct a set of ideas and beliefs in opposition to the dominant belief system. As we shall see in Chapter 6, the construction of new ideologies is one of the key activities of new social movements.

In summary, the Marxian analysis of ideology contains a very simplistic view of 'representation'. Representation is concerned with how something we see or hear reminds us of something else: for example a heart shape may remind a person of love and romance, while a smile is a representation of happiness. These are issues of 'cognition', meaning that something happens inside our brain (the process of cognition) which suggests that we think about a person, place or thing when a representation of it presents itself to us. In the Marxian analysis of ideology, people have their ideas manipulated. This means that the bourgeoisie are able to redefine meaning for us. The bourgeoisie are said to be capable of taking any object, idea or belief and substituting a new representation in our consciousness, a representation that supports capitalism, is against our own interests, and legitimises both the position of the bourgeoisie and the exploitation of the working class.

How can the bourgeoisie intervene in the processes of cognition, substituting representations and planting new meanings in our heads?

Activity

Below are a number of evaluative statements about the Marxian concept of ideology. Briefly explain if you agree or disagree with the comment and state at least one reason why.

Evaluative statement	Agree	Disagree	Reason
1 The concept explains why a revolutionary working class has not emerged within capitalist society.			
2 The structure of the argument is 'functionalist' in nature.			
3 The argument places too much emphasis on shared values and beliefs.			
4 There is an overemphasis upon class interests.			
5 It is not clear if the bourgeoisie accept the dominant ideology or simply impose a set of known false beliefs upon the proletariat.			

Marxism: modernist perspectives

For Ralph Miliband (1974), there is a coherent, well organised capitalist class, who hold top positions in both industry and the state, most of whom were privately educated before going to Oxbridge. These privileged individuals use the state as an **instrument** for continued bourgeois domination.

In contrast, Nicos Poulantzas (1973) argues that the class background of individuals in top state positions is unimportant. The structure of society is capitalist, and the role of the state is to maintain that structure. The state must have a high degree of autonomy, or independence, from individual capitalists in order to choose effectively between the competing demands for state action by different capitalists. In other words, the state is always functional to the needs of capital, even though individual members of top state institutions do not come from a top class background.

Antonio Gramsci (1957) rejected the economic determinism contained in the type of argument that Poulantzas is putting forward. Writing from his prison cell in the 1930s, Gramsci made a distinction between two parts of the state:

o **political society**, which contained all the repressive state institutions, such as the police and the army; and

o **civil society**, which contained all the institutions, such as the mass media, which attempt to manipulate our ideas.

The state rules by consent although it has the ability to use force if necessary. However, the state would always prefer to use negotiating skills to produce a compromise. The state attempts to form a historic bloc, which involves making compromises with different groups, in an effort to maintain solidarity. Consent is maintained by **hegemony**, a body of ideas which becomes part of our consciousness and which we accept as right. Capitalism can only be overthrown by challenging and reformulating hegemony and establishing a new historic bloc.

David Coates (1984) has built upon this analysis by Gramsci, and suggests that the state must make compromises with various bodies both at home and overseas. New forms of ideology have to be created in an effort to maintain legitimacy; Thatcherism may be an example. Thatcherism was populist: it attempted to appeal to the people by identifying similarities between key elements of common sense and Thatcherite ideology.

Abercrombie, Turner and Hill (1980) reject approaches that overemphasise the ideological aspects of state power. There are numerous studies, claims Abercrombie, which show that working-class individuals reject a dominant ideology. Paul Willis's study *Learning to Labour* (1977), for example, shows how a group of working-class 'lads' attempt to import masculine shop-floor culture into the classroom in an effort to reject the dominant ideas that the teaching staff attempt to impose. Abercrombie and his colleagues argue that it is economic factors such as fear of unemployment that form the key factor in maintaining the structure of inequality within capitalism: many people fear to rebel, as this might result in the loss of their job.

Marx on ideology

For Marx the relationship between a person's economic interests and attitudes could be one of two types:

o A person could have 'true' consciousness – this is where a person is aware of their economic interests, and their attitudes support those interests. An example is a factory owner guided by their own interests, such as the need to make profits.

o   A person could have a 'false' consciousness – the person is unaware of their economic interests and therefore may hold views that contradict their true interests: for example working-class people who are hostile to the trade union movement.

The Frankfurt School

The scholars who made up the Frankfurt School were all directly associated with the Frankfurt Institute of Social Research: Theodor W. Adorno, Walter Benjamin, Herbert Marcuse, Max Horkheimer and, later, Jürgen Habermas. The school accepted the central assumptions of the Marxian analysis, but wanted to reconcile Marxist theory to the changed economic and political conditions of the twentieth century. The work of the school became known as 'Critical Theory'.

Critical Theory was one of the most significant developments in Marxian theorising. The Frankfurt School adopted an interdisciplinary approach to understand the 'industrialisation' of culture, claiming that culture was becoming commodified, standardised and massified. In *The Jargon of Authenticity*, Adorno explains that within capitalist societies, language, in the form of 'jargon', is a key factor in maintaining the class division. By 'talking down' to people in an effort to humiliate them and raise our own standing, we manipulate language to further the needs of capitalism.

If we are to create a more open and equal society this problem of communication has to be overcome. People should be able to open their minds, become receptive to new perspectives on the world and communicate their own personal truths. For this to happen we need to break down the structures and institutions of what became for the Frankfurt School the 'culture industry', which propagated and maintained capitalist ideology through stereotypes, advertisements and lies. It was by manipulation of the culture industry that the Nazis were able to make their inhuman programme appear reasonable.

However, it is easier to outline the notions of culture that the school reject. They did agree that artistic culture should be regarded as something more than simply the reflection of class interests. For the director of the school, Max Horkheimer, culture originated in the organisational basis of society. The Marxist approach – which regarded culture as something that simply emerged from the economic base – was rejected as too simplistic. In *The Eclipse of Reason* Horkheimer argues that in modern society *reason* came to be defined as **rationality**. Moreover, we have moved away from the use of 'objective' reason, which places a great deal of emphasis on the search for right or wrong by reference to universal truth, and towards 'subjective' reason in which the personal, unsubstantiated opinions of the individual and the situation they are in are given greater emphasis. Subjective reason makes it difficult for people to identify and remove delusions. Therefore, we need 'critique' to maintain our freedom and safety.

The Frankfurt School believed it was important to develop a sociology of 'mass culture', in order to fully understand the changes that had taken place since the 1930s, such as:

o   the emergence of the 'mass media';
o   the emergence of an entertainment industry;
o   the manipulation of culture by the Nazis.

All these factors pointed to significant changes in patterns of culture. The school focused on assessing how ideas were transmitted by the culture industry, and how this influenced our personal and private life. Horkheimer and Adorno rejected the idea that 'culture' could arise spontaneously from the masses. Culture was not something which emerged from the demands of people: it was brought about by manipulation. Local and folk cultures are destroyed in this process. The culture industry, via commercial entertainment, aims to gain an attentive but passive welcome from the masses. The culture industry reproduces and reinforces the dominant interpretations of reality. At the same time the audience responses are standardised, as each product contains cues as to the appropriate response, for example 'canned' laughter to induce laughter from the audience. The culture industry was said to prevent individual people from developing into independent individuals capable of critical thought. The media develops a state of dependence and weakness, which helps to reinforce the status quo. David Held (1980) gives the following summary of one of the leading figures in the school, Herbert Marcuse on the culture industry. 'The development of mass culture', he wrote:

o   establishes a (false) harmony between public and private interests
o   reinforces privatisation and consumption orientations
o   spreads an advertising aesthetic
o   undermines indigenous working class culture
o   increases the domination of instrumental reason, and
o   manipulates sexuality – leading to general pursuit of false and limited wants and needs. (Held, 1980: 108)

The Frankfurt School argued that the culture industry has a significant effect upon the formation of our identity. Again Marcuse suggests that the individual, as understood by Freud, is likely to become extinct. According to Held this is because:

o   severe limits are placed on ego development
o   there is a decline of the position of the father
o   individuals do not develop an autonomous conscience
o   values and prohibitions become less central to the individual's concerns and reflections
o   there is a transference of the ego ideal to a group ideal – now itself being undermined
o   repressive desublimation reinforces social control. (Held, 1980: 138)

Walter Benjamin

Benjamin (1892–1940) expressed his dislike of the concept of a 'system' and was critical of the distinction between 'high' culture and 'low' culture. In his critical sociology he developed Marx's conception of ideology into a theory of aesthetics and mass culture. He argued in contrast to many in the Frankfurt School, that the aesthetic imagination, could be both a critical and a liberating faculty, if one could overcome ideological and utopian thinking. Art was created in a specific period and under social pressures and Benjamin attempted to understand these relations of artistic production.

In summary, the early Frankfurt School argued that the function of the culture industry was to legitimise capitalist society by ideological means.

Jürgen Habermas

Habermas (1929–present) was not a contemporary of the other members of the Frankfurt School, but he is included in the school of thought because his work continues its critique. Taking his starting point from Weber's (1922) theory of rationalisation, Habermas argues that the **life-world** or **the world of lived experience** – the taken for granted world of everyday common sense – is in danger of being destroyed by the rational economic and bureaucratic systems within modernity which destroy local cultures.

Weber discussed 'rationalisation' in three contexts:

o   'ongoing rationalisation' as the dominant cultural trend in the West, as part of his philosophy of history;

o   the rationality of his ideal-type, as part of his scientific method/ philosophy of science;

o   as representing the 'disenchantment' of life and its devaluation, in the sense of substituting purely technical, instrumentalism for value-oriented conduct, as part of his philosophy of life. In other words, as part of a moral critique.

What Habermas has to say relates to the first and the third contexts. Rationalisation is the motive force behind bureaucracy; and Weber's conception of 'rational legal authority' is an example of what society would be like if rationalisation, as a process, was taken to its extreme.

Weber's discussion of rationalisation is rife with value judgements about what constitutes 'the good life'.

According to Habermas:

Rationalization means, first of all, the extension of the areas of society to the criteria of rational decision. Secondly, social labour is industrialized, with the result that criteria of instrumental action also penetrate into other areas of life (urbanization of the mode of life, technification of transport and communication). Both trends exemplify the type of purposive-rational action, which refers to either the organization of means or choice between alternatives. Planning can be regarded as purposive-rational action of the second order. Moreover the progressive 'rationalization' of society is linked to the institutionalization of scientific and technical developments. (Habermas, 1971: 87)

The predominant concept in Weber's *Weltanschauung* (world philosophy) is rationalisation, which he saw as far reaching and accelerating. Rationalisation signified the fundamental character of the occidental style of life. As Dennis Wrong explains:

> By 'rationalization' Weber meant the process by which explicit, abstract, intellectually calculable rules and procedures are increasingly substituted for sentiment, tradition, and rule of thumb in all spheres of activity. Rationalization leads to the displacement of religion by specialized science as the major source of intellectual authority; the substitution of the trained expert for the cultivated man of letters; the ousting of the skilled handworker by machine technology; the replacement of traditional judicial wisdom by abstract, systematic statutory codes. Rationalization demystifies and instrumentalizes. (Wrong, 1970: 26)

Rationalisation is the product of the scientific specialisation and technical differentiation peculiar to Western culture. According to Freud it is the organisation of life by the division of, and coordination of, activities on the basis of an exact study of people's relations with each other, with their tools and their environment, for the purpose of achieving greater efficiency and productivity. Weber also described rationalisation as a striving for perfection, an ingenious redefinement of the conduct of life and the attainment of increasing mastery over the external world. The development of rationalisation instrumentalises life: everything can be calculated and appropriated. Weber analysed the evolution of rationalisation in all areas of human activity – religion, law, art, science, politics and economics. Increasing rationalisation is far from representing progress; although it is based on scientific techniques, it cannot be said to constitute an advance in knowledge in the sense of a better understanding of our way of living. As Weber explained in 'Science as a vocation':

> Does it mean that we, today, for instance, everyone sitting in this hall, have a greater knowledge of the conditions of life under which we exist than has an American Indian or a Hottentot? Hardly. Unless he is a physicist, one who rides on a streetcar has no idea how the car happened to get into motion. And he does not need to know. He is satisfied that he may 'count' on the behaviour of the street car, and he orients his conduct according to this expectation; but he knows nothing about what it takes to produce such a car so that it can move. The savage knows incomparably more about his tools. When we spend money today I bet that even if there are colleagues of political economy here in the hall, almost every one of them will hold a different answer in readiness to the questions How does it happen that one can buy something for money – sometimes more and sometimes less? The savage knows what he does in order to get his daily food and which institutions serve him in this pursuit. The increasing

intellectualization and rationalization do *not*, therefore, indicate an increased and general knowledge of the condition under which one lives.

It means something else, namely, the knowledge or belief that if one but wished one could learn it at any time. Hence, it means that principally there are no mysterious incalculable forces that come into play but rather that one can, in principle, master all things by calculation. This means that the world is disenchanted. (Weber, 1918: 139)

For Weber then, the techniques and social structures created by and originally expressing our rationality and mastery of the environment become a self-maintaining process no longer dependent on the rationality that created them but actually stunting and constricting the rational capacities of the people they dominate. Habermas (1975) takes this point further; it would be an even more grievous error to believe that rationalisation brings reason in its train, in the sense not only of enlightenment but also of individual or collective moral progress. Reality has become dreary and flat – as a direct result of the ongoing rationalisation process – leaving a great void in the souls of people that they seek to fill by furious activity and through various devices and substitutes.

Weber sought to elucidate the historical foundations of rationalisation, and to show how historically it may assume different forms. He saw rationalisation as the basis of the distinction between capitalism and traditional society. These are 'types' which are based on two different 'spirits', modern capitalism being a great complex of interrelated institutions based on rational rather than speculative 'types' of economic pursuit. It is with the advent of modern capitalism, and its essential element of bureaucratisation, that we find the 'legal' form of business corporation. These are based on long-range capital investment, a planned division of labour that is voluntary in supply and a similar 'division of labour' of production functions, and they exist in a market economy.

Weber identifies the following as capitalism's 'value relevant' characteristics of the modern productive institutions of capitalism: a rationalistic spirit or economic ethic (as outlined in *The Protestant Ethic and the Spirit of Capitalism*), and the apparent indispensability of this spirit as well as rationalisation of the conduct of life in general which involves a specific form of calculable activity. These factors can be described as being 'formally' rational in nature.

Although it could be claimed that rationalisation was significant for Weber because it was the major factor contrasting modern society with traditional society, we could argue that he was interested in it because he was also concerned with its effects upon human existence and dignity. Weber was critical of formal rationality as an end in itself, especially calculability becoming both the standard of achievement and the criterion for defining what is problematic. This perhaps is Weber's 'point of departure' for his discussion of bureaucracy.

From Weber's point of view as a 'scientist of society', formal rationality is synonymous with capitalist rationality, the motivating force being the pursuit of forever renewed profit as an end in itself, but not itself a value.

For Habermas, this rationalisation process with its bureaucratic structures and formal rule-based systems is changing the process of social
integration – our everyday assumptions and the beliefs we share that
intertwine to form the relations and communications between members of
a social community: how people bond together into communities, local
processes of socialisation, ways of informally teaching children and young
people the culture and other informal rules about living within a community. In other words, all forms of locally produced culture are becoming
incorporated within a universal rational process. This is what Habermas
terms the 'colonisation of the lifeworld'. The process of rationalisation
significantly undermines people's quality of life. The impact of this
'colonisation of the lifeworld' can be resolved only if people are able and
willing to establish a 'public sphere', to listen and talk to each other in
what Habermas termed the ideal speech situation – a form of shared
communication between people who want to resolve their differences.

Douglas Kellner (1997) has made some critical comments about the
position of the Frankfurt School:

o   The school made a number of assumptions about the rigid distinction
    between high culture and low culture: such a distinction is blurred.
o   The school argued that only high culture can be critical, subversive
    and emancipatory: popular mass culture can also have critical
    moments.
o   The school assumed that all popular culture is ideological in nature.
o   The school did not take into account that audiences can produce their
    own meanings of the products of the culture industry; the audience is
    not totally passive.

British cultural studies

From the early post-war period to the present day, a group of British writers
from Richard Hoggart (1957) to Raymond Williams and the Centre for
Contemporary Cultural Studies at the University of Birmingham (CCCS)
have attempted to develop an understanding of culture. British cultural
studies rejects the elitism of the Frankfurt School and in particular their
distinction between **high culture** and **popular culture**. Richard
Hoggart, who also rejected the Marxian approach, argued that Marx had

> A middle class Marxist's view of the working classes . . . He pities the betrayed
> and debased worker, whose faults he sees as almost entirely the result of the
> grinding system which controls him. He admires the remnants of the noble
> savage . . . Usually, he succeeds in part-pitying and part-patronising working-class
> people beyond any semblance of reality. (Hoggart, 1957: 16)

Hoggart described the Hunslet area of Leeds without over-romanticising it,
but pointed out that the territory was mapped and familiar to residents. He

argued that since working-class communites grew up around industry, people living and working closely together formed strong social bonds and had a distinct sense of social solidarity. As well as sharing leisure pursuits, cultural groups celebrated rituals and festivals, many rooted in their shared experience of work. This culture was passed on by singing in clubs and other rituals. The culture of Hunslet was based on the belief in 'us' and 'them', with 'us' being the working-class community and 'them' the 'hegemonic leadership': '"Them" is a composite dramatic figure, the chief characteristic in modern urban forms of the rural peasant–big-house relationships. The world of them is the world of the bosses' (Hoggart, 1957: 62).

Hoggart's model presents the Hunslet residents as passive and receptive to the culture they found themselves in, and he saw the working-class culture he described in the 1950s as disappearing because of the 'interplay' of material improvement and cultural loss, and the effect of popular culture. Free from hardship, people no longer needed the security that loyal membership of working-class groups once gave:

> No doubt many of the old barriers of class should be broken down. But at present the older more narrow but also more genuine class culture is being eroded in favour of mass opinion, the mass recreational product and the generalised emotional response . . . The old forms of class culture are in danger of being replaced by a poorer kind of classless . . . 'faceless', culture, and this is to be regretted. (Hoggart, 1957: 280)

The community Hoggart described now no longer exists: it was razed to the ground to make way for the M621 motorway.

Unlike Hoggart, Raymond Williams believed that popular culture had an active and critical audience who could evaluate everything from sporting events to film. However, drawing upon Gramsci's notion of hegemony, he still argued that culture was used to reproduce capitalist society and induce consent.

This approach was built upon by Stuart Hall, who argued that with the transformation of traditional society into modern society new communities emerged which developed their own identity in ideas, religion, symbols, views of the art and traditions: for example the French national identity developed from the 1789 Revolution which overthrew the old regime and rejected the monarchy, whereas the British monarchy is a national symbol. Hall and the others at the CCCS distanced themselves from the traditional Marxian approach to ideology, on the grounds that it was too deterministic.

In place of ideology Hall and his colleagues put forward the notion of the 'relative autonomy' of the superstructure, which allowed young people in particular to develop their own forms of **cultural resistance** to authority. One of the many interesting books that came out of the CCCS was Dick Hebdige's *Subculture: The Meaning of Style* (1979) which made use of semiological concepts to *read* youth subcultures as a form of resistance, from Teddy boys in the 1950s to punks in the late 1970s. These groups, although radically different in the styles that they adopted, were concerned with the same thing: showing their contempt for authority and capitalist ideology by developing forms of resistance in the form of loud music with radical lyrics, styles of dress and aggressive behaviour. Youth culture was then a deliberate resistance to capitalist ideology. However, there were problems with the CCCS's position on youth culture. If youth culture is a form of resistance to capitalist ideology, how do we theorise conflict between working-class youths, such as mods and rockers? In addition, the CCCS tended to ignore middle-class youth cultures. Overall the CCCS did not look at youth culture from the point of view of the youths who were actually involved in the youth culture. Many young people did not see youth culture as a form of resistance to capitalism, rather it was simply about having a good time.

In the 1980s Stuart Hall developed the 'New Times' thesis, which was a sign of a loss of confidence in Marxism and the growing significance of **post-Fordism**. Hall saw Thatcherism as 'authoritarian populism', where Thatcher recreated common sense in the minds of the working class by the use of 'hegemonic messages'.

Post-Fordism

o   a shift to new 'information technologies';
o   the emergence of a more flexible, specialised and decentralised labour force, together with a decline of the old manufacturing base and of sunrise, computer-based, hi-tech industries;
o   a contracting-out of functions and services hitherto provided 'in house' on a corporate basis;
o   a leading role for consumption and a greater emphasis on choice and product differentiation, on marketing, packaging and design, on the 'targeting' of consumers by lifestyle, taste and culture;
o   a decline in the proportion of the skilled, male manual working class and a corresponding rise of the service and white collar class;
o   more flexi-time and part-time working, coupled with feminisation and ethnicisation of the workforce;
o   a new international division of labour and an economy dominated by multinationals;
o   globalisation of the new financial markets;
o   an emergence of new patterns of social division – especially between 'public' and 'private' sectors and between the 'new poor' and under-class of the one third that is left behind. (Adapted from Ashley, 1997: 95–6)

In the 1990s Stuart Hall, in particular, moved away from what he saw as increasingly redundant Marxian concepts towards concerns with identity which have a more postmodern feel to them. In 'New ethnicities' (1992) he argues that the notion of 'black' is now uncertain. Black politics in the 1970s and 1980s was based upon the notion of an essential black subject, or fixed black identity. However, there are significant differences within the black community in ethnic background, religion and culture, and significant political differences between 'black' people, based upon these. This deconstruction of the category 'black' has generated substantial literature which points out that although racism is based upon skin colour, 'racial formations' or the 'process of racialization' should include factors such as religion and nationality.

A number of people have attempted to save the Marxian analysis. Raymond Williams, for example, argued that within the Marxian analysis individual people were responsible for producing culture, but to remain within a Marxian framework he still had to make comments such as this:

> At one level, 'popular culture' . . . is a very complex combination of residual, self-made and externally produced elements, with important internal conflicts between these. At another level, and increasingly, this 'popular' culture is a major area of bourgeois and ruling-class cultural production, moving towards an offered 'universality' in the modern communications institutions. (Williams, 1981: 228)

In other words, people have an active role to play in culture, even popular culture, but underneath it all people are pushed about and have the ideas inside their heads manipulated by the capitalist media.

Activity

Ideology is an interesting concept but how do we gather information about it? Is the notion of ideology something which we can discover in everyday life? Read the polemic below about the Glasgow University Media Group and come to some conclusions about the empirical usefulness of the concept of ideology.

An evaluation of the Glasgow University Media Group

For over twenty-five years the Glasgow University Media Group have argued that both BBC News and ITN cannot refrain from editorialising and fall short of their legal obligation to present political and industrial news in a balanced, neutral and objective fashion. They argue that television news:

o   does not reflect the full range of views;
o   is undemocratic in its choice of who is allowed to speak;
o   defies notions of accuracy and impartiality.

The Group argued that: 'the dominant ideology works in the production of television news' (GUMG, 1980: 497). In addition, the Group made a clear distinction between the distorted false consciousnesses generated by the media and the independent reality of events found in true consciousness: 'Our argument in *Bad News* Volume 1 of this study was that routine news practices led to the production of bad news. For example, viewers were given a misleading portrayal of industrial disputes in the UK when measured against the independent reality of events' (GUMG, 1980: xiii).

One of the key problems with the Group's research is concerned with the manner in which they gather the data for their arguments. The group rejected conspiracy theories of the media; instead they have always argued that *news* was 'structured and organised' by 'taken for granted professional routines' of journalists. Their initial research made use of content analysis in an effort to identify and measure ideology and its consequences. John Eldridge has strongly supported the use of the content analysis by the Group. Eldridge (1995) argues that content analysis is a methodologically unobtrusive measure, which can be used to analyse data without influencing what is produced.

However, there are issues about how the Group define and measure ideology and if conceptual and methodological devices the Group used can support their conclusions. When asked to explain what the Glasgow University Media Group understood by ideology Greg Philo and David Miller recently explained: 'We define ideology as social perspectives or ways of understanding which are linked to class or other interests'. Their work does not simply reproduce the Marxian conception of ideology: 'Our studies have gone a long way beyond traditional models of the Bourgeoisie and the Exploited classes . . . We have been centrally concerned with the role of media in the mass production of misunderstanding and ignorance . . . We have also shown how the media do have a role in the legitimisation of powerful interests and how ideologies can actually work to convince populations' (Philo and Miller, 2001: 17). Philo and Miller also argue that the content analysis can be used effectively to describe and measure ideology.

Content analysis

Positivists, such as the Glasgow University Media Group, who use content analysis, assume that numbers and number systems have a logic and meaning. Positivists also assume that human behaviour has a logic and meaning. Most importantly, the assumption is that the logic and meaning of number systems can be applied to human behaviour in order to fully describe and explain it in a way that non-positivists never could.

The Glasgow University Media Group's content analysis involves producing a set of analytical categories in advance, which are then objectively applied to recorded television news programmes. The information from the news programmes is fitted into the categories. The number of times each category appeared in the news programmes is counted and the numerical quantification is said to reveal the true meaning of the news.

In 1982 the Group argued:

> Public broadcasting . . . is committed to an ideological perspective which is founded on the view of consensus, 'one nation' and 'the community' . . . The broadcasters attempt to relay ideas which are already more or less present and interpret them for what they mistakenly see as a 'mass audience'. (GUMG, 1982: 134)

The important question here is: how did the Group get from the numerical quantification of the content analysis to that conclusion? Similarly, Eldridge has argued: 'But we did suggest that unspoken, unacknowledged assumptions, practices or perspectives help to constitute what *Goffman* had called the "primary framework", whereby news talk becomes meaningful' (Eldridge, 1995: 22).

The question here is: how can content analysis capture this?

In his discussion of media institutions and journalists Greg Philo claims that 'the routine working practices of journalists are informed by class assumptions of the society in which they live' (Philo, 1995: 181). And: 'They usually wish to claim that their reportage is accurate and trustworthy, although as we show in the case studies of our original work the unconscious political assumptions which they hold produce selection and distortion which often invalidate these claims' (1995: 182).

Apart from the obvious objection that the production of news and current affairs programmes is not performed in an 'unconscious' fashion, content analysis cannot measure such things as 'unconscious political assumptions'. What is happening here is the imposition of an analysis rather than the objective discovery of data. The Group simply present a set of complex-looking numbers to enhance the appearance of their arguments, which were formed and well rehearsed in advance of the data collection. The analytical categories were also defined in advance of data collection and were then used as evidence to support a theory that was already in the minds of the Group. The content analysis was never more than a projective test to reinforce the researchers' own analysis.

In addition, content analysis can never tell us anything about 'the mass production of misunderstanding and ignorance' because it can tell us nothing about how the audience consume the meaning of the *news*. Again as Eldridge makes clear in his discussion of the findings of the Group: 'This does not imply that television viewers interpret the news in the same way' (Eldridge, 1995: 22).

In response to the argument that they are simply propagating the myth of the passive viewer, the Group gave the unconvincing response that: 'The argument outlined above is nothing more than a restatement of the classic reinforcement view' (GUMG, 1980: 140). However, they continued to assume that media audiences passively accept often-repeated messages with no justification.

Even if we accept the Group's argument that *news* was 'structured and organised' by 'taken for granted professional routines' of journalists, what Philo and the Group need to do is to explain why their perspective of news events is superior to that of the journalistic accounts. Ironically, in support of their arguments the group regularly make use of what they consider to be authoritative news sources such as the *FT* or *Management Today*. Surprisingly, although the Group spend a great deal of time telling their readers what is *news* and what is *not news*, what is *due impartiality* and what is *distortion*, they shy away from placing the truth at the centre of their analysis.

The Group develop a critique of postmodernism that is clearly outlined in *Message Received* (1999) edited by Greg Philo. In this volume Greg Philo argues:

> much of this subject area (and much else in social science) has lost the ability to engage critically with the society in which it exists and has drifted into irrelevance. We argue that this was in part the result of the growth of post-modernist approaches and the adoption of their inadequate philosophical assumptions about the relationship between language and reality. The most important assumption here has been that the 'real' world is understood through language, but because language changes its meaning in use (and between cultures and groups) therefore 'reality' also changes and is never absolutely defined or agreed upon.
>
> Within the post-modern vision, there can be no agreed reality or 'facts' because meanings are not fixed but are re-negotiated in the constant interplay of the reader and the text. (Philo, 1999: ix)

Here Philo is assuming that there is an objective reality which can be grasped by a 'true' consciousness and is also objecting to the argument that audiences are proactive in their consumption of media texts. Not only do members of the Glasgow University Media Group – including Greg Philo himself – regularly argue against the idea of a 'true' consciousness and the idea of a passive audience. Most importantly, for his critical comments about postmodernist positions, Greg Philo and the Group have a tendency to 'drift off into the mists of relativism'. At the centre of their analysis is the Deleuzian notion of the rhizome – the assumption that no account of the world is superior or inferior to any other conception of the world. The only reason why the work of the Group has any critical edge to it is because of these postmodern assumptions. (For a full discussion of Deleuze and other key postmodernists see Chapter 6.) As Philo explains:

> Reality is not, therefore, something which is simply 'out there' waiting to be measured – a neutral set of 'facts'. Rather, what can be seen in the reality depends in part upon assumptions that are held of what the reality is, and of what are the relations which produce it as it is. (Philo, 1990: 229)

The Group argue that due impartiality is impossible to achieve, and criticise both BBC News and ITN for not achieving it:

> We find it difficult, indeed unhelpful, to assign labels like 'objective', 'impartial' or 'neutral' to such a manufactured product. (GUMG, 1985: 237)

> [We] . . . realise the inadequacies of using a term like bias, as though there were a wholly objective account of the world that can be reported on a news bulletin instead of different ways of constructing the account. (Eldridge, 1995: 13)

Apart from the obvious embracing of full-blown postmodernism by Greg Philo and other members of the Group, content analysis is an inappropriate research method for reading ideologies; this probably explains why the Group initially supplemented it with more semiological and thematic approaches and eventually moved away from gathering empirical data by research methods, opting instead for producing political tracts from a distinctly 'Old Labour' perspective which relied on print and broadcasting products that the Group approved of: *Panorama*, *Dispatches*, *The Observer*, *The Guardian*, *Marketing Week*. For an example of this 'newspaper/ political campaigning' approach and the drift of the Group away from their token attempt at empirical research and into mere speculation, see Philo's 'Television, politics and the rise of the New Right' (Philo, 1995: 198–233).

In *More Bad News* (1980) the Group did make a brief defence of content analysis, including a claim that it can be used to make empirically valid statements about the process of news production and ideology. The Group argue: 'It has been a basic contention of our approach that the detailed examination of the output of television journalism can be used to demonstrate its ideology and practices' (GUMG, 1980: 407).

How is this possible? The justification of the Group is that 'Since the output clearly has meaning, then the production of that meaning can be as clearly studied on the screen as it can be by interviewing either producers or audiences' (GUMG, 1980: 409).

There are several problems with this argument. The Group assume that any text has only one meaning for an audience. In other words, the Group mistakenly see a 'mass audience' in the same way as the journalists they accuse. Moreover, the Group assume that the reading of the audience is one and the same as the imposed reading of the Group, which is clearly not the case. Some of the assumptions that the Group make about the process of news production, such as the key role played by 'unconscious political assumptions', cannot be studied either by content analysis or interviewing, but can only be inferred from responses. The meaning of the output generated by the content analysis is dependent upon the analytical categories used in the process of data collection. These categories merely reproduce news output in a form that mirrors the prejudices of the researchers. Again, meaning is inferred and imposed but never discovered by the Group.

What is a thematic analysis?

Throughout their work the Group make unjustified assumptions about the enduring nature of class and class cultures. In the later books this approach – of imposing a form of class analysis on the data prior to numerical quantification – was described as thematic analysis. Greg Philo sees this process as: 'A key issue . . . to show the meaning of individual words or statements in their specific contexts' (Philo, 1990: 167).

Setting the context as one of enduring class structures and cultures is simply the imposition of class analysis by fiat. On the whole this class-based assumption of the relationship between class interests and belief is shared by all members of the Group, but not always by Greg Philo. In *Seeing and Believing* he argues: 'But class experience was not synonymous with political belief' (Philo, 1990: 153). Similarly, Philo has argued: 'Firstly, the beliefs of an individual are not a single coherent entity derived in a linear fashion from one aspect of their class position' (1990: 185).

Greg Philo is unclear and uncertain about the relationship between truth, class and ideology.

Countering ideology

Philo (1990) does give the reader an indication of how to combat *the mass production of misunderstanding and ignorance*. Protection from ideological distortion of the media can be achieved by

- drawing upon one's direct experience;
- drawing upon direct contacts;
- drawing upon political culture;
- drawing upon our class experience;
- drawing upon processes of logic;
- drawing comparisons between different accounts (Philo, 1990: 154).

On this last point Greg Philo argues: 'A second major reason for doubting television news was the comparison of it with other sources of information, such as the "quality" and local press or "alternative" current affairs programmes and radio' (1990: 150). This raises the question of why Philo holds some journalistic accounts in such high regard, but not BBC and ITN accounts. The basis of this privileged positioning of some accounts needs some justification. In addition, he seems to be suggesting that people who read the same quality and local press, watch the same Channel Four documentaries, share the same friends, political culture and logic as Greg Philo are liberated from ideology. Greg may be a legend in his own mind, but the rest of us would like to see some explanation of how he claims to have knowledge that the rest of us do not possess and to be able to adjudicate between competing cognitive claims. How does he justify his claim to hold such a position of epistemological privilege?

Conclusions

The Glasgow University Media Group do not pose interesting questions because they have their answers in advance. Greg Philo has no concept of ideology. Ideology is merely news and views that he disagrees with. The whole argument of the Group is wrapped up in a romantic package about what life was like before the New Right. One of the reasons why many people have embraced post-modern ideas is because of the total and complete intellectual collapse of Marxism as the basis of an explanatory framework for anything.

Eldridge, J. (ed.) (1995) *Glasgow University Media Group Reader Vol. 1: News content, language and visuals*. Routledge: London.

Glasgow University Media Group (1976) *Bad News*, foreword by Richard Hoggart. Routledge: London.

Glasgow University Media Group (1980) *More Bad News*. Routledge: London.

Philo, G. (1990) *Seeing and Believing: The Influence of Television*. Routledge: London.

Philo, G. (ed.) (1995) *Glasgow University Media Group Reader Vol. 2: Industry, Economy, War and Politics*. Routledge: London.

Philo, G. (1999) *Message Received: Glasgow University Media Group Research, 1993–1998*. Longman: Harlow.

Philo, G. and Miller, D. (2001) 'Market killing: a reply to Shaun Best', *Social Science Teacher*, 31 (1): 17.

Baudrillard, postmodernity and Marxism

Jean Baudrillard (1929–present) is a postmodernist who is critical of all forms of 'enlightenment' thinking – Marxism and Critical Theory. He rejects all epistemology (theories which attempt to answer the question, 'How do we know what we know?'), all truth claims and *a priori* concepts (concepts which are true for all time). All of the theories mentioned are based upon 'metanarratives' or 'foundations', which are used by their authors and followers to distinguish between 'the truth' and various forms of non-truth, notably ideology.

The postmodern condition casts doubt upon all grand narratives, and as such all the key assumptions of Marxism are brought into question. Enlightenment values – especially claims to have found 'the truth' – are seen by Baudrillard as a source of error and evil. The special place that Marx gave to labour power and that other thinkers, notably Weber, give to rationality as a foundation of truth he sees as themselves without foundation.

Jean Baudrillard has argued that imagery has evolved through a number of stages, over the course of history:

o   Initially, any sign once stood for a truth, for example a pain in the chest could be a sign of heart disease.

o   In the nineteenth century with the development of Marxism, signs began to be seen as concealing or deliberately distorting the truth: the Marxian conception of ideology.

o   As we moved into the twentieth century, signs then became seen as masking the absence of the truth: this is the idea that style is used to make up for the lack of substance.

o   Finally, in the contemporary world, we believe that there is no link between an image and truth: in other words, in the postmodern condition there is no representation, what you see is what there is. The image is real.

For Baudrillard, reality is a human creation made by media products and our feedback of these products, for example our feedback on what we have seen on television. Our values are created by consumer demand that is itself influenced by an endless rotation of interpretations, reflections and advertising codes. There is no clear division, and no objective criteria that can be used to distinguish between what is true and what is ideological. It is no longer possible to state the difference between what is seen on television, and the world it is meant to represent. As we shall see below, there are similarities between what Baudrillard suggests and what Rorty (1998) suggests is the nature of truth.

In *The Mirror of Production* (1973) Baudrillard casts doubt upon the Marxian distinction outlined above, between 'use value' and 'exchange value'. In Baudrillard's opinion, 'use value' is seen by Marxists as based upon genuine need, whereas 'exchange value' is brought about by capitalists distorting the consciousness of the population by ideology and alienation. By alienation, Marx means that as individual people we are essentially creative in nature; however, within capitalism work is dull and boring to such a degree that we are unable to express our creativity. In contrast, in a socialist society people would work for the common good. Making use of Marxian concepts we could say that a socialist society is based upon the principle, 'from each according to his ability, to each according to his needs'. In other words, solely taking care of our 'use values' would satisfy all our needs. For the Marxist, the concepts of 'value' and 'labour' are non-negotiable: they cannot be questioned, and they are essential for any analysis of the world.

In contrast, for Baudrillard genuine need is impossible to identify, without taking into account how our needs are manipulated, explained and even created by the mass media. It is at this point that Baudrillard introduces us to his concept of **simulacra**, which is explained by David Ashley as follows:

> In the same year [1992], the line between image and reality became so confused that TV viewers were able to watch a sitcom character ('Murphy Brown') pose as a real journalist criticising an allegedly real vice president (Dan Quayle) for condemning her fictional pregnancy. (The baby's TV shower was, of course, attended by 'real' reporters.) Viewers were subsequently treated to the spectacle of Quayle discussing with 'real' journalists Murphy Brown's criticism of him as if this attack had been launched by a real newswoman on a real news show. Needless to say, the vice president's increasingly bizarre behaviour – which included persistent attempts to send flowers to a character he seemed not to understand was fictional – was itself covered as a major news event about which the public needed to be kept fully informed. (Ashley, 1997: 27)

Thus, people make use of the media, both fictional and news programmes, not only to make sense of the world but also to give their own views, beliefs and feelings enhanced validity. Baudrillard uses the term **hyper-reality** when he discusses the simulacra.

Baudrillard's argument rests upon three points:

o The truth is an 'unreal' creation and the search for the truth by Marxists and others doomed to fail.
o All arguments are ideological and distorted; there can be no rational argument, because all ways of thinking, including rationality, are ideological in nature.
o There is no truth.
o There is no distinction between the 'real' and the 'unreal' or ideo-logical.

By way of criticism however, we could argue that Baudrillard's argument purports to be a correct explanation of what goes on in the world. He appears to offer what his analysis suggests he cannot offer: a true account! In other words, his argument is self-refuting.

Baudrillard's work has generated a very mixed response.

Activity

Take a look at the two quotes below, and give a brief account of which one you find the most convincing, and why:

(A)

Baudrillard is a first-rate diagnostician of the postmodern scene, but thoroughly inconsequent and muddled when it come to philosophising on the basis of his own observations. For it just doesn't follow from the fact that we are living through an age of widespread illusion and disinformation that *therefore* all questions of truth drop out of the picture . . . (Norris, 1990: 140)

(B)

It is no longer possible for us to see through the appearance of, for instance, a 'free market' to the structuring 'real relations' beneath (e.g. class conflict and the expropriation by capital of surplus value). Instead, signs begin increasingly to take on a life of their own referring not to a real world outside themselves but to their own reality – the system that produces the signs. (Hebdige, 1990: 141)

Post-communism

A communist society is a society that attempts to base itself upon the ideals outlined by Marx. However, contrary to the views of many Marxists, these regimes have often been seen as anti-democratic, because of their imposition of rigid state control over areas of social life.

The anti-communist rebellion started in 1989 and was most apparent in Eastern Europe. In August 1991, Latvia, Lithuania, Estonia and Georgia became independent sovereign states. Communist regimes had been overthrown in Poland, Bulgaria, Czechoslovakia, East Germany, Hungary and Romania. In addition, four of the six republics that made up Yugoslavia had non-communist governments. Communists were also falling from power in countries throughout the rest of the world: in Benin, Mongolia, Ethiopia, Mozambique, Angola and Congo, to name a few. By December 1991 the Soviet Union no longer existed. Finally, the anti-communist movement was brought to an end in China by a massacre of protesters at Tiananmen Square in Beijing on 4 June 1989, and the imposition of martial law.

Zygmunt Bauman (1992) argues that communism pushed the project of modernity to its very limits. It involved grand social engineering projects that attempted to control nature in the perceived interests of the working class. However, individuals within the communist societies wanted to share in the 'lavish consumption enjoyed under capitalists' auspices':

It was the postmodern, narcissistic culture of self-enhancement, self-enjoyment, instant gratification and life defined in terms of consumer styles that finally exposed the obsoleteness of the 'steel per head' philosophy stubbornly preached and practised under communism. (Bauman, 1992: 179)

So communism collapsed because individuals behind the Iron Curtain wanted to participate in the processes of making unhindered and highly personal lifestyle choices which people in the West enjoyed. Consumer culture brings pleasure. State socialism, in the former Soviet Union, may have pushed modern rationality to its very limits but it could never understand the pleasure of shopping!

John A. Hall (1994) argues that sociologists have 'largely failed to understand the collapse of state socialism' and he suggests that a 'variety of regimes will follow the immediate post-communist period' (1994: 538). Some post-communist societies made the break early, for example Slovenia, which also has close links with Austria and is one of the next countries most likely to gain European Union membership. The Baltic states could further develop their links with Scandinavia. These societies have managed to avoid the 'symbolic politics' of nationalism and have made a speedy transition to liberal democracy.

Most post-communist societies have so far had great difficulty constructing a constitutional political system, and have yet to develop legitimacy in legal and political rules. This lack of legitimacy creates a political vacuum. As Hall suggests: 'Civil society has not yet been born' (1994: 537).

Political vacuums tend to be highly unstable. In post-communist societies:

o   people have no fixed identity;
o   they have suffered a loss of trust in possible political arrangements;
o   lost trust shows itself in low turnout in voting, for example in Poland and Hungary;
o   people have an inability to cooperate politically.

These factors have created a democratic deficit. People's lack of trust and cooperation is so great that they are unable to generate the volition needed to build an agreed set of rules about how to organise a democratic society, with competing political parties. 'It is hard to take a venal and weak state and to turn it into a body capable of co-ordinating and co-operating with society' (Hall, 1994: 537).

This situation is made worse, claims Hall, because – except in the case of the reunification of Germany – North America and Western Europe have chosen to have little or no active involvement in the reconstruction of post-communist societies. The end result is that the political vacuum is filled by nationalism, a violent and highly emotionally charged ideology that claims that one's country is always right.

What is significant for social and political theory about the collapse of the Soviet Union and other communist societies? Most importantly, that the people who live in these countries were said to have lost faith in both socialism as a form of society and in the ability of the Marxian analysis to describe and explain the world. However, a number of writers have attempted to maintain the credibility of the Marxian analysis in the face of the postmodern condition: we shall look first at the work of Ernesto Laclau and Chantal Mouffe (1984) and then at that of Fredric Jameson (1991).

Laclau (1935–present) and Mouffe (1943–present)

Since the mid-1980s Ernesto Laclau and Chantal Mouffe have been developing a social theory which is explicitly post-Marxist in nature and which draws upon Gramscian notion of hegemony, poststructuralism and Lacanian subject theory in order to explore the question of how our social and political identity is constructed. Laclau and Mouffe reject what they call the rationalist 'dictatorship' of the Enlightenment and attempt to devise a form of postmodern theorising. This overcomes the two central problems of traditional Marxism: **epiphenomenalism** – the idea that legal, political and ideological factors are determined by the economic base; and **class reductionism** – the idea that all aspects of a person's life can be reduced to their class location. For Laclau and Mouffe neither our identity nor our values are fixed; both are constituted by reference to politics and to the problems that we face. The two problems of epiphenomenalism and class reductionism are brought together in the phrase *the problem of essentialism*. These *essential* elements can be identified in the work of Poulantzas (1979) on ideology, when he argues that:

o   all people are class subjects;
o   all ideology is class based;
o   all classes have pure and coherent ideologies.

For Poulantzas and others, such as Althusser (1981), ideology is never independent of the economic base and is always a distorted reflection of social reality. The failure of Marxism to account for a politics that is independent of the determining force of class leads to the disappearance of politics in the Marxian analysis. Laclau and Mouffe draw upon Gramsci's notion of the **integral state** to give their theorising an ethical and political dimension. The integral state is built upon civil society, and in the widest sense of the word the state educates the people by forming attractive moral and political ideas, which the people are made to feel are necessary for the continued existence of civilisation. Hegemony, for Gramsci, takes the form of intellectual and moral reform, which is achieved only when the ruling class have created an **historic bloc** – a set of institutional arrangements and ideas that wins the consent of the people because it is believed to give both moral and intellectual leadership and successfully eliminates the opposition. For Laclau and Mouffe the discursive construction of hegemony ceases to be a superstructure and is independent of the economic base. Identity is also constructed independently of the economic base, and is formed through a process of struggle within hegemony. This struggle for the successful articulation of an identity, and the antagonism that it generates, replaces class struggle for Laclau and Mouffe.

In *Hegemony and Socialist Strategy* (1984) Laclau and Mouffe cast doubt upon the whole Marxian tradition, claiming that its 'totalising' logic – its attempt to theorise about the whole of society – is both flawed and anti-democratic. In contrast, they argue that society is highly plural in nature and people have an identity that is independent of economic forces. New social movements provide the basis for bringing about social change and the source on which individuals can build an identity. Marxists took up many of these ideas in the 1990s.

Fredric Jameson (1934–present)

For Fredric Jameson (1991) postmodernity is at the end of the process of modernisation. What he finds striking about the postmodern condition is the way in which many diverse articles, objects and ideas come together into a new 'discursive genre', or distinct perspective or notion of what reality consists of. Postmodernism is a 'systemic modification of capitalism itself' (Jameson, 1991: xii). Capitalism has undergone a radical change and is now built upon assumptions that Marx was unaware of. This distinct stage in capitalism is described by Jameson as a 'schizophrenic present', by which he means that there is not one accepted theory of the nature of reality but many, and this represents a significant break with the modernity of late capitalism.

Society appears to be very different, but in its essential features it is still the same; postmodernity is a capitalist society with more choice of commodities, ideas and lifestyles.

Unlike most postmodern writers, Fredric Jameson has attempted to absorb postmodern insights into the Marxian analysis. Jameson sees postmodernity as the third great stage in the global expansion of capitalism:

o   The first stage was the national market, in which we have capitalism in one country but limited international trade.
o   The second stage was the older imperialist system in which countries were colonised for economic reasons.
o   The third stage is postmodernity, which he views as a historic socio-economic reality.

Postmodernism is described as a 'broad cultural logic'; a new stage in the cultural development of capitalism which has new forms of consciousness and is dominated by fragmentation, pastiche and simulacra. For Jameson, postmodern culture has a high level of class content. However, he departs from the fundamental presuppositions of the Marxian analysis in that he rejects the distinction between 'base' and 'superstructure' outlined above. In the postmodern condition we need to think about cultural phenomena before we think about the economy: so, contrary to the traditional Marxian analysis, 'superstructure' becomes more important than the 'economic base' as the factor bringing about future social change. Moreover, the superstructure is a source of conflict and the basis for formulating radical political positions. In Jameson's eyes the relationship between base and superstructure is no longer coherent in the way that Marx described, and this is partly because in the postmodern condition people feel that nature has been abolished. Everything is cultural and is understood by reference to earlier cultural products: you may notice how in Steven Spielberg films there is often reference to Saturday morning cartoons.

Jameson's account of this new stage of capitalism has the following characteristics:

o a new depth-ness, which is found in both current social theory and in a new culture of the simulacrum;
o a weakening of historicity (our idea of history), both in our relationship to public history and in the new forms of our personal lives;
o a new 'schizophrenic' structure which inclines us towards new types of syntax or syntagmatic relationship, especially in the more short-lived arts, such as popular music;
o a whole new type of emotional foundation for people;
o the deep and creative relationship of the above points to new technology;
o a completely new world economic system;
o a confusing new deregulated space in the world for multinational capital to do as it pleases, outside of the control of governments.

In contrast to Lyotard (1984), Jameson argues that grand narratives have not evaporated or otherwise gone away. And for Jameson it is still possible to view the world in terms of class struggle. All areas of personal and social life, he argues, have become dependent upon commodities, as through advertising people are made to feel that they can only be happy through consumption. Jameson goes on to argue that the fragmentation of the working class, because of the development of new occupations and the deskilling of others, has not altered the organisation of class relations or politics. However, there is a need for what Jameson calls **cognitive mapping**. Individuals are unable to place themselves within the network of classes that make up capitalism; they cannot define themselves as part of a collectivity which has a class identity. Radical politics is about cognitive mapping, enabling people to define their place in the world. Novels could provide such cognitive maps, and could also help people to formulate political demands. In the postmodern condition, radical politics is built upon the activity of new social movements. Radical politics is no longer about the proletariat but about finding commonality and building alliances between groups who have experienced oppression within capitalism: women, ethnic minorities, gays and lesbians, etc.

What is the cognitive map meant to do? Jameson's answer is far from clear. It is

to enable a situational representation on the part of the individual subject to that vaster and properly unrepresentable totality which is the ensemble of society's structures as a whole. (Jameson, 1991: 51)

In other words, cognitive mapping gives us a heightened sense of our place in the global system. This involves the mapping of the social space in terms of our class position and where we stand in both a national and international context, how we view our individual social relationships in terms of class. This process should raise in our minds practical issues that prompt us into taking political action.

The problem here is that the groups that Jameson has in mind (women, ethnic groups, gays etc.), may have little if anything in common with each other, and could even be in conflict. Women can be racist; ethnic minorities can be homophobic. Moreover, the oppression that these groups may experience often predates capitalism, and as such may have little or nothing to do with the existence of capitalism. In addition, these groups may favour a form of capitalism which is deeply embedded in the postmodern condition, where individuals are free to define and redefine themselves in any way they wish – sexually, ethnically, morally, whatever.

Jameson also redefines the relationships contained within the 'labour theory of value' into a 'linguistic account'. In the traditional Marxist analysis outlined above, the value of very different things (e.g. hammers, linen, television sets) will be the same if they contain the same amount of labour power. In Jameson's view, 'value' emerges as something independent of the labour power that went into making it. This 'value' is an 'abstraction' or 'concept' and the market place becomes a place of the 'symbolic exchange' of value.

So 'value' is said by Jameson to be independent of the labour power that produced it. 'Value' is a concept, it is an idea, and must be explained in cultural terms: terms that are free of the terminology of the traditional Marxists, such as economic exploitation. The significance of this is that Jameson has collapsed the economic base into the superstructure and suggested that we can only make sense of the world in cultural terms. The economic base, including the relations of production, is irrelevant in the postmodern condition. The economic base is no longer the force which moves history forward: it is culture and ideas that generate future social change.

Although Jameson does not reject the labour theory of value, he rejects its traditional form and redefines it as a cultural or superstructural concept. We could argue that he places the labour theory of value outside of the traditional Marxian analysis.

Activity: can Fredric Jameson be described as a Marxist?

From the information in the text above:

1 Outline the traditional Marxist position and the Jameson position on the issues presented below.
2 Write a short paragraph in which you provide an answer to the question: can Fredric Jameson be described as a Marxist?

Traditional Marxist view	Jameson view
The nature of class conflict:	
The role of the economic base:	
The role of the superstructure:	
The source of ideas, culture and ideology:	

3   Construct a table in which you outline the strengths and the weaknesses of Jameson's analysis.

Alex Callinicos

On postmodernism and socialism

In contrast to Jameson, Alex Callinicos (1991) argues that there has been no radical break with modernity and that the notion of postmodernism is politically or ideologically motivated. It is a right-wing attempt to save capitalism by diverting attention from the class struggle. He points to the many contradictions in the contributions of postmodern writers:

> Postmodernism corresponds to a new historical stage of social development (Lyotard) or it doesn't (Lyotard again). Postmodern art is a continuation of (Lyotard) or a break from (Jencks) modernism. Joyce is a modernist (Jameson) or a postmodernist (Lyotard). Postmodernism turns its back on social revolution, but then practitioners and advocates of a revolutionary art like Breton and Benjamin are claimed as precursors. (Callinicos, 1994: 384)

He then goes on to quote approvingly the comment that postmodernism is 'another of those period descriptions that help you to take a view of the past suitable to whatever it is you want' (ibid.).

In *The Revenge of History: Marxism and the East European Revolutions* (1991) Callinicos attempts to outline what he sees as the implications for socialism of the collapse of Stalinism. Stalinism was a doctrine named after the Soviet dictator Joseph Stalin who maintained the enforcement of his rule by 'liquidating' people who were seen as a threat to his domination. Callinicos's argument is that the collapse of Stalinism cannot be used to justify the argument that Marxism is irrelevant to explaining the modern world. In addition, Callinicos points out that as long ago as 1947 socialists such as Tony Cliff had argued that Stalinist regimes such as the Soviet Union would be brought down by the working classes. Hence Callinicos argues: 'The East European revolutions and the turmoil in the USSR itself are thus the vindication, rather than the refutation, of the classical Marxist tradition' (Callinicos, 1991: 20).

Activity

Read the following passages from Callinicos (1991) and use them to write a paragraph which outlines his position on why the Soviet Union collapsed.

Item A

The industrialization of the USSR could only proceed by pursuing economic autarky . . . that is 'by exploiting the peasants, by concentrating resources of the peasantry in the hands of the state'. (p. 31)

Item B

Real wages in 1932 were at most 50 per cent of their 1928 level. If this analysis is correct, then 'socialist' industrialization in the USSR was made possible not simply by the destruction of the peasantry but by the intense exploitation of the very class which in theory ruled the country and was supposed to be the main beneficiary of the changes involved. (p. 32)

Item C

Strikes were quite frequent in the period 1928–34, but, given the very harsh methods used to crush them . . . (p. 33)

Item D

the class structure of the Soviet society was crystallising around the intensive exploitation of the mass of workers and around intensive exploitation of the mass of workers and peasants. (p. 35)

Item E

the historical record leaves little doubt of the qualitative difference between Bolshevism and Stalinism. (p. 37)

In the late 1980s the Soviet leader Mikhail Gorbachev attempted to introduce greater openness and reform into the Soviet system, on both the political and the economic fronts. The economic reforms involved attempting to implant market mechanisms into the state planning systems. In the view of Callinicos, this produced the worst of both systems, with little or no benefits.

For Callinicos, a socialist society need not have a Stalinist-style planned economy and an absence of democracy. In a socialist economy, individual workers would direct production and this would be in the interests of providing people with the consumption that they believed they needed. In addition, claims Callinicos, Soviet democracy can achieve much greater accountability than is possible within liberal democracy, because in a socialist society people are active politically rather than passive. Moreover, people make their political decisions face to face in the workplace, rather than by being lulled into passivity by a mass media which distorts reality in the interests of capitalists.

Callinicos on Marxism

Activity

Read the following statement from Callinicos and write a short paragraph outlining why you agree or disagree with it:

Marxism is the only tradition with the theoretical and political resources needed to confront the issues currently facing us . . . it is radically at odds with its monstrous Stalinist distortion . . . Marx and his successors developed a perfectly feasible strategy for overthrowing capitalism and constructing a better society in its place. (Callinicos, 1991: 135)

Activity

'Political progress' is brought about in the Marxian analysis by class action; the proletariat rising up and smashing capitalism; in other words by revolution.

Do you find the Marxist view of 'political progress' by revolution convincing? Outline the reasons for your answer

---

In contrast to Callinicos's view of postmodernism, we could argue that the lack of any agreement on the basic assumptions of postmodernity is in itself an aspect of postmodernism. But what is the difference between postmodernism and postmodernity?

o **Postmodernity** is an epoch of history that is on the far side of modernity.
o **Postmodernism** is a collection of theories about what life is like on the far side of modernity.

However, we could also point out that individual writers within any perspective often disagree about the fundamental concepts of the perspective. This, as we have seen above, is most clearly the case with Marxism.

Karl Mannheim: the transition from the theory of ideology to the sociology of knowledge

Karl Mannheim (1893–1947) provides one of the earliest and most well informed critiques of Marxism and is regarded by many as the founder of the sociology of knowledge. In his most influential text *Ideology and Utopia* (1936), Mannheim argued that there were two distinct meanings of the term 'ideology': the **particular conception** of ideology: this is where individuals are sceptical of the opinions and ideas of opponents and believe that opponents are telling lies; and the **total conception** of ideology: this has its origins in the work of Marx and is concerned with the ideology of an age or the ideology of a class.

Mannheim rejects the distinction in Marx between a true consciousness – which is free of ideology; and a false consciousness – in which working-class people are unaware of their true class interests because they have had their ideas and beliefs manipulated. In Mannheim's view all ways of thinking are ideological in nature. In many respects, what Mannheim is describing is similar to thinking about politics; it is not possible to think about politics without taking up a position – in other words, without thinking ideologically. For Mannheim, there are only competing ideo-logical ways of thinking. Mannheim, therefore, uses Marxian concepts against Marxism, and in this sense he moves beyond Marx. Once we all come to view ways of thinking as ideological, rather than as true or false, then we experience a major shift in our thinking.

The relationship between the criteria of truth (the things that we use to verify to ourselves that we have come across the truth, such as a scientific method) and the historical situation is mediated by the **existential situation**. In the modern world knowledge is said to be *seinverbundernheit* knowledge. What this means is that knowledge is produced cooperatively between people. This new knowledge also contains an *activistic* element: this means that people have basic interests, for example economic interests, and these influence the way individuals play a role in defining the nature of the world.

Mannheim refers to the notion of cooperative knowledge as a 'syn-thesis'. The synthesis can be used to organise the economic and political system in the interests of the population. This involves drawing upon all the different political perspectives in order to generate a form of knowledge that is better than any one political perspective. The idea of synthesis is usually associated in Mannheim's work with the idea of a free-floating intelligentsia, a group of intellectuals who are above politics and who create the synthesis. For a commentary on the intelligentsia in Mannheim's work see 'Karl Mannheim: the myth of the free-floating intelligentsia' (Best, 1990: 55–7).

Marxists would respond to Mannheim's argument by claiming that it is 'relativist' in nature. In other words, Mannheim is claiming that there is no such thing as objective knowledge or truth, because he is arguing that all ways of thinking are ideological in nature. Mannheim responded to this criticism by arguing that his position was 'relationist' in nature rather than 'relativist'. Relationism involves producing a dynamic synthesis of partial truths, taken from competing ideologies, rather than denying the existence of truth. The reader may like to note that in recent years Richard Rorty has taken up the themes that Mannheim addressed.

Activity

The Marxist analysis is based upon the assumption that 'the truth is out there'.

1 Outline Richard Rorty's argument as to why the truth may not be 'out there'.
2 What implications does Rorty's argument have for the Marxist distinction between 'true' consciousness and 'false' consciousness?

According to Richard Rorty, political progress is brought about by the 'accidental coincidence' of a private obsession with a public need (Rorty, 1989: 37).

3 What do you think Rorty means by this statement? (*Hint*: to answer this question you must look at the relationship between the individual and the society.)

Activity: What is wrong with Marxism?

1 Write down a reason why you agree or disagree with each statement made.

Giddens's critique of Marxism   *Agree*   *Disagree*   *Reason*

Marxists do not have a satisfactory
account of power; in particular they
have no real analysis of military power

Within the Marxian analysis there is no
real account of administrative power
or what is distinctive about
administrative power within the
nation state.

Marxists do not take into account
non-economic sources.

Marxists do not take into account
conflicts which are not related
to class issues.

Marxists do not take into account
non-class-based politics – such as
the green movement or gender politics.

2 Now imagine how a Marxist might respond to the points you
   have made.
3 In your opinion, would Jameson accept or reject Giddens's
   critique of Marxism?

From post-industrial society theory to network society theory

One of the most influential post-Marxist analyses is that of Manuel Castells's 'network society' which forms his description of the social structure of the information age. Its various cultural and institutional *flows* pass through both rich and poor countries alike. In contrast to Marx, Castells argues that the means of production in the postmodern world are informational rather than industrial. Capitalism is constituted as a series of flows: of labour, capital, information, leisure, flexible manufacturing systems, deregulation and privatisation of financial power and the decline of the state. In the twentieth century industrial society was characterised by the social structure of capitalism and statism, organised around relationships of production/consumption and power, with rigidly established personal identities operating within a culture which was itself generally shaped by the industrial society. In contrast, fundamental to the social structure of the information age is its reliance on networks as the key feature of social morphology. Castells acknowledges that networks may be

'old forms' of social organisation, but says that new information/
communication technologies have significantly empowered them. Networks are brought into being, acted out and transformed by people, often
within non-class-based new social movements that openly challenge social
practices, engage with flexible decentralisation, or with focused decision-
making, the consequences of which may be unpredictable.

The information society

According to William J. Martin: 'the information society is an advanced
post-industrial society characterised by a high degree of computerisation
and large volumes of electronic data transmission, and by an economic
profile heavily influenced by the market and employment possibilities of
information technology' (Martin, 1988: 37).

Like many people who use the terms 'information society' and 'post-
industrial society' Martin argued that he was living at a time of
information-driven social change and he projected possible future changes
on the basis of a number of indicators. He speculated that an information
society would be characterised by:

o   change in the nature of the workforce;
o   increased awareness of the value of information as a resource;
o   appreciation of the need for widespread computer literacy;
o   wholesale diffusion of information technologies;
o   government intervention in support of the key enabling technologies
     of computing, microelectronics and telecommunications.

The information society was a place where economic well-being, including
living standards, the type of work available, education and opportunities in
the increasingly global market place, was dependent upon the exploitation
of information. Martin divides the theorists on the information society
into the *optimists* who believe industrial societies will experience an
orderly and peaceful transition into information societies and the
pessimists who believe that the transition will see the further expansion
of Tayloristic rationalisation and the subordination of social needs to the
needs of market.

The transition from the industrial society to the information society has
been summed up by John Naisbitt and Patricia Aburdene (1990) as five
mega-trends that add up to 'large social, economic, political, and technological changes' (Naisbitt and Aburdene, 1990: xvii):

o   In the economic sphere, there has been a shift from industrial pro-
     duction to service provision, and as a consequence the occupational
     structure has changed.

o   The 'service class' has become much more significant in the stratification system.
o   Technology has become mainly concerned with processing information rather than processing raw materials.
o   Self-sustaining economic growth becomes central to the process of social change.
o   The lifelong acquisition of knowledge becomes one of the central elements of the value system of the information society.

However, Naisbitt and Aburdene have an over-optimistic vision of life at the start of the new millennium, which they describe as a world where nationalism and ideological struggles have been brought to an end by processes of globalisation. Moreover, the *rapprochement* between the USA and the Soviet Union in the 1980s has reduced 'the chance of a regional conflict escalating into a world war' (Naisbitt and Aburdene, 1990: 337).

Yoneji Masuda (1980) also presents a very optimistic vision of the information society, which he describes as a form of society 'with highly intellectual creativity where people may draw future designs on invisible canvas and pursue and realize individual lives worth living' (1980: 3). Drawing upon social evolutionary assumptions Masuda explains its characteristics:

o   Information is to become the axis of socio-economic development, and this will be produced by 'the information utility', an infrastructure of IT and communication networks which provide inexpensive and easily accessible information.
o   Self-production of information will increase.
o   A *synergetic economy* will emerge in which 'each person cooperates and acts from his or her own standpoint in solving common problems' (Masuda, 1980: 104).
o   Politically the information society is a participatory democracy, which places an emphasis upon 'the realisation of time value' (1980: 33), a form of society in which all people can enjoy a worthwhile life.
o   Morally, the information society is built upon a spirit of globalism and living together ethically with each other and nature.

Masuda goes on to explain that in the information society the expanding 'knowledge frontier' will be the driving force behind an expansion in the 'information market'.

Daniel Bell is one of the best-known theorists of the 'post-industrial society'. In *The Coming of Post-Industrial Society* (1973), Bell argued that we were moving beyond the industrial model of society analysed by Durkheim, Marx and to a lesser extent Weber. For Bell we were on the brink of an 'information society' characterised by:

o   a shift from manufacturing to services;
o   centrality of new science-based industries;

o the rise of a new technological elite and transformed forms of stratification.

In the early 1970s Bell, like most people in the social sciences, was obsessed by modernist theories of determinism. Bell's work is underpinned by Weberian conceptions of evolutionary social change in the direction of greater rationalisation and technological determinism. As we moved through the 1990s and the work of Anthony Giddens became more influential, social scientists came to the opinion that societies do not determine the lives of individual people; individuals are skilled and knowledgeable human agents actively involved in the creation of the structures that are used to organise their lives. In a similar fashion, technology is now less likely to be viewed as a sphere separate from society: technology is a resource that human agents can draw upon in their interaction with other people. As Strum and Latour (1987) make clear, technology is part of what makes society possible: in social relations we almost always make use of artefacts (things that people have made) in our interaction with others. Are we becoming technologically dependent cyborgs? It is only when we have unprotected sex, argue Strum and Latour, that we socially interact without technology, 'baboon-like' relying on our naked bodies and voices alone. Answers to the central sociological questions, 'How is society possible?' 'How is sustained social interaction possible?' should always make reference to technology. Debates about the 'information society' place technology at the centre of social relations and give it a significant role in any conception of structuration.

In this chapter we will look at the possible connections between the formation of self, identity and technology. Are central elements of our self and our identity such as our gender and our ethnicity shaped by technology, or is technology itself shaped by gender and ethnicity?

In contrast to traditional Marxian approaches, in Bell's information society 'theoretical knowledge' became the key source of value as information technology was applied to all aspects of society. The concept of a post-industrial society was popularised by Peter Drucker in *The Age of Discontinuity* (1969) and Alvin Toffler in *Future Shock* (1970).

For many commentators the notion of an information society fits well into the liberal, progressive tradition of Western thought. However, there are other conceptions of the post-industrial, knowledge-based, information society.

What is information?

Humans are information-processing creatures. We maintain our social relationships by various forms of communication, and information is the material of communication. In the late 1940s a number of publications, such as Shannon and Weaver's *The Mathematical Theory of Communication* and Wiener's *Cybernetics*, defined 'information' as anything which reduced uncertainty within a given situation. Information theory, for Shannon and Weaver and others, was about devising ways to calculate the level or amount of **entropy** or complexity within systems, in order to make complex systems appear simple and organised. Information was seen as something that we use to describe and understand our situation and as a resource that we draw upon in order to act effectively. Theorists in the 1940s assumed that societies were evolving into more complex structures and because of this the level of entropy would increase. The assumption was that new and more effective mediums of communication would be needed to pass on the greater amounts of information and that people needed in order to come to terms with higher levels of complexity and uncertainty. The evolution of the industrial society into the more complex post-industrial society should also involve the emergence of the information society, with the complex networks of communication that people need to service their greater need for information.

Daniel Bell: the coming of post-industrial society

The theory of the post-industrial society that Daniel Bell (1973) proposed was based upon the idea that the industrial society was going through a series of social transformations, possibly brought about by technological factors, that had consequences in all areas of our social life. The central theme running through his book is that scientific and technological change have resulted in 'ideology' being replaced by 'technical decision making' in society. There has been a change in knowledge and in the character of knowledge – more theoretical knowledge, more 'codification of knowledge into abstract systems' (Bell, 1973: 20), algorithms rather than intuitive judgements. Decision-making has become much less emotional and expressive and much more calculating and instrumental in nature. The impact of this shift can be seen in social relations, power structures and culture. 'The concept of a post-industrial society is not a picture of a complete social order; it is an attempt to describe and explain an axial change in the social structure of the society' (Bell, 1973: 119).

Bell argues that from the middle of the nineteenth century onwards there were 'social tensions' which could be identified with 'social frameworks'. These social tensions came about because of the contradictory impulses of equality and bureaucracy, which are found in the social structure and the political structure of a modern industrial society. There is a widespread desire for greater participation and a greater degree of control being exercised by more organisations staffed by professionals.

'Social frameworks' are not empirical reflections of the world. In Bell's analysis they are conceptual schemata that are built upon an axial principle and axial structure which provide an *organisational* frame, allowing

Bell to suggest answers to key questions such as 'how a society hangs together' (Bell, 1973: 10).

Axial principles are institutions, such as property relations. Because there are several such key institutions, this way of theorising allows Bell to avoid deterministic accounts of social change. Social frameworks do not *determine* in Bell's analysis; rather they suggest questions and pose management problems.

Society for Bell is divided into three parts:

o   the **social structure**, which is composed of the economy, technology and occupational system, which has the axial principle of *economising*, ensuring the optimum distribution of resources;

o   the **polity**, which distributes power and resolves conflict, which has the axial principle of *participation*;

o   the **culture**, 'the realm of expressive symbolism and meanings' (Bell, 1973: 12), which has the axial principle of *fulfilment and enhancement of the self*.

In Parsons's analysis these elements of the social structure would have been held together by a common value system. However, by the 1970s a distinct disjunction had appeared between the three.

There are five dimensions to Bell's post-industrial society:

1   economic sector: the change from a goods-producing to a service economy;
2   occupational distribution: the pre-eminence of the professional and technical class;
3   axial principle: the centrality of theoretical knowledge as the source of innovation and of policy formulation for the society;
4   future orientation: the control of technology and technological assessment;
5   decision-making: the creation of a new 'intellectual technology'. (Bell, 1973: 14)

The changes that Bell identifies have a significant impact on class and class analysis. In contrast to Marx, who argued that the working class were the key agents in social change, Bell argues that it is science and technology that are the key agents in change. Moreover, whereas in the industrial society wealth, power and status defined the boundaries of classes in the post-industrial society, classes – with the main axis of stratification becoming knowledge – seek wealth, power and status. The major class within the post-industrial society is a professional class, who have knowledge rather than property. In addition, Bell explains that this professional class is made up of four *estates*: the scientific, the technological, the administrative and the cultural. Each estate may have internal bonds themselves, based upon *situses* (a shared identity and ethos) that provide 'corporate cohesiveness' (Bell, 1973: 377), but there is no bond between the four estates.

Table 2.1 *General schema of social change*

	Pre-industrial	Industrial	Post-industrial	
Regions:	Asia Africa Latin America	Western Europe Soviet Union Japan	United States	
Economic sector:	Primary Extractive: Agriculture Mining Fishing Timber	Secondary Goods producing: Manufacturing Processing	Tertiary Transportation Utilities	Quaternary Trade Finance Insurance Real estate
			Quinary Health Education Research Government Recreation	
Occupational slope:	Farmer Miner Fisherman Unskilled worker	Semi-skilled worker Engineer	Professional and technical Scientists	
Technology:	Raw materials	Energy	Information	
Design:	Game against nature	Game against fabricated nature	Game between persons	
Methodology:	Common sense experience	Empiricism Experimentation	Abstract theory: models, simulation, decision theory, systems analysis	
Time perspective:	Orientation to the past Ad hoc responses	Ad hoc adaptiveness Projections	Future orientation Forecasting	
Axial principle:	Traditionalism: Land/resource limitation	Economic growth: State or private control of investment decisions	Centrality of and codification of theoretical knowledge	

Source: Bell (1973: 117)

Bell outlined what he considered to be the significance of post-industrial society:

1 It strengthens the role of science and cognitive values as a basic institutional necessity of the society.
2 By making decisions more technical, it brings the scientist or economist more directly into the political process.
3 By deepening existing tendencies toward the bureaucratisation of intellectual work, it creates a set of strains for the traditional definitions of intellectual pursuits and values.
4 By creating and extending a technical intelligentsia, it raises crucial questions about the relation of the technical to the literary intellectual. (Bell, 1973: 43)

Table 2.2 *Structure and problems of the post-industrial society*

Axial principle	The centrality of and codification of theoretical knowledge
Primary institutions:	University Academy institutes Research corporations
Economic ground:	Science-based industries
Primary resource:	Human capital
Political problem:	Science policy Education policy
Structural problem:	Balance of private and public sectors
Stratification: Base – Access –	Skill Education
Theoretical issue:	Cohesiveness of 'new class'
Sociological reactions:	The resistance to bureaucratisation The adversary culture

Source: Bell (1973: 118)

Giddens (1989) has outlined several critical points about Bell's analysis. First, Giddens questions the assumption that information is becoming the main basis of the economic system and that this has resulted in a shift from manufacturing occupations to service occupations. Giddens argues that a majority of workers have always worked outside of manufacturing, either in agriculture or services. The important change in the occupation structure has been the shift from agriculture to other types of employment. Secondly, Giddens argues that Bell assumes that the service sector is a heterogeneous group in the population. In Giddens's view, many service sector employees have manual occupations, for example petrol pump attendants. In addition many white collar workers are experiencing 'deskilling', which causes damage to their market and work situation and places them in a position similar to many people in manufacturing occupations. Thirdly, the distinction between 'service' and 'manufactur-ing' occupation is often arbitrary, as many service occupations are found within manufacturing companies. Fourthly, Giddens claims that Bell's analysis tends to overemphasise changes in the economic sector as factors bringing about social change. Finally, Bell uses the United States as his model of the post-industrial society; however, the USA has many specific characteristics that make it unsuitable as a typical model. Giddens has listed these differences in an earlier text: the size of the USA, its largely immigrant population, greater possibilities for upward social mobility, the absence of a feudal past, rich material resources, a large underclass (Giddens, 1973).

Frank Webster and Kevin Robins (1986) were also highly critical of Bell's post-industrial society thesis. They argue that although Bell's book is a very long one, he never explains the origins of 'intellectual technology'; he simply assumes that it is an inevitable product of a Weberian process of rationalisation. Bell presents in their eyes 'a catalogue of effects with causes'. In addition, he assumes that the process of rationalisation is socially neutral and independent of the social, but at the same time socially significant. They describe Bell's work as technologically deterministic in nature. Bell offers no justification for his conception of the social structure. He assumes that the post-industrial society will be politically directed in a different fashion from the industrial society but again there is no explanation of how this change will come about.

Manuel Castells

Castells argues that the advanced societies are going through major social transformation based upon changing information-communication technologies, cultural change, transformation in the role of women, the rise in an ecological consciousness and a transformation of the global economy. These changes represent the formation of an information society. Changes in the world political order, including the collapse of the Soviet Union and the demise of Marxism as an intellectual branch of learning, are also perceived by Castells as consequences of the rise of the information society.

Manuel Castells: the network society

According to Castells (2000) the end of the twentieth century saw the emergence of a new global economy. This is a new form of capitalism with three essential features:

o The core economic activities – strategically crucial activities, from capital markets to specialised labour, management and entertainment, are global in nature.
o Productivity and competitiveness are a function of knowledge generation and information processing – these network-oriented communication and information technologies provide the infrastructure for the global economy.
o Firms and territories are organised in networks of production – the financial aspect is one of the key features. As Castells explains, the financial dimension of the network economy 'has the ability to extend or retrench its geometry without excessive disruption, simply by reconforming the networks of investment and trade. This occurs in instants, in an endless flow of circulation' (Castells, 2000: 68).

Networks, argues Castells, rather than countries or economic areas, form the true architecture of the new capitalist global economy. Through the process of financial globalisation, following the deregulation of the City of

London in October 1987, new technologies became crucial in the management of the deregulated system and allowed quasi-instantaneous global financial trading. The outcome of this was the creation of 'an Automation' at the centre of our economies. AI machines monitor the electronic transactions that form the network of capital flows.

Financial markets were the first to become globally interconnected. Castells makes it clear that the remarkable expansion of tradable value that we saw over the last decade of the twentieth century was possible only because of the use of highly developed mathematical models, made operational by impressive computer systems provided with constantly updated information communicated electronically from all over the world. However, contrary to the pessimists that Martin described, Castells believes that there is nothing inherently subordinating about the technology in itself. Information technology can be used either to liberate people, providing new opportunities for individuals to share information and influence the political process, or to enhance the needs of capitalists and increase inequality.

However, Castells argues that there needs to be a full reassessment of the key assumptions and arguments of Bell and other post-industrial society theorists.

Such theorists draw their analyses exclusively from North American and Western European experience. As we saw above, Bell discusses only the United States. According to Castells, we have to consider the interaction between the advanced societies and dependent societies. In discussing the emergence of the information society we must take into account the development of a network of informational flows, which forms a key element in the interdependent global economy. We also need to take into account the distinct development of places such as Japan. Many other commentators on social development have discussed the notion of *Japanisation*.

Japanisation demonstrates that there is not one single path to the information society. In the nineteenth century Japan adopted Western technology but maintained traditional Japanese culture and beliefs. Japan's development path diverges significantly from that of Western Europe and North America. Tim Leggatt (1985) in his comparative study of social development maintains that both Russia and Japan industrialised in the twentieth century and both were deliberate followers of the first industrialising nations. However, each society had its own distinct form of industrial evolution, very different that of the earlier industrial nations.

From November 1871 until September 1873, the Meiji government of Japan had sent the Iwakura mission, a diplomatic team, to Europe and North America to investigate all features of Western industrial societies. The purpose of the mission was to give guidance to the Meiji government about development paths the Japanese could take in their modernisation. The report of the Mission was published in 1878 under the title of *Tokumei zsenken taishi Bei-O Kairan jikki* (Journal of the Envoy Extraordinary Ambassador Plenipotentiary's Travels through America and Europe), which is commonly known as the 'Jikki'.

The Meiji government wanted a planned process of modernisation. The Jikki suggested that Japan should adopt Western technology but not Western values. The Mission's belief was not simply that Japanese culture and values were superior, but that there was a danger of causing major social disorder if changes to traditional cultural patterns were introduced. This is contrary to the modernisation theory of Parsons and Rostow (1962), which suggests that traditional cultures are a brake on the modernisation process.

Nakane Chie makes a distinction between modernisation as a universal process, and cultural features of a society that are independent of the modernising process. As Nakane Chie comments: 'Japanese working in all types of organisation are significantly different from their counterparts in the West and have not essentially changed since the Meiji period' (1985: 15).

Kozai shows the possible development paths faced by the Japanese at the end of the nineteenth century, as follows:

Spirit (Kon)

wakon
(Japanese culture)

yokon
(Western culture)

Japan (wa) _____ West (yo)

wasai
(Traditional Japanese)

yosai
(Western technology)

Technology (sai)

Source: Kozai 'Wakon-ron-noto' (Tokyo, Iwanami shoten 1984)

Wakon is the 'spiritual power' or 'ideological core' of a people; *yosai* the rational technology of the West. *Wakon* is not anti-modern and *yosai* is not peculiar to the West. What is the traditional Japanese culture? Ruth Benedict's *The Chrysanthemum and the Sword* (1946) claims that dominant Japanese cultural patterns are to be found in all regions and amongst all classes in Japanese society. The 'sword' symbolises Japanese militarism, and the 'chrysanthemum' the culture of Japan. Her argument is that Japanese culture is a planned mixture of primitive militarism that can give way to violent forms of ultra-nationalism, yet the Japanese people have an appreciation of things of great beauty deeply embedded in their culture.

Castells argues that the concept of 'information society' (*Johoka Shakai*) is a Japanese invention. This society not only makes use of information technology, its social structure is shaped by the informational paradigm.'

Castells argues that the Japanese Ministry of Education was responsible for preserving Japanese cultural identity, and coordinating the rigid examination system which determined recruitment to the University of Tokyo, particularly its Faculty of Law, and the other elite private universities; this selection process underpinned the stratification system. In addition, the Emperor system reinforced traditional culture, particularly the universal belief in the superiority of the Japanese nation.

However, by the 1990s Japan had become a *network society*. Japan, Singapore, Hong Kong and Taiwan not only became interdependent in the Pacific, but became intensely entwined with the networks of global informational capitalism.

The constant financial flows in and out of the Japanese economy were diminishing the control over the economy by the Bank of Japan, and the Ministry of Finance had less control over interest rates, which had been the cornerstone of Japanese industrial policy. Deregulation of utilities, telecommunications and media was opening up opportunities for foreign sources of investment. The political crisis caused by this had a significant effect on Japanese national identity. In the last years of the twentieth century Japan was becoming an increasingly confused society; this applied particularly to younger people. There was growing affluence, but a decline in traditional values, as the influence of familial patriarchalism and ritualistic Japanese traditions declined whilst American icons, distributed by high-tech consumption, became more influential.

In his discussion of *Aum Shinrikyo*, a Japanese cult that was responsible for poison gas bomb incidents on the Japanese underground, Castells argues that it is a 'horror caricature' of the Japanese information society because of its mixture of respect for advanced technology and traditional Japanese spiritualism.

Most importantly, claims Castells, post-industrial theorists have undervalued the role and position of women in post-industrialisation. In the information society women have entered the informational workforce and undermined the structure of the traditional patriarchal family. Castells argues that a number of basic elements of traditional patriarchal families have been questioned:

o   Interpersonal relationships between the two members of the couple
o   The professional life of each member of the household
o   The economic association of the members of the household
o   The distribution of domestic work
o   The raising of the children
o   Sexuality (Castells, 1999: 53)

In addition, because they relate to important determinants of our personality, the critical probing and questioning of family structures and sexuality bring about the possibility of new forms of personality. Feminism, for Castells, is the redefinition of a woman's identity and a degendering, in order to end male domination. Sexuality increasingly becomes the possession of the individual, which leads to a more diverse notion of desire, of partnership in sharing a life and to greater diversity in the raising of children: 'It is characterised by the de-linking of marriage, family, heterosexuality, and sexual expression' (Castells, 1997: 235).

New forms of socialisation are taking individuals out of the traditional pattern of the patriarchal family and bringing about a redefinition of roles and of interpersonal relationships as an expression of self.

For Castells the whole world becomes interconnected in its economic functions through selective information and communication flows, 'the purposeful, repetitive, programmable sequences of exchange and inter-action between physically disjointed positions held by social actors in organisations and institutions of society' (Castells, 1999: 57). Many regions and countries are connected, but networks of organisations and institutions bypass many more.

The networks of flows are unstable and constantly change, but generally they work within the social structure at several levels. Networks shape the distinctions of power, wealth and prestige within societies and determine the positions of actors, organisations and institutions and the position of the society within the global economy. Moreover, networks have a structural hierarchy, and position within them is related to the amount of influence an individual or institution can have on the direction of the flow within the network. Editors have more influence over the flow of news than does the viewer or listener. However, power within such networks can never be total; central governments have control over huge financial reserves but their power over key economic indicators is often influenced or directed by speculators.

> The structural domination of the organizational logic of the networks and of the relational logic of flows has substantial consequences that are often considered as indicators of the new informational society. In fact, they are the manifestation of a deeper trend: the emergence of flows as the stuff from which our societies are made. (Castells, 1999: 60)

Knowledge is also a flow. The power of institutions, our personal prosperity, our ability to generate new knowledge and to gather strategic information are dependent upon access to the flows of knowledge and information, for example between major research centres. However, Castells's argument is that there is no single, privileged source of information: no researcher, or research centre, for example, can survive in isolation in modern science. Similarly, no financial investment can be made without specialised information about the market – that is, about the flow of transactions.

Economic units such as firms, regions or cities, have to position themselves within the networks of the global economy. The network is more than a global market place; it also includes the movement of labour and capital and companies' strategies, which come together as networks of networks. Dominance within the network is dependent upon the ability to manipulate and manoeuvre within and between the flows of information.

The media have a key role to play in shaping representations and flows of communication. In particular, through the use of *spin*, politics becomes mediated experience and politicians attempt to use media representation to shape our conceptions of reality. There has been a reduction in the number of politically active social organisations that are based upon achieving or defending a material interest. Political action is constructed around messages and symbols, as the *materiality* of our identity is made up of flows, and resistance to flows comes from communities who feel that their identity is under threat. People have to construct and reconstruct their identity in an effort to manage the flows of information.

People who are excluded from, or who attempt to resist, global networks draw upon religious, nationalist or territorial communities to construct an identity. Castells argues that such identities are necessarily **defensive identities**, organised around a shared set of values that provide safe haven from a hostile world. Defensive identities express resistance to three threats:

o globalisation, which dissolves the independence of institutions and the traditional communication systems that people would have used to conduct their lives;
o networks that blur the boundaries of social relationships;
o the crisis in the traditional patriarchal family that previously provided a sense of security.

In the information society, flow of information is the most dominant of all social processes and now forms the substance of human activity: 'networks of wealth, technology, and power, are transforming our world. They are enhancing our productive capacity, cultural creativity, and communication potential. At the same time, they are disfranchising societies' (Castells, 1997: 68–9).

However, within the information society there is a fundamental opposition between two spatial logics:

o the space of flows – which organizes the simultaneity of social practices by information and telecommunication systems; and
o the space of places – which is concerned with physical contiguity of institutions and social interaction; in other words people have a desire to control their living space.

The information society contains a fundamental division between the **globalists**, who are generating flows which are timeless and which have no respect for national borders; and **localists** who are constantly defending their local community.

Information and power – a powerless state?

According to Manuel Castells (1997) the information society is moving towards a supranational order of governance. State control over space and time is increasingly bypassed by global flows of capital, goods, services, technology, communication and information. The nation state has lost much of its sovereignty because its power has been destabilised by the flows of wealth, information and power coming from transnational organisations. In particular, Castells points to the nation state's inability to maintain a welfare state. The state's attempt to reassert its power in the global arena by developing supranational institutions further reduces its sovereignty. Castells takes as his starting point Giddens's (1985) definition of the nation state and argues that Giddens's definition has been undermined by the impact of globalisation on economic activities, the media, electronic communication and crime.

Globalisation threatens the state's ability to run a welfare state. Significantly different levels of regulation, cost and social benefit are difficult to maintain in the face of global flows. This matters, argues Castells, because for much of the post-war period the legitimacy of the state was dependent upon the provision of generous social welfare.

Information and citizenship

For Castells (1997) the reconstruction of political meaning within the information society challenges the modernist notion of citizenship, which was one of the foundations upon which the nation state rested throughout the twentieth century. The traditional modern nation state was faced by two conflicting principles in relation to the nature of citizenship:

o   Legitimate mechanisms had to be put in place to exclude people from using up scarce resources.
o   There was a need for solidarity amongst the people.

For T.H. Marshall (1964) there were three types of citizenship rights that nation states guaranteed:

o   **civil rights or our legal citizenship** – rights associated with individual freedom, such as the right to free speech, to own property, to have equality before the law;
o   **political rights** – rights associated with democracy, such as the right to vote;
o   **social rights** – mainly our welfare rights, such as the right to education, health care and social security. This philosophy underpinned the welfare state and provided the nation state with a degree of legitimacy.

Marshall recognised that those citizenship rights were not based upon a universal standard:

> citizenship is a status bestowed on those who are full members of a community. All who possess the status are equal with respect to the rights and duties with which the status is endowed. There is no universal principle that determines what those rights and duties shall be, but societies in which citizenship is a developing institution create an image of an ideal citizenship against which achievement can be measured and towards which aspiration can be directed. The

urge forward along the path thus plotted is an urge towards a fuller measure of equality, an enrichment of the stuff of which the status is made and an increase in the number of those on whom the status is bestowed. Social class, on the other hand, is a system of inequality. And it too, like citizenship, can be based on a set of ideals, beliefs and values. It is therefore reasonable to expect that the impact of citizenship on social class should take the form of a conflict between opposing principles. (Marshall, 1964: 84)

In other words, *citizenship* based upon residence within the boundaries of a nation state provided individuals with a foundation for their cultural and political identity. Castells's argument is that because of the dynamics of global flows of wealth, information and power, this concept is now inadequate for understanding the problems surrounding issues of citizenship in information societies.

Nation states cannot fulfil their obligations to maintain citizenship rights. It was for this reason, argues Castells, that by the end of the twentieth century there was a significant rise in the number of fundamentalist nationalist, ethnic and religious movements, localism, symbolic politics and single issue mobilisations. There is a severe crisis in credibility affecting the political systems of all nation states, as they face a growing fragmentation of their political systems. People formed their own political and ideological constellations, which made little use of the traditional political structures. Political debate moved away from issues of redistribution of wealth, over which the individual nation state had diminishing control, and towards personalised leadership and scandal politics. As Castells makes clear: '*I contend that scandal politics is the weapon of choice for struggle and competition in informational politics*' (Castells, 1997: 337, italics in original).

However, the emergence of political movements around what were previously considered to be non-political issues is seen by Castells as reconstitution of democracy within the information society. New social movements attempt to manipulate images and codes of information in an effort by people to reassert their identity, build their lives and decide their behaviour. Within the information society the key features of the social structure are globalisation, capitalist restructuring, organisational networking and the primacy of technology. For Castells these are the forces against which communal resistance is focused. However, he claims, it does not follow that nation states have become irrelevant, or that they will disappear. Nation states can build upon 'communalism' and can resist global flows. In other words, for Castells the information society has a profound impact upon identity and class relations: 'the information society is not the superstructure of a new technological paradigm. It is based on the historical tension between the material power of abstract information processing and society's search for meaningful cultural identity' (Castells, 1997: 67). In addition, *statism*, including government planning and other forms of state intervention that were common within modern state socialist societies, was unable to grasp the new history. Statism suffocates the capacity for technological innovation, and takes over and attempts to redefine individuals' historically rooted identities in an effort to dissolve those identities so that people will come to identify themselves with the state rather than their past. This process of identity dissolution and redefinition becomes increasing difficult when people have the ability to constantly renew information. Statism was unable to generate legitimacy for its preferred identity.

Changing class divisions

For Castells, within the network society, class divisions are no longer generated by the Marxian labour theory of value; instead stratification is founded upon the process of *social exclusion*, which Castells defines as: '*the process by which certain individuals and groups are systematically barred from access to positions that would enable them to earn an autonomous livelihood within the social standards framed by institutions and values in a given context*' (Castells, 1997: 73, italics added). Although the boundaries of exclusion shift, and there are changes in who is excluded and included at any time, exclusion is usually associated with education, demographic characteristics, social prejudices, business practices and public policies. The consequence of these processes is that households contain no people who have access to regular well-paid employment. In addition, because of the movement of capital, the processes of social exclusion affect not only individual people, but also regions of countries and larger territories. Hence, the network society brings with it accelerated and uneven development, together with a growth in extreme poverty for many people in the world. The increasing assimilation of markets, and firms, into a shared informationalised global economy makes it difficult for non-informationalised countries to become part of the new affluent global economic environment.

However, in the advanced societies Castells claims that empirical evidence supports the view that increasing informationalisation is associated with:

o deindustrialisation: as a consequence of globalisation of industrial production, labour and markets, geographical shift (not disappearance) of industrial production to other areas of the world is not uncommon. These geographical shifts eliminate decently paid manufacturing jobs.

o individualisation and networking of the labour process, which is an important factor generating inequality. Because workers have highly specialised skills they often are left to bargain on an individual basis for better pay and conditions of service.

o incorporation of women into paid labour in the informational economy, under conditions of patriarchal discrimination causing a

o crisis in the patriarchal family.

o sociopolitical factors, such as pro-capitalist policies and ideologies that ensure the domination of unrestricted market forces and heighten inequality.

The black holes of informational capitalism

For Castells there is a systemic relationship between what he calls the structural transformations of the network society and the increasing decay of the ghetto, because the informational global economy brings with it constant economic restructuring; an increasing irrelevance of nation states, hence continual crisis within welfare states bringing about political alienation, which manifests itself in feelings of becoming disfranchised; and a growing need for communal retrenchment in the face of global forces which are seen to be taking control over people's lives. The decline of the patriarchal family, without any obvious replacement, raises issues about the socialisation of children; and finally the network society has seen the surfacing of a global criminal economy, infiltrating society at all levels.

One of the 'black holes' of the network society is the exploitation of children. There has been a turnaround in children's rights across the globe because deregulation gives companies the opportunity to bypass governments' legal protection of children. Without the systems of protection previously provided by their patriarchal families or the state, children are open to various forms of exploitation. In Pakistan, for example, children now weave carpets for worldwide export, and through a network of suppliers these carpets are sold in large department stores in affluent markets. Many children in the world are also subject to mass global tourism organised around paedophilia or electronic child pornography supplied via the Internet. According to Castells:

> it is frequent to find in the economic development field, experts' views accepting, and supporting, the spread of child labor, as a rational market response which, under certain conditions, will yield benefits to countries and families. The main reason why children are wasted is because, in the Information Age, social trends are extraordinarily amplified by society's new technological/organizational capacity, while institutions of social control are bypassed by global networks of information and capital. (Castells, 1997: 161)

Marx himself invented none of these key concepts: class, socialism, the labour theory of value, dialectic, base–superstructure, ideology or alienation. What he did while he was in the British Museum Reading Room was to bring these ideas and concepts together to produce a coherent theory very different from the sum of its parts. Even the prediction that Marx made about the long-term tendency for the rate of profit to fall was first argued by David Ricardo. Marx was a nineteenth-century political economy Fat Boy Slim.

These are interesting times if you are a Marxist. When Corus, Motorola, Dunlop, Goodyear, Coats-Viyella, Ford and Vauxhall announced mass job losses in 2001, the 'value' of these companies rose on the stock market. We live in a brutal and brutalising global capitalist system in which it appears that global companies have developed the ability to generate value without the need to extract surplus value from labour.

It is the lumpenproletariat (which *is* one of Marx's terms) that suffers most in the context of global capitalism. Should we continue to share Marx's contempt for these people? What is the nature of exploitation now? Can Marxists still accept the view that 'labour is the source of all wealth' or not? Following on from Gunder-Frank and Wallerstein, what Marxists seem to object to about globalisation is what Marx termed the 'exchange value of labour', which he rightly dismisses as nonsense. Labouring activity generates value, as explained via the labour theory of value, but labour itself has no value. Making complaints about low wages in the world is a perfectly honourable moral stance, and I applaud Marxists such as Gunder-Frank for taking it, but we should not confuse that moral stance with Marxism. Empathic understanding has no role to play in the Marxist analysis. Moreover, in the context of globalisation, it is not possible as a Marxist to make ethical distinctions between the activities of nation states or corporations. Marxism places a high emphasis upon the class struggle. However, beyond the slogan 'The class struggle as the motor of history', Marx gives a detailed analysis of the changing relationship between forces and relations of production, which clearly explains that 'class struggle' is not a significant explanation of social change. The proletariat defeat the bourgeoisie as a consequence of social change; the class struggle is not the cause of this change. According to Marx: 'The conditions under which definite productive forces can be applied are the conditions of the rule of a definite class of society' (Marx and Engels, 1970: 85). Similarly in *The Poverty of Philosophy* Marx explains that 'a change in men's productive forces necessarily brings about a change in their relations of production' (Marx, 1846: 137).

The clearest statement is in *Capital*:

> To the extent that the labour process is solely a process between man and nature, its simple elements remain common to all social forms of development. But each specific historical form of this process further develops its material foundations and social forms. Whenever a certain stage of maturity has been reached, the specific historical form is discarded and makes way for a higher one. The moment of arrival of such a crisis is disclosed by the depth and breadth attained by the contradictions and antagonisms between the distribution relations, and thus the specific historical forms of their corresponding production relations, on the one hand, and the productive forces, the productive powers and the development of their agencies, on the other hand. A conflict then ensues between the material development of production and its social form. (Marx, 1867: 861)

A given class dominates a mode of production because the productive forces develop in such a way as to allow this to happen. The question then becomes: why don't 'relations of production' come to dominate 'forces of production'? Also, how much productive force is needed to bring about change and why is that change always in one direction? Why is it that Marx places so much emphasis upon productive forces yet classifies societies by their social forms?

Marx places the labour theory of value at the very heart of his analysis; it provides the theory of exploitation, which is the foundation of the theory of power and the basis of the Marxian conception of class. Without an understanding of this theory you will be unable to understand what Marxism is about. However, the labour theory of value is the Achilles' heel of Marxism; it is seriously flawed.

As we saw above, Jameson redefines the relationships contained within the 'labour theory of value' into a 'linguistic account'. In contrast to the traditional Marxist analysis of the labour theory of value, Jameson's view is that 'value' emerges as something independent of the labour power that went into making it. This 'value' is an 'abstraction' or 'concept' and the market place becomes a location for the 'symbolic exchange' of value.

In other words, 'value' is said by Jameson to be independent of the labour power that produced it. 'Value' is a concept, it is an idea, and must be explained in cultural terms. Concepts which are free of the terminology of the traditional Marxists, most notably the concept of economic exploitation; the significance of this is that Jameson has collapsed the economic base into the superstructure, and suggested that we can only make sense of the world in cultural terms. The economic base, including the relations of production, is irrelevant in the postmodern condition. The economic base is no longer the force that moves history forward; it is culture and ideas that generate future social change.

So although Jameson does not reject the labour theory of value, he rejects its traditional form, and redefines it as cultural or superstructural. There are serious problems with Marxism that clearly need to be addressed. The terminology in Marx is unclear, even with fundamental concepts such as 'base' and 'superstructure'. Do these refer to 'processes' or 'relations'? Is everything that we understand as 'social' either 'base' or 'superstructure'? E.P. Thompson rejected the base–superstructure metaphor completely, whereas Raymond Williams regarded the economic base as a process.

Productive forces develop over time and condition the character of relations of production. A key element in this process is our knowledge of how to control and transform nature. However, what are these productive forces? Is what *enables* production a productive force or should we also include things that *stimulate* production, such as ideological factors? Science and knowledge produced by universities are classed by Marx as a mental productive force; but is such knowledge 'base' and/or 'super-structure'? Productive forces are made up of the means of production and labour power. What are the means of production for Marx? Should we include space, premises and fuel? Why is the means of subsistence for working animals – what working animals eat – classed by Marx as part of the means of production, whilst what working people eat is not classed as part of the means of production?

Many Marxists make a distinction between Marxism and Stalinism. The problem with this is that Stalin wrote at great length about Marxism and for the argument to be convincing Marxists need to explain what was wrong with Stalin's revision and explain why we should reject it. Ross Abbinnett's argument sounds very convincing when he explains that: 'The labour camps of the former Soviet Union did not exist as "transitional" institutions; rather, they attested to the economy of domination-resistance produced by the administration of "proletarian democracy"' (1998: 123).

However, the fundamental difficulty with Marxism is reification and the consequent loss of subjectivity. Nothing is attributed to individual people, who are classed as merely supports of the 'places and functions determined by the mode of production' (Althusser, 1977: 180). How is it possible for individual people to act independently when the world they live in is externally determined? How is it possible for Marx to sustain the notion of an autonomous individual? The notion of a 'species being' – which is the essence of what it means to be a person for Marx – is limited and stated in purely functional terms. The autonomy of the individual is reduced to an instrumental function of economic life. In addition, whilst Marxists place a strong emphasis upon functional interdependence when explaining class divisions, at the same time many Marxists firmly reject the functional interdependence that underpins Talcott Parsons's work.

Summary

In this chapter we have outlined the central assumptions and evaluated the various contributions to Marxism and post-Marxism.

o   Marxism argues that there is a small ruling class that holds power, and a large group of powerless people.
o   Marxism is a zero-sum conception of power; in other words Marxists assume that there is a fixed amount of power in society.
o   Marxism assumes that the ruling class maintain their power by manipulating the ideas of the powerless.
o   Marxian analysis assumes that the ruling class is always an economic class.
o   Marxism is a very optimistic theory – the powerless will one day rise up and take power.
o   Marxian analysis argues that the relationship between the bourgeoisie and the proletariat is one of economic exploitation.
o   Marxism is a political justification for socialism.

The Marxian contribution to social theory is essentially *economic* in nature and the power of the bourgeoisie is legitimised by the use of ideology, which takes the form of a false consciousness. We assessed the effect of the postmodern condition in bringing about the end of communist regimes across the world. We also looked at the contribution of a number of Marxists who have attempted to maintain the validity of the Marxian analysis in the face of the postmodern condition, such as Fredric Jameson and Alex Callinicos, who argues that with the fall of the Soviet Union a new dawn for Marxism is possible. With the world now largely free from Stalinism, a true Marxism can develop.

We also examined a number of 'modernist' critiques of Marxism and its underlying assumptions in the work of Karl Mannheim and Anthony Giddens. Finally we looked at the claim, by post-Marxist Castells, that we now live in an information-based network society.

References

Abbinnett, R. (1998) *Truth and Social Science: From Hegel to Deconstruction*. Sage: London.

Abercrombie, N., Hill, S. and Turner, B. (1980) *The Dominant Ideology Thesis*. Allen & Unwin: London.

Adorno, T. (1973) *The Jargon of Authenticity*, trans. K. Tarnowski and F. Will. Routledge & Kegan Paul: London.

Althusser, L. (1981) *Montesquieu, Rousseau, Marx: Politics and History*, trans. B. Brewster. Verso: London.

Althusser, L. and Balibar, E. (1977) *Reading Capital*, trans. B. Brewster. Left Book Club: London.

Ashley, D. (1997) *History without a Subject: The Postmodern Condition*. Westview Press: Boulder, CO.

Baudrillard, J. (1973) *The Mirror of Production*. Telos Press: St Louis.

Bauman, Z. (1992) *Intimations of Postmodernity*. Routledge: London.

Bell, D. (1973) *The Coming of Post-Industrial Society: A Venture in Social Forecasting*. Basic Books: New York.

Benedict, R. (1946) *The Chrysanthemum and the Sword*. Houghton Mifflin: Boston.

Best, S. (1990) 'Karl Mannheim: the myth of the free-floating intelligentsia', *Social Science Teacher*, Spring: 55–7.

Boyne, R. and Rattansi, A. (eds) (1990) *Postmodernism and Society*. Macmillan: Basingstoke.

Callinicos, A. (1991) *The Revenge of History: Marxism and the East European Revolutions*. Polity Press in association with Basil Blackwell: Oxford.

Castells, M. (1997) *The Power of Identity*. Blackwell: Oxford.

Castells, M. (1999) 'Flows, networks, and identities: a critical theory of the informational society', in P. McLaren, *Critical Education in the New Information Age*. Rowman & Littlefield: Lanham, MD.

Castells, M. (2000) *The Network Enterprise*. Oxford University Press: Oxford.

Coates, D. (1984) *The Context of British Politics*. Hutchinson Education: London.

Drucker, P. (1969) *The Age of Discontinuity*. Harper & Row: New York.

Giddens, A. (1973) *The Class Structure of the Advanced Society*. Hutchinson: London.

Giddens, A. (1985) *The Nation State and Violence*. Polity: Cambridge.

Giddens, A. (1989) *Sociology*. Polity: Cambridge.

Giddens, A., Held, D., Hubert, D., Seymour, D. and Thompson, J. (eds) (1994) *The Polity Reader in Social Theory*. Polity: Cambridge.

Gramsci, A. (1957) *The Modern Prince and Other Writings*. International Publishers: New York.

Habermas, J. (1971) *Toward a Rational Society: Student Protest, Science and Politics*. Heinemann Educational: London.

Habermas, J. (1975) *Legitimation Crisis*. Heinemann Educational: London.

Hall, J.A. (1994) 'After the fall: an analysis of post-communism', *British Journal of Sociology*, 45(4): 525–42.

Hall, S. (1992) 'New ethnicities', in J. Donald and A. Rattansi (eds), *'Race', Culture and Difference*. Sage: London.

Hebdige, D. (1979) *Subculture: The Meaning of Style*. Methuen: London.

Hebdige, D. (1990) in R. Boyne and A. Rattansi (eds), *Postmodernism and Society*. Macmillan: Basingstoke.

Held, D. (1980) *Introduction to Critical Theory: Horkheimer to Habermas*. Hutchinson: London.

Hoggart, R. (1957) *The Uses of Literacy: Aspects of Working Class Life with Special Reference to Publications and Entertainments*. Chatto & Windus: London.

Horkheimer, M. (1947) *The Eclipse of Reason*. Oxford University Press: New York.

Jameson, F. (1991) *Postmodernism: or, the Cultural Logic of Late Capitalism*. Verso: London.

Kellner, D. (1997) 'Social theory and cultural studies', in D. Owen (ed.), *Sociology after Postmodernism*. Sage: London.

Kozai (1984) *Wakon-ron-moto*. Iwanami shoten: Tokyo.

Laclau, E. and Mouffe, C. (1984) *Hegemony and Socialist Strategy: Towards a Radical Democratic Politics*. Verso: London.

Lyotard, J.-F. (1984) *The Postmodern Condition: A Report on Knowledge*, trans. G. Bennington and B. Massumi. Manchester University Press: Manchester.

Mannheim, K. (1936) *Ideology and Utopia*. Routledge & Kegan Paul: London.

Marshall, T.H. (1964) 'Citizenship and social class', in T.H. Marshall (ed.), *Sociology at the Crossroads*. Heinemann: London.

Marx, K. (1965) *Capital, Volume 3*, trans. D. Fernback. Penguin: Harmondsworth.

Marx, K. (1976, orig. 1867) *Capital*, Vol. 1, trans. B. Fowkes, Penguin: Harmondsworth.

Marx, K. and Engels, F. (1970) *The German Ideology* (1846) (students' edition) ed. and introduced by C.J. Arthur, trans. W. Lough, C. Dutt and C.P. Magill. Lawrence & Wishart: London.

Masuda, Y. (1980) *The Information Society as Post-Industrial Society*. World Future Society: Washington, DC.

Miliband, R. (1974) *The State in Capitalist Society*. Weidenfeld & Nicolson: London.

Naisbitt, J. and Aburdene, P. (1990) *Megatrends 2000: New Directions for Tomorrow*. Avon Books: New York.

Norris, C. (1990) in R. Boyne and A. Rattansi (eds), *Postmodernism and Society*. Macmillan: Basingstoke.

Poulantzas, N. (1973) *Classes in Contemporary Capitalism*, trans. D. Fernbach. New Left Books: London.

Poulantzas, N. (1978) *State, Power, Socialism*, trans. P. Camiller. New Left Books: London.

Poulantzas, N. (1979) 'The problem of the capitalist state', *New Left Review*, 68, November–December.

Rorty, R. (1989) *Contingency, Irony and Solidarity*. Cambridge University Press: Cambridge.

Rostow, W.W. (1962) *The Stages of Economic Growth: A Non-Communist Manifesto*. Cambridge University Press: Cambridge.

Shannon, C.E. and Weaver, W. (1949) *The Mathematical Theory of Communication*. University of Illinois Press: Urbana, IL.

Strum, S. and Latour, B. (1987) 'The meanings of social: from baboons to humans', *Social Science Information*, 26: 783–802.

Toffler, A. (1970) *Future Shock*. Random House: New York.

Weber, M. (1948) 'Science as a vocation' (1918), in C. Wright Mills (ed.), *From Max Weber: Essays in Sociology*. Routledge & Kegan Paul: London.

Weber, M. (1976) *The Protestant Ethic and the Spirit of Capitalism*, trans. T. Parsons. George Allen & Unwin: London.

Weber, M. (1978) *Economy and Society: An Outline of Interpretive Sociology*, ed. G. Roth and C. Wittich, trans. E. Fischoff. University of California Press: Berkeley, CA.

Webster, F. and Robins, K. (1986) *Information Technology: A Luddite Analysis*. Ablex: Norwood, NJ.

Wiener, N. (1948) *Cybernetics or Control and Communication in the Animal and the Machine*. MIT Press: Cambridge, MA.

Williams, R. (1981) *Culture*. Fontana: London.

Williams, R. (1990) *What I Came to Say*, ed. N. Belton, F. Mulhern and J. Taylor. Hutchinson Radius: London.

Willis, P. (1977) *Learning to Labour: How Working Class Kids Get Working Class Jobs*. Saxon House: Farnborough, Hants.

Wrong, D. (1970) *Max Weber*. Prentice-Hall: Hemel Hempstead.

Chapter contents

3 The Action Perspectives: Theorising Social Action and Self

By the end of this chapter you should:

- have a critical understanding of the central concepts within the action perspectives: self, agency, social action, intention;
- have a critical understanding of the work of the central symbolic interactionists, Herbert Blumer, G.H. Mead, Charles Cooley, William James, Erving Goffman;
- be familiar with the contribution of the Chicago School, pragmatism and Freudian psychoanalysis to the development of the action perspectives;

- have a critical understanding of Alfred Schutz's phenomenology and Harold Garfinkel's ethnomethodology;
- have an understanding of contributions to our understanding of self which are derived from the action perspectives: Charles Taylor, Christopher Lasch and Richard Sennett.

The focus of the action perspectives – symbolic interactionism, ethnomethodology, and phenomenology – is on an understanding of how sustained social interaction is possible. This often involves observing people in their natural settings and examining particular instances of behaviour in a way that is sympathetic and sensitive to people's view of the world.

In essence we understand social action because it is symbolic and reciprocal in nature. Social actions are human behaviours that have an intention behind them: we as members of a society can observe, read and understand the meaning of behaviours that we observe. Behaviour has meaning for us because the words we use, the movements of our bodies and the gestures we make are symbolic in nature: they are representations of our intentions. We learn to read and understand symbols and representation because in our processes of socialisation, where people learn how to become members of society, we internalise a stock of meanings of words, gestures and behaviour. In addition, people are reflexive and to varying degrees have the ability to put themselves in the position of 'the other' and look at the world through the eyes of 'the other'. Although symbolic interactionism, for example, is not a unified perspective within the social sciences, there is an emphasis on pragmatism in the work of all symbolic interactionists. Moreover, for the symbolic interactionists society is more than a collection of individuals yet there is no such thing as society that exists independently of the people who exist within the society.

Blumer and symbolic interactionism

For Herbert Blumer what is distinctive about human relationships is our ability to construct and share our social worlds. As Blumer explains:

> The term 'symbolic interaction' refers, of course, to the peculiar and distinctive character of interaction as it takes place between human beings. The peculiarity consists in the fact that human beings interpret or 'define' each other's actions instead of merely reacting to each other's actions. Their 'response' is not made directly to the actions of one another but instead is based on the meaning that they attach to such actions. Thus, human interaction is mediated by the use of symbols, by interpretation. Or by ascertaining the meaning of one another's actions. (Blumer, 1962: 139)

Blumer assumes that:

o society is a framework within which interaction takes place, but society does not determine social action;
o social change is a product of interpretation, not brought about by factors outside of the person.

In Blumer's eyes no factors can influence social action, outside of this process of self-indication. Only interpretation precedes the act. Human beings identify things within their surroundings that they believe to be of use in guiding what they do. When we identify something in this fashion, Blumer argues, we disentangle it from its setting and give it meaning. We act on the basis of such symbols, attempting to identify their possible significance for our future actions. This approach stands in sharp contrast to Marxism and functionalism: in these perspectives, claims Blumer, human behaviour is seen to be a product of stimulus–response variables such as social class:

> The individuals who compose a human society are treated as the media through which such factors operate, and the social action of such individuals is regarded as an expression of such factors . . . If a place is given to 'interpretation', the interpretation is regarded as merely an expression of other factors (such as motives) that precede the act, and accordingly disappears as a factor in its own right. (Blumer, 1962: 143)

Symbolic interactionism has it origins in the work of a diverse group of theorists and researchers at the University of Chicago between 1890 and 1940, all of whom would describe themselves as pragmatists. In the early years of the twentieth century sociology in the USA was dominated by Park, Burgess and the other members of the Chicago School, who developed a perspective known as 'human ecology'. Human ecology drew upon Darwinian principles of natural selection and adaptation in order to explain the nature of social solidarity within the city.

Human ecologists argued that the city was organised on two levels:

o   the biotic – the impersonal forces and forms of dominance used by people in the competition for space in the city;
o   the cultural – a set of ideas and values which rest upon the biotic level.

For Louis Wirth (1897–1952) (1938), one of the leading figures in the school, rural areas and urban areas are at opposite ends of a spectrum. The city is a 'relatively large, dense and permanent settlement of socially heterogeneous individuals'. Social life in cities is very different from that in rural areas. There is a distinct 'urban way of life'. The size of the city suggests that people cannot know one another personally, so contacts are more impersonal in nature. These impersonal urban relationships can become anomic: people feel isolated, without the support of the community. Relationships in cities are almost always competitive and almost never cooperative, and the subsequent friction between individuals has resulted in the loss of a feeling of community. The heterogeneity, which Wirth mentions in his definition of the city, means that there is a greater division of labour (people specialise in their occupation), the class structure becomes more complex and there is greater social and geographical mobility.

Critics have cast doubt upon the distinction between the biotic and the cultural levels and suggest that Wirth overstated the impersonality of modern cities. Moreover, Wirth generalises from the experiences of American cities, notably Chicago, while cities in other parts of the world may have very different forms of urban social life. Pragmatism is an approach to social theory which emphasises the direct correspondence between meaning and action. Pragmatists place a great deal of stress upon understanding the meaning of any action by looking at the consequences of that action in terms of the practical significance it has on the everyday life experiences of people. Pragmatists assume that knowledge is always incomplete, uncertain, subject to error, and that our ideas, concepts and judgements are merely symbols. Charles Horton Cooley (1864–1929), for instance, argued that our central moral ideas such as justice and freedom, upon which the moral unity of society was built, were derived from face-to-face relationships in primary groups such as families, neighbourhoods and children's play groups. Although the influence of Darwinian principles has largely declined, in the latter part of the twentieth century pragmatism was popularised by postmodernists such as Richard Rorty.

William James (1842–1910) was the first theorist to develop what has become known as the symbolic interactionist conception of the 'self'. James recognised that individuals have the ability to perceive themselves as others see them and to make use of these ideas in how they think about themselves. James developed three overlapping conceptions of the self:

o   **material self** – which consists of the roles that people play, such as undergraduate or lecturer, and physical objects, such as wearing glasses, the type of clothes we wear, our hairstyle and other things that help to make us 'who we are';

o **social self** – the feelings we acquire about ourselves because of the associations we have with other people, for example who we choose as friends;
o **spiritual self** – the cognitive style and capacities that typify our personality.

One of the central theorists who contributed to symbolic interactionism by building upon the work of James was George Herbert Mead (1863–1931). Mead's analysis starts with his conception of the 'action', which can take one of two forms:

o *the act-as-such* – which refers to our organic activity as animals (for example, eating);
o *the social act* – which is relevant to the interpretation of people's behaviour in society.

In *The Philosophy of the Act* (published in 1938, after his death), Mead explains that the 'act' develops in four stages:

o The impulse to action – in which the individual feels the need to respond to what they believe to be a problematic situation. The individual consciousness is then *intentional* in nature.
o The perception of the problem – in which the individual defines the nature of the problem that they face. In this sense Mead assumes action is future oriented and that the self has a time-consciousness in which problems can be anticipated and unpleasant consequences identified.
o The manipulation stage – in which the individual takes action to change the problematic situation.
o The consummation stage – in which the problematic situation is resolved.

Mead's work can be considered as central to the symbolic interactionist tradition. Under the influence of John Dewey (1859–1952) – who can also be considered an early symbolic interactionist – the social constitution of meaning is often referred to as 'situational meaning'. For Dewey, results are not evidential but provisional (hypotheses) and he placed a great deal of emphasis on 'experience'. Knowledge is always tentative and has to be constantly 'tested' and reworked in an ongoing discourse. For Dewey, underpinning epistemology is a method by which one experience is made available to another experience by giving direction and meaning, which he described as 'reflective thinking'.

In 1891 Dewey, Head of the Department of Philosophy at the University of Michigan, recruited Mead to work there. Dewey and Mead were friends and informed each other's theorising.

Mead accepted the assumptions that Dewey made about human agency:

o That what makes humans different from other animals is their ability to think.

- That 'mind' is a process not a structure that comes out of our attempt to organise and make sense of the situations we are in.
- That coming to terms with the situations we are in is a reflexive process in which we anticipate possible responses and their consequences, before we select our social action.

From these propositions Mead developed the idea of a 'conversation of gestures'. One famous example he outlined was that of the dog-fight:

> Dogs approaching each other in hostile attitude carry on such a language of gestures. They walk around each other, growling and snapping, and waiting for the opportunity to attack . . . The act of each dog becomes the stimulus to the other dog for his response. There is then a relationship between these two; and as the act is responded to by the other dog, it, in turn, undergoes change. The very fact that the dog is ready to attack another becomes a stimulus to the other dog to change his own position or his own attitude. He has no sooner done this than the change of attitude in the second dog in turn causes the first dog to change his attitude. We have here a conversation of gestures. They are not, however, gestures in the sense that they are significant. We do not assume that the dog says to himself, 'If the animal comes from this direction he is going to spring at my throat and I will turn in such a way.' What does take place is an actual change in his own position due to the direction of the approach of the other dog. (Mead, 1934: 14, 42–3)

In 1934 G.H. Mead defined the 'self' as that which is designated in common speech by the words 'I' and 'Me'. For Mead, 'mind' and 'self' are social in nature and language is the key factor in their formation. Language gives the individual the ability to replace behaviour with ideas. Moreover, the individual can view himself or herself as an object that they have control over. What guides an individual's perception of himself or herself is the perception of others. This is how 'society' has an influence over the individual self, and how we acquire a 'social self'. 'Society' is found in the mind of the individual as 'the generalised other', which Mead defines as 'The organized community or social group which gives to the individual his unity of self' (Mead, 1934: 154). In addition, individuals can ask for information from 'significant others', people who are close to them and are regarded as part of a primary group.

In a similar fashion, Cooley (1922) argues that the self should be viewed as a social construction, arising out of social experience and built by reference to other people's responses to the behaviour of the self. Cooley referred to this in *Human Nature and the Social Order* (1922: 184), as the 'looking glass self'.

Social reference in Cooley's analysis is first of all how the individual self appears in one's own imagination. As he explained:

> Each to each a looking-glass
> Reflects the other that doth pass.

As we see our face, figure, and dress in the glass, and are interested in them because they are ours, and pleased or otherwise with them according as they do or do not answer to what we should like them to be; so in imagination we perceive in another's mind some thought of our appearance, manners, aims, deeds, character, friends, and so on, and are variously affected by it. (Cooley, 1922: 185)

The self-concept has three main parts in Cooley's analysis, all of which link the self to society:

o   We look at our appearance from the perspective of the other.
o   We attempt to imagine the judgement of the other about us.
o   We use the above information to develop feelings about our self, such as self-respect or embarrassment.

In a similar fashion to Cooley, for Mead, selves can exist only in definite relationships to other selves; moreover, the essence of self is cognitive. In other words, the self is formed through knowledge acquired by mediated experience. This is the basis of the distinction that Mead makes between the 'I' and the 'Me'. The 'I' is the acting self that is free, unique and can exercise initiative. In contrast, the 'Me' is the internalisation of the attitudes of others, represented by the notion of 'the generalised other'. The 'I' and the 'Me' form a cognitive structure, with the concept of 'the generalised other' allowing the individual self to organise its cognitive experience. Individual selves reflect upon themselves, by use of 'the generalised other' – which Mead understood to be 'the attitude of the whole community' to which a person belongs; it is the 'essential basis and prerequisite of the fullest development of that individual's self' (Mead, 1967: 219).

Mead explains the 'social self' by claiming that 'until one can respond to himself as a community responds to him, he does not genuinely belong to the community' (Mead, 1934: 265).

For Mead, the self is a reflective project, and this reflexivity distinguishes human consciousness from animal consciousness and differentiates the self from other objects and from the body.

It is perfectly true that the eye can see the foot, but it does not see the body as a whole. We cannot see our backs; we can feel certain portions of them, if we are agile, but we cannot get an experience of our whole body. There are, of course, experiences which are somewhat vague and difficult of location, but the bodily experiences are for us organized about a self. The foot and hand belong to the self. We can see our feet, especially if we look at them from the wrong end of an opera glass, as strange things which we have difficulty in recognizing as our own. The parts of the body are quite distinguishable from the self. We can lose parts of the body without any serious invasion of the self. The mere ability to experience different parts of the body is not different from the experience of a table. The table presents a different feel from what the hand does when one hand feels another, but it is an experience of something with which we come definitely into contact. The body does not experience itself as a whole, in the sense in which the self in some way enters into the experience of the self. (Mead, 1934: 136)

Consciousness indicates, first, 'a certain feeling consciousness' in relation to environment and secondly an awareness of 'I' as our *self*-consciousness. The distinction that Mead makes between the 'I' and 'Me' has a great deal in common with the work of Sigmund Freud on the self.

Mead's social analysis

Society – All group life is essentially a matter of cooperative behaviours	Cooperation is brought about by a process whereby: (a) persons ascertain the intentions of others (b) they respond on the basis of their perception of those intentions	*Necessary conditions* (a) Able to understand the lines of action of others (b) Able to guide own actions to fit in with those lines of actions
Self – Formed through the definitions made by others. 'I' – the impulsive tendency in the individual 'Me' – the incorporated 'other'	Person comes to see him/herself as an object, by stepping outside him/herself, and seeing as others see them	*Necessary conditions* (a) Language development (b) Ability to take role of 'other'
Mind – The mental images that emerge out of communication	(a) All behaviour involves selective attention and perception (b) Mind is present only when significant symbols are being used by the individual	*Necessary conditions* Imagination
Acts – Encompasses the total process involved in human activity (attention, perception, reasoning, emotion, etc.)	The culmination of all of the foregoing processes (society, self and mind)	

The key concepts of Mead's social analysis (adapted from Turner, 1991: 388–9)

Sigmund Freud

Perhaps the most obvious starting point for any discussion of the self-concept would be the work of Sigmund Freud (1856–1939). In Freudian psychoanalysis, the substance of self is an imprint of the significant other people, notably parents, upon the protoplasm (the very cells which form the basis of life in all plants and animals) of the young child's psyche. The boundaries of self, for Freud, are established through a complex interface between four key concepts: **projection**, **introjection**, **repression** and **regression**. Projection is commonly viewed as a form of rationalisation:

an individual disowns something mentally intolerable by projecting it on to another person or object. Introjection is the opposite. Repression can be viewed as a form of 'motivated forgetting', with repressed thoughts pushed deep into the unconscious mind. Any unpleasant thoughts, ideas or expressions can simply be repressed – we deny their existence. The effect of this may be to stop individuals from understanding their own intentions. People in a repressed state may experience fears but have no understanding of their cause. Regression is a process in which an individual reverts to former ways of behaving in order to satisfy needs. Individuals, for example, may choose to smoke when they are under pressure, in an effort to gain pleasure similar to the young child sucking at its mother's breast.

The structure of the self, for Freud, is made up of three systems: the **id**, the **ego** and the **superego**. The id is biological in nature, and is the home of the libido, a set of biological drives which are pleasure seeking and primarily sexual. The ego is a social entity that develops to keep the id under control, and attempts to find a form of compromise between id and superego, on the basis of a **reality principle** that is itself the product of identifications with others. The ego curbs the need for immediate satisfaction that our id demands, in order to fit in with the demands of the wider society. Finally is the superego: this has been described as the 'internalised representative of society' or the 'parent within'. The superego can be viewed as the repository for social values within the self and is concerned with prohibitions and restrictions imposed upon us by the outside world. A key concept in the Freudian analysis of self that still has significance in present debates about self is the notion of 'incongruence': our need for positive regard on the basis of conditions laid down by others. As individuals we have a tendency to hide or reject elements of our self that fail to receive the positive regard of others. This is clearly related to the Freudian notion of **narcissism** that, as we shall see below, has been transformed by Lasch from the 'libidinal investment of the self' (Lasch, 1978: 36) to the 'projection of inner anxieties' (1978: 51).

Within psychology, even within psychoanalysis, many people were unhappy with the Freudian conception of the id: that it was biologically driven and solely sexual in nature. Within sociology, most notably in what was to become symbolic interactionism, at the turn of the century we find a different conception of self emerging, although still concerned with individuals having to face up to modernity.

The Mead conception of 'I' is similar to the Freudian id, the impulsive/ unorganised part of the individual self, while the 'Me' is a situated self that we find playing roles within a structured environment. In other words, the 'Me' is the self that we present within a group and the 'I' the subjective reflection upon ourselves, by the use of the 'generalised other' which is made up of what we understand to be accepted attitudes and beliefs. For Mead: 'It is a structure of attitudes which makes a self' (Mead, 1967: 226). However, the self is not passive in Mead's analysis and does exercise agency. It has to respond to the generalised other, but the behaviour of the self is not determined by the generalised other. Moreover, it is the individual that constructs the generalised other and the individual can include new others.

Mead represents the first example of what was to become known as the 'linguistic turn' in sociology, as he places language at the very centre of his analysis of self-formation. Communication using language is a precondition for the emergence of self. It is only when an individual can organise their thoughts in language that they become a self. Language allows people to reflect upon themselves in an objective fashion, which is essential for the formation of the 'Me'. A number of recent accounts of the self fall within this 'linguistic turn', notably those of Jürgen Habermas, Rom Harré and Charles Taylor.

Alfred Schutz on action, interaction and sociological phenomenology

Alfred Schutz (1899–1959) put the individual human agent at the centre of his analysis. Schutz's phenomenology assumes that all our knowledge is drawn from phenomena: that which is directly experienced by our senses. The phenomenological approach is based upon the careful description of these phenomena. Whatever lies behind phenomena – what is referred to as *noumen* – always remains unknowable. Phenomenologists have produced subtle analyses of how individuals create categories of thought and how reality is put together within social processes.

In 1935, Austrian-born Schutz emigrated from Germany to the United States. In the later years of his life he integrated many of the ideas of the Chicago School and pragmatism into his work. Schutz's ideas had a significant impact on a generation of American social scientists, such as Peter Berger and Thomas Luckmann (see *The Social Construction of Reality*, 1967).

For Schutz we live in the *Lebenswelt* or *lifeworld* – 'the world of lived experience', which is made up of the life experiences of other people and how they impact upon us as individuals. The *Lebenswelt* consists of physical and social objects which are experienced by us as already existing and already organised. We assume that the *Lebenswelt* was there before we were born; we take it for granted and suspend doubt that things might be otherwise. According to Schutz, we adopt 'the natural attitude' towards the *Lebenswelt*.

Our everyday experiences, our personal direction, social action and the many other dealings that we have with people are found within the *Lebenswelt*. However, unlike many philosophers Schutz wanted to develop an analysis of social action which was objective but not deterministic in nature and allowed individuals to have a completely free choice in their social action.

Schutz's contribution to phenomenology developed out of a close reading and critique of Max Weber's analysis of social action. According to Weber a social action is any action which has an intention behind it. Weber identified four types of intention:

o *Zweckrationalität* – social action which is motivated by a goal;
o *Wertrationalität* – social action which is motivated by a value;
o *Affect* – social action which is motivated by emotion;
o *Tradition* – social action which is motivated by customs or other well established ways of behaving.

Schutz was concerned by the lack of serious philosophical basis for Weber's work. For Schutz, social action is much more subjective than Weber had described and has a much richer variety of intentions underpinning it. For Schutz, the meaning of an action is constituted by the agent.

The focus of Schutz's analysis is *intersubjectivity* – *how* we understand each other and how we come to have similar perceptions and conceptions of the world. Whilst interacting with others within the *Lebenswelt* we assume a *reciprocity of perspectives*. In other words we assume that, if we changed places with the other, we would view the world as the other does. This assumption is similar to Mead's notion of taking the role of the other.

According to Schutz, there is a distinction between *action* and *act*: 'action is a spontaneous activity oriented toward the future' (1972: 57). In contrast act occurs when the individual agent reflects upon the completed action. Individuals can choose to carry out any social action they wish, based upon an infinite range of possible intentions. However, for Schutz all people have a life project, a thing that they are aiming for which is of their own choosing. Accordingly, all individual social actions should be viewed as mini-projects, which are carried out in order to allow the person to fulfil their overall life project. All social actions have an *in-order-to motive*, in which a person justifies to themselves that they are about to carry out a social action *in order to* achieve something. After the completion of the social action, people reflect on the action and justify it with a *because motive*. Here the person says to themselves, 'I did that social action *because* I want to achieve something.'

An important component that we use for understanding our social setting is our **stock of knowledge at hand**. A large amount of this stock consists of our reflections on actions we have carried out, what we did the action for and the motives we had for carrying out the action. If we have done something once, we know how to do it again in the same fashion. Schutz refers to this stock of knowledge as 'typifications': these are the 'rules of typicality' that we use to organise the social world and that make us feel able to act with confidence. As Schutz explained in a discussion of language:

> The typifying medium *par excellence* by which socially derived knowledge is transmitted is the vocabulary and syntax of everyday language. The vernacular of everyday life is primarily a language of named things and events, and any name includes a typification and generalization referring to the relevance system

prevailing in the linguistic in-group which found the named thing significant enough to provide a separate term for it. (Schutz, 1964: 14)

This 'knowledge at hand' is socially constructed as *the natural attitude* and forms the foundation of the intersubjective understanding that we experience as 'we-relationships', and/or 'they-relationships'. Moreover, because we communicate with others about their respective meanings, we come to experience this social reality as having an 'objective' meaning, made up of customs, habits, laws and regulations.

Schutz assumes that individuals who have chosen the same 'life project' will also have to choose similar 'in order to motives' and similar 'because motives'. Therefore although the individual human agent has a completely free choice over the social actions they involve themselves in, and have a whole range of subjective human experiences, it is possible to predict the actions and intentions of an individual on a given life project. On the basis of this Schutz constructs 'ideal type' people, which he terms *homunculi*. These ideal type people have all the 'in order to motives' and all the 'because motives' of a person on a given life project. The individual may construct their own world, but they must do this with the materials that are available to them in the lifeworld, which are often shared by others. Individuals absorb the contents of the lifeworld, interpret and make sense of their experience on the basis of the natural attitude, the typical ways of behaving, which is found within the lifeworld itself.

Erving Goffman: the ethnographer of the self

Erving Goffman (1922–1982) is regarded by many as one of the best exponents of symbolic interactionism. He was primarily concerned with understanding 'face-to-face' interactions, or what he called 'the interaction order': situations where people are 'physically in one another's presence'. He looked at social action as a theatrical performance, in which social actors played roles within a 'front region', which had a great deal in common with the stage front of a theatrical performance. As people we attempt to stage-manage the impressions that others receive of us. Hence, Goffman argued, social actors present themselves in everyday life as people performing for their social audiences with the appropriate props and costumes in an effort to convince observers that they genuinely had the skills and ability to perform the role.

Like Mead, Goffman believed the self to be reflexive and a product of the internal conversation we have with ourselves, taking into account exchange of gestures, the ability to read the meaning of gestures and symbols that people present about us, and the ability to manipulate the perception that others have of us. In Goffman's approach, social actors always attempt to control what they consider to be the central aspects of a setting in order to present a coherent front. At the same time people attempt to conceal anything about themselves that they believe to be inconsistent with successfully performing the role. Goffman's approach was later described as dramaturgical in character. In developing his dramaturgy, in his early work Goffman argued that there were social rules and rituals which people drew upon to 'define the situation'; in his latter works he developed the notion of *frame*, which moved away from the type of analysis that Mead had pioneered and rested on a structuralist approach.

Goffman's work involves the examination of particular instances of social life as they occur in their usual settings. His work is characterised by partisanship. Goffman's research is neither objective nor value-free, is anti-positivistic, and uses methods of data collection such as participant observation and case studies. His aim was to see the world in the same way as those people under investigation and his research gave a sympathetic and sensitive understanding of their worldview. The basic concepts used by Goffman are outlined in the following sections.

The self

In *The Presentation of Self in Everyday Life* (1959) Goffman explains that selves reside in social roles, and that the self can be divided in two. First there is the official self: 'During interaction the individual is expected to possess certain attributes, capacities, and information which, taken together, fit together into a self that is at once coherently unified and appropriate for the occasion' (Goffman, 1956: 263).

Behind this official self is the unsocialised self, which is referred to by Goffman as the 'self as perfomer', 'our all too human selves', the 'self as player'. If the official self is disrupted in some way then, according to Goffman:

> The individual who performs the character will be seen for what he largely is, a solitary player involved in a harried concern for his production. Behind many characters each performer tends to wear a single look, a naked unsocialised look, a look of concentration, a look of one who is privately engaged in a difficult treacherous task. (Goffman, 1959: 235)

All social behaviour, Goffman believed, is based upon intentionality; every social action has meaning for the social actors.

Activity

Do the concepts of 'official self' and 'unofficial self' apply to you? Explain to yourself how your 'official self' differs from your 'unofficial self'.

If you have a job, is there a distinction between 'front region' and 'back region'? If you have ever worked in a restaurant, for example, did the waiters ever behave differently when dealing with the public than they did in the kitchen?

Activity

Do people choose their **identity** or is it imposed upon them? Ask people to adopt any identity that they wish. You could ask a sample of people if they would incorporate the role of miniskirt-wearer into their identity. Would any people feel unable to incorporate this lifestyle choice into their identity? Make a list of people who said no and give an indication of their reasons.

Moral career

All social roles constitute a 'moral career'. For Goffman each person can be viewed as having a moral career which is two sided:

o   Internally, the moral career involves image of self and felt identity.
o   Externally, the moral career involves social location, style of life and 'is part of a publicly accessible institutional complex' (Goffman, 1961c: 127)

Moral career refers to the progression through a number of social roles. In everyday language, we use the word *career* to describe the progression and development of an individual in their chosen job or profession. In a similar fashion a mental patient goes through a number of stages: they may be said to have a career as a mad person beginning with a complaint about behaviour and ending with hospitalisation. They develop the characteristics of the mad person, accepting pressures which influence behaviour and limit further choice.

Alvin Gouldner, in Chapter 2 of *For Sociology*: 'The sociologist as partisan: Sociology and the welfare state', is highly critical of this position of partisanship. Gouldner accuses the symbolic interactionists of sentimentality, saying that their work produces 'essays on quaintness':

> The danger is, then, that such an identification with 'the underdog' becomes the urban sociologist's equivalent of the anthropologist's (one-time) romantic appreciation of the noble savage. (Gouldner, 1974: 37)

> It is a sociology of and for the new Welfare state. It is the sociology of young men with friends in Washington. It is the sociology that succeeds in solving the oldest problem in personal politics: how to maintain one's integrity without sacrificing one's career, or how to remain liberal although well-heeled. (Gouldner, 1974: 49)

The revelation of rationality

Goffman attempted to demonstrate that the behaviour of 'underdogs' was not irrational. The most often quoted example is the hoarding behaviour of mental patients. Goffman argued that in the abnormal situation of the mental hospital, hoarding is the normal reaction to an abnormal situation, because of the almost total lack of a secure place for personal possessions to be kept; yet this behaviour is regarded by the staff as evidence of mental illness.

Defining the situation, social occasion, frame

If social actors define the situations in which they find themselves as real, then for Goffman the situation *is* real. Social situations are a 'negotiated order': the definition of the situation is created by a process of negotiation between the social actors involved:

> When persons come into each other's immediate presence they tend to do so as participants in what I shall call a social occasion. This is a wider social affair, undertaking or event, bounded in regard to place and time and typically facilitated by fixed; a social occasion provides the structuring social context in which many situations and their gatherings are likely to form, dissolve and reform while a pattern of conduct tends to be recognised as the appropiate and often official intended one. (Goffman, 1963a: 18)

In his later work Goffman develops these themes into the notion of a frame. In *Frame Analysis* (1975), he explains:

> I assume that definitions of the situation are built up in accordance with principles of organization which govern events – at least social ones – and our subjective involvement in them; frame is the word I use to refer to such of these basic elements as I am able to identify. That is the definition of frame. My phrase 'frame analysis' is a slogan to refer to the examination in these terms of the organization of experience. (Goffman, 1974: 10–11)

Goffman divides up what he refers to as 'primary frameworks' into two types:

1 *Natural primary frameworks*:

> Natural frameworks identify occurrences seen as undirected, unoriented, unanimated, unguided, 'purely physical'. Such unguided events are ones understood to be due totally, from start to finish, to 'natural' determinants. It is seen that no wilful agency causally and intentionally interferes, that no actor intentionally guides the outcome. (Goffman, 1975: 22)

2 *Social primary frameworks*:

> provide background understanding for events that incorporate the will, aim and controlling effort of an intelligence, a live agency, the chief one being the human being. (Goffman, 1975: 22)

For Goffman, these primary social frameworks constitute the central element in a social groups' culture.

Keys and keyings

From his notion of the primary framework, Goffman develops the notions of 'key' and 'keyings'. The key is a set of conventions. This term means more than simply a 'rule'; the concept also involves issues such as necessity, obligation and interdependence, by which: 'a given activity, one already meaningful in terms of some primary framework, is transformed into something patterned on this activity but seen by the participants to be something quite else. The process of transcription can be called keying' (Goffman, 1975: 43).

Goffman explains that a rough musical analogy is intended: 'A keying then, when there is one, performs a crucial role in determining what it is we think is really going on' (Goffman, 1975: 45).

Goffman's argument is that definitions of the situation are neither static nor simplistic, having potentially different meanings for participants, new participants and observers. Unless one is on the same wavelength as the social group one will never fully understand – as they do – what is going on.

If we take our example of mental patients and hoarding behaviour again, on one level it is possible to say this is evidence of mental illness: the staff keying. On another level, from the point of view of the mental patient – a mad keying – it is reasonable behaviour, something one would not normally do if one were in a different social situation. In other words, unless the staff are familiar with the key used by the inmates, they will not be in a position to fully understand the primary framework of the social relationship.

The notion of keying means that social activity is vulnerable to fabrication: 'the intentional effort of one or more individuals to manage activity so that a party of one or more others will believe about what it is that is going on' (Goffman, 1975: 83).

Fabrication is a common theme in Goffman's work and he discusses a number of types, for example 'benign fabrications' of which there is a rich variety, ranging from practical jokes to the 'purely strategic'; where a benign fabrication is engineered in the basic interests of the one who is deceived. Fabrications can also be of an exploitative kind.

Goffman explains how a legitimate key can be used as a cover for a deception, as for example in the case of using medical procedures as a front for improper action. He quotes the following example:

> Los Angeles – A housewife has filed a $100,000 malpractice suit against a psychiatrist. She claimed he prescribed sexual relations with himself as therapy and then charged her for the 'treatments'.

In the suit the 33-year-old mother of two said she had held the doctor in 'complete confidence and trust'. He persuaded her, she said, that her problems stemmed from lack of sexual activity and suggested himself as a sexual partner. She said she agreed to the 'treatments' for several months and then became 'worried and remorseful' because he had stopped charging for the visits. Mrs. Keene said that when she implored him to stop the treatments, he criticized her sexual abilities and told her he was intimate with her only because she was so available. Then he billed her for $225. (Goffman, 1975: 160)

Keying and fabrications are referred to by Goffman as 'basic transformations' of the untransformed activity of the primary social framework, which set the terms for experience.

Let us have a closer look at some of Goffman's central texts.

Erving Goffman: The Presentation of Self in Everyday Life *(1959)*

In this book Goffman describes the ways in which people present an image of themselves to others:

> some of the common techniques that persons employ to sustain such impressions and common contingencies associated with the employment of those techniques . . . In their capacity as performers, individuals will be concerned with maintaining the impression that they are living up to the many standards by which they and their products are judged. Because these standards are so numerous and so pervasive, the individuals who are performers dwell more than we might think in a moral world. But *qua* performers, individuals are concerned not with the moral issue of realizing these standards, but with the amoral issue of engineering a convincing impression that these standards are being realised. (Goffman, 1959: 26, 243)

The research for the book is based largely upon Goffman's unpublished Ph.D. thesis 'Communication conduct in an island community' (1953); this was a study of a crofting community in the Shetland Islands, together with many case studies from sociology, fiction and journalism. For Goffman, the expressiveness of the individual involves two types of sign activity: **traditional communication**, used simply to convey information; and **action symptomatic of the actor**: this is action performed for reasons other than the conveying of information. *The Presentation of Self in Everyday Life* is mainly concerned with the second type of communication.

All communication takes place within a definition of the situation, and within groups of social actors there is a 'division of definitional labour':

> Each participant is allowed to establish the tentative official rule regarding matters which are vital to him but not immediately important to others, e.g. the rationalizations and justifications by which he accounts for his past activity. In exchange for this courtesy he remains silent or non-committal on matters important to others but not immediately important to him . . . a 'working consensus'. (Goffman, 1959: 21)

Any definition of the situation will have a moral character, according to Goffman. Individuals who have particular characteristics may feel that they have the right to be treated in the recognised and appropriate way. Moreover, any individual who implicitly or explicitly signifies that they have particular characteristics ought to be what they say they are. Individuals, and groups (which Goffman refers to as *teams*) present a *front* when they are carrying out any social action. The front is the 'expressive equipment' used to make social action and communication more effective. Front is made up of two basic elements:

- o   *Setting*: the geographical aspects of a situation in which a performance is given.
- o   *Personal front*: aspects like rank, sex, age and race.

In order for communication to be possible, observers stress the abstract similarities that are seen to exist, for example all doctors may be viewed in a similar fashion and treated accordingly. This allows the individual social actor to deal with a number of fronts in a wide variety of situations:

> it is to be noted that a given social front tends to become institutionalized in terms of the abstract stereotyped expectations to which it gives rise, and tends to take on a meaning and stability apart from specific tasks which happen at the time to be performed in its name. The front becomes a 'collective representation' and a fact in its own right. (Goffman, 1959: 37)

'Fronts' for Goffman are selected, not created. Goffman also gives us a clear idea of what the individual behind the front is like:

> Behind many masks and many characters, each performer tends to wear a single look, a naked unsocialized look, a look of concentration, a look of one who is privately engaged in a difficult, treacherous task. (Goffman, 1959: 228)

In an effort to maintain front individual social actors are involved in audience segregation: this is an attempt by the social actor not to present contradictory fronts to the same audience, and therefore lose face.

Goffman is not simply concerned with individual social action; he is also concerned with team performance. Within any group of people with a common purpose (team), individuals will be involved in regional behaviour. Goffman defines a region 'as any place that is bounded to some degree by barriers to perception' (1959: 109). Front region is the place where the performance for the audience is given. In contrast, back region 'may be defined as a place, relative to a given performance, where the impression fostered by the performance is knowingly contradicted as a matter of course' (1959: 114).

All groups appear to have a front region and a back region, as Goffman explains:

Since we all participate on teams we must all carry within ourselves something of the sweet guild of conspirators. And since each team is engaged in maintaining the stability of some definitions of the situation, concealing or playing down certain facts in order to do this, we can expect the performer to live out his conspiratorial career in some furtiveness. (1959: 108)

Erving Goffman: *Stigma: Notes on the Management of a Spoiled Identity* (1963)

In this book Goffman is concerned with three different types of stigma:

First there are abominations of the body – the various physical deformities. Next there are blemishes of individual character perceived as weak will, domineering or unnatural passions, treacherous and rigid beliefs, and dishonesty, these being inferred from a known record of, for example, mental disorder, imprisonment, addiction, alcoholism, homosexuality, unemployment, suicidal attempts, and radical political behaviour. Finally, there are the tribal stigmas of race, nation, and religion, these being stigmas that can be transmitted through lineages and equally contaminate all members of a family. (Goffman, 1963a: 14)

For Goffman individual social actors with very different stigmas are in a similar situation *vis-à-vis* the rest of the population, and stigmatised individuals, irrespective of the type of stigma they have, respond to the wider population in a very similar fashion. We all have the capacity to play the role of stigmatised and normal. Both sets of social actors acknowledge that a stigma means possessing shameful differences regarding identity. This Goffman refers to as the 'normal–stigmatized unity' (1963a: 155). Normals regard stigmatised individuals as not fully human, and not only subject them to a variety of forms of discrimination, but also construct an ideology to explain why the stigmatised are inferior and why they pose a threat: this is 'rationalizing an animosity' (1963a: 15). It is important to understand that the categories of stigmatised and normal are *not* concrete groups of people, but *perspectives*. Almost all individual social actors carry with them some degree of stigma, but some have lifelong attributes that give them very high visibility, which causes them to be typecast as stigmatised in all social situations, continually in opposition to normals. Such a person progresses along a socialisation path which Goffman refers to as a *moral career*: a process by which the stigmatised learns the normal point of view, and that they are excluded from it. The rest of us, successfully on the whole, use a variety of techniques to restrict information about our minimal stigma. However, we live in constant fear that it will be exposed. Goffman gives examples of girls who examine themselves in the mirror after losing their virginity to see if their stigma shows, only slowly accepting that they look no different. One such technique of information control Goffman refers to as *covering*; this usually takes the form of not displaying the things about ourselves which we know are abnormal, if this is at all possible. Name-changing is one of the most often used covering techniques. Handicapped people too learn to behave in such a way as to minimise the obtrusiveness of their stigma.

Although the major epistemological break in Goffman's work – the shift from symbolic interactionism to structuralism – did not come until near the end of his life; in *Stigma* Goffman uses a number of *semiological* concepts in order to understand stigma; most notably referring to the stigmatised individual as the *signifier*. Stigma is explained in terms of the presentation of *signs*, and the ability of the normals to decode those signs.

We can see in this work the influence of Talcott Parsons. Consider the following examples:

> It can be assumed that a necessary condition for social life is the sharing of a single set of normative expectations by all participants, the norms being sustained in part because of being incorporated. When a rule is broken restorative measures will occur; the damaging is terminated and the damage repaired, whether by control agencies or by the culprit himself. (Goffman, 1963a: 152)

> in an important sense there is only one complete unblushing male in America: a young, married, white, urban, northern, heterosexual Protestant father of college education, fully employed, of good complexion, weight and height and a recent record in sports. Every American male tends to look out upon the world from this perspective, this constituting one sense in which one can speak of a common value system in America. (ibid.)

Alvin Gouldner argues that Goffman's sociology is ahistorical and that it fails to confront the matter of hierarchy. He also believes Goffman pays no attention to power: that is, his microsociology fails to explain how power affects the individual's abilities to present selves effectively. This critique is found in *The Coming Crisis in Western Sociology* (1971: 179–90) and in *For Sociology* (1974: 347ff.).

Mary F. Rogers in 'Goffman on power, hierarchy, and status' (1981) takes up the critique that Goffman's analysis is poor on understanding power relationships. Rogers argues that Goffman's sociology contains very few open references to power; power relationships are present, but are treated almost entirely implicitly. Individuals use power to affect the behaviour of other actors in society, by the use of resources. Rogers describes these as *instrumental resources* and *infra resources*.

Instrumental resources include interpersonal skills like character, presence of mind, perceived fateful circumstances (Goffman, 1967: 216ff.), knowledge (Goffman, 1961c: 219–20), and information control (Goffman, 1959: 102).

Infra resources, according to Rogers, focus 'largely on perceptions, information and access'. She quotes Goffman: 'Control of people results from shaping their definitions of a situation' (1959: 30), and from shaping 'what they perceive' (1959: 6). Negative stereotypes, labels and ideologies constitute mechanisms generating control. According to Rogers, it appears that for Goffman power is a form of collusion between people who have a minimal stigma and who can pass as normals, against others who for a variety of reasons are unable or unwilling to accept the definition of the situation.

Various theorists have taken up a number of the themes in relation to 'self' and 'culture' that were first devised by symbolic interactionists, but who are not part of the symbolic interactionist tradition. I would like to conclude the chapter by looking at some of these contributions.

Charles Taylor on the self

Although Goffman's work on the self has had a great influence within sociology, he does not examine in any detail the notion of 'agency'. Goffman is only concerned with our performance as people, with manipulating self-image. Alister MacIntyre (1981) argues that success in Goffman's universe is nothing but what passes for success. Goffman has identified the self with mere role-playing, the self being no more than 'a peg' on which the clothes of the role are hung.

In contrast to Goffman, Charles Taylor is concerned with the question: what is it to be a human agent? He explains: 'We talk about a human being as a "self" . . . meaning that they are beings of the requisite depth and complexity to have an identity' (Taylor, 1989: 32). The self has a 'strategic capacity' and as such requires some form of reflective awareness. In addition, for Taylor: 'One is a self only among other selves. A self can never be described without reference to those who surround it' (1989: 35).

The notion of the self is peculiar to the modern world and would not have been understood by individuals who lived in the distant past. Our modern self has a distinction between inside and outside. The inside contains our inner thoughts, desires and intentions, which requires a 'radical reflexivity' and constantly reviews what it does and thinks and why it does what it does and thinks what it thinks in the way that it does. The outside is the public domain, the image we present to the outside world.

Taylor's work also falls within what sociologists call the 'linguistic turn' within sociology. For Taylor, we find sense in our life by talking about it. In addition, Taylor introduces the notion of moral frameworks, which people use in order to create a self that they find acceptable. We define who we are from the position we speak from and whom we speak to. Our skill as speakers – Taylor uses the term 'interlocutors' – allows us to form relationships with others and to be involved in shared activities, which are essential to becoming an individual self. 'It's as though the dimension of interlocution were of significance only for the genesis of individuality' (Taylor, 1989: 36).

Christopher Lasch on the self

In *The Culture of Narcissism* (1991, first published 1978), Christopher Lasch attempts to explain how a culture of competitive individualism has developed into a 'narcissistic preoccupation' with the self and with how we look as individuals.

Individuals who are narcissistic rely upon expert systems such as various forms of therapy like counselling or psychoanalysis. Practitioners present these therapies as means of emancipation from the repressive burdens of the past. In the modern world, individuals are ridden with anxiety, together with a feeling of inner emptiness and deeply anti-social impulses. Individuals are living in a state of personal unrest and constantly attempt to fulfil unsatisfied desires. Narcissism makes people psychologically dependent, for the narcissist needs others to provide her/him with self-esteem; hence the world becomes a mirror. Moreover, the self becomes an 'egomaniacal, experience devouring imperial self . . . [which] regresses into a grandiose, narcissistic, infantile, empty self: a "dark wet hole"' (Lasch, 1991: 12) with only a 'pseudo-insight' expressed in psychiatric clichés, which are used merely to deflect criticism.

In *The Culture of Narcissism* Lasch outlines two sources of narcissistic culture in the contemporary world:

o *Bureaucracy*, which he describes as a 'dense interpersonal environment . . . in which work assumes an abstract quality almost wholly divorced from performance'; and

o the *mass media*, and other media of mass tuition, for example the health service and welfare services, all of which: 'not only transcribe experience but alter its quality', making life appear as a 'hall of mirrors': 'Modern life is so thoroughly mediated by electronic images that we cannot help responding to others as if their actions – and our own – were being recorded and simultaneously transmitted to an unseen audience' (Lasch, 1991: 47).

In his earlier book, *Haven in a Heartless World* (1977), Lasch explains the origin of narcissism by using arguments from the psychoanalysis of Sigmund Freud. Many parents who rely upon experts lose their skills as parents. Children who believe that their parents are weak, because of their parents' over-reliance upon experts, create another set of parents in their minds that are mainly the creation of unconscious thought. These constructed parents are projections of the child's unconscious wishes and fears, and are unjust, punitive and dictatorial to a terrifying degree. Because the child's real parents tend to be remote, these unconscious projections go largely unchecked. The child incorporates these constructed parents into its own psyche and believes that she/he contains an alien aggressor that threatens to destroy the child from within.

Narcissism has a major psychological impact on the love relationship between a man and a woman. In an intimate relationship individuals try to protect themselves from emotional injury, while at the same time attempting to manipulate the emotions of their partners. Lasch described this as an attempt to 'cultivate a protective shallowness' (Lasch, 1977: 194). In addition, the family is undermined. Lasch argues that the same forces deskill workers in the factory or office, based as they are upon expert systems. Modernist ideas have damaged parental authority: parents have become unsure of what to do or how to do it, so individuals feel much more comfortable outside of marriage in non-binding commitments. Instead of serving as a 'haven in a heartless world' the family has taken on the form of relations that we find in places of work. Most notably, in the struggle for moral advantage, one individual attempts to impose their will upon the other, while also trying to generate guilt in that person. As Lasch explains:

> Conditions in the family thus mirror conditions in society as a whole, which have created an ever-present sense of menace and reduced social life to a state of warfare, often carried out under the guise of friendly cooperation. (Lasch, 1977: 157)

Richard Sennett on the self

Before we look at the contribution of Richard Sennett to our understanding of 'self' we need to review what sociologists understand by 'community'.

What do we mean by 'community'? The word is popularly and sociologically used in many different ways:

o the local community; community schools; community policing; care in the community; the Sikh community; the gay community; occupational communities.

 A community is then any form of social relationship within genuine boundaries. These boundaries allow people to define who is a member, and who is not a member. According to Richard Sennett (1996), people believe that they can maintain their dignity and form a common identity, through communal solidarity.

Similar pessimistic views to that of Lasch are found in Richard Sennett's book, *The Fall of Public Man* (1977). Sennett also makes use of the notion of narcissism. He argues that 'public life' has gone into decline since the end of the nineteenth century and has been replaced by the widespread belief that all problems in the world are caused by impersonality or coldness. The world of personal intimate feelings has lost its boundaries, so that for example political leaders are judged on what kind of person they are, rather than on policy or action. Public space in the city is viewed as 'dead' and the inhabitants of the city are isolated; inhibited from fulfilling personal relationships, transported in cars, which diminishes our relationship with the surroundings, and isolated in buildings which place the individual under a high degree of constant surveillance. Sennett refers to this society as 'the Intimate Society' and it is organised on the basis of two principles:

o Narcissism: 'the search for gratification of the self which at the same time prevents that gratification from occurring' (Sennett, 1977: 230).

o Destructive *Gemeinschaft* or 'a market exchange of intimacies' in which individuals are encouraged to make revelations on the grounds that this activity is a moral good in itself.

However, Sennett warns, 'when people today seek to have full and open emotional relations with each other, they succeed only in wounding each other. This is the logical consequence of the destructive gemeinschaft' (Sennett, 1977: 223).

If we accept Richard Sennett's views then it is little wonder that people want to move away from the cities. Outside of the city, people can develop their own self in a reflexive fashion, making choices about how they want to live their lives; they can create an identity of their own choosing. It is possible then to point to the suburbs as places of diversity. This is particularly the case if we accept the idea of the postmodern condition, in which people are much more likely to be free from constraints on their lifestyle choices.

The culture of the contemporary world puts pressure upon people to act narcissistically and when we disclose our feelings to others it becomes destructive. This is because narcissism makes a person attempting to form an intimate relationship feel that 'this isn't what I wanted'. The end result is a withdrawal of commitment.

Ethnomethodology

Ethnomethodology is a perspective in sociology which has a strong link with phenomenology. Like the other approaches we have looked at in this area, ethnomethodology is based upon the assumption that people are not pushed about by forces outside of their control but shape, create and recreate their own social world. This perspective is built upon the attempt to understand everyday life by systematically defining, then drawing upon, the techniques that we make use of on a daily basis. This process involves the clarification of the ways in which people, as members of a common culture, create the rules and routines that constitute the social structure of the everyday through their own practice, activities and relations of interaction, which come together in a shared conception of 'membership'. As Stephen Pfohl explains:

Ethnomethodology extends the phenomenological perspective to the study of everyday social interaction. It is concerned with the methods which people use to accomplish a reasonable account of what is happening in social interaction and to provide a structure for the interaction itself. Unlike symbolic interactionists, ethnomethodologists do not assume that people actually share common symbolic meanings. What they do share is a ceaseless body of interpretive work which enables them to convince themselves and others that they share common meanings. (Pfohl, 1985: 292–3)

The central theoretical assumptions of ethnomethodology are:

o **Members' methods** – these are informal rules that individuals draw up in order to make sense of the world around them. The members' methods allow people to recognise events and situations that they come across in everyday life. In order to identify and describe these taken-for-granted members' methods, Garfinkel encouraged his students to conduct 'breaching experiments' in which they would deliberately attempt to break the methods in an effort to get people to fully describe them. Garfinkel's students had to pretend that they were strangers in their own homes, asking if they could use the toilet. Not surprisingly, parents became alarmed and believed that their children were taking drugs or having a breakdown.

o **Indexicality** – our behaviour, actions, conversation etc. are part of the setting in which the behaviour takes place. This means that every action and situation is unique and in order to pass on information about an event we have to 'repair' indexicality by producing a short-hand description and imposing it upon the unique situation or event. If two people are shouting at each other and making threatening gestures we could describe this as an 'argument'. When we repair indexicality we make general statements which can be applied to a range of situations and which have an objective feel to them.

o **Reflexivity** – when we come into contact with the social world it has an organised and structured feel to it. According to Garfinkel we experience the world as a 'factual order'. However, this impression of a factual order is a product of the members' methods. When we encounter an event or a situation we have to place it into an appropriate context: this Garfinkel refers to as reflexivity.

o **Membership** – because we share members' methods we have a common culture and a common conception of the world as a factual order. In other words, we are members of a common culture, with shared concepts and beliefs.

A word of warning: Garfinkel is an ethnomethodologist and he is attempting to make visible the commonsense notions which we take for granted in our everyday lives. He is trying to move *beyond* common sense in an effort to explain common sense. However, this feeling of a factual order is a product of the members' methods and according to Garfinkel we do not have members' methods to identify and fully explain the workings of the members' methods. This often makes his work feel incomprehensible, because there do not seem to be words in the language to explain common sense: after all, it needs no explanation. Garfinkel always has to use inappropriate tools for the task he has set himself.

Perhaps Garfinkel's most influential study was that of Agnes. This study clearly outlines the ethnomethodological perspective.

The ethnomethodological self: Agnes the transsexual

Identity is concerned with questions of who we are as individuals and who we are as a people. Our identity defines which groups we belong to. The philosopher A.J. Ayer (1956) suggested that the general criteria of personal identity might be solely physical in nature – that our personal identity may be based upon our physical appearance. In contrast to this view, the philosopher David Hume (1711–1776) (1777) viewed the self as a 'bundle of perceptions', and in this sense our identity may be built upon such experiences. However, Ayer argues that only persons can have experiences and one must be a person before one can do any experiencing. Hume's argument suggests that our identity can exist as a disembodied spirit, and as a memory trace. Ayer's conclusion is that 'we would appear to have no alternative but to make people's identities depend upon the identity of their bodies' (1956: 192).

In 1967 these arguments were taken to the limit by the ethnomethodologist Harold Garfinkel in his case study, 'Passing and the managed achievement of sex status in an intersexed person' (Garfinkel, 1967, ch. 5: 116–85) which is more commonly known as his study of Agnes the transsexual.

In Western society the transfer of sexual status is not possible. The legal change of the birth certificate is not allowed. As Garfinkel explains: 'our society prohibits wilful or random movement from one sex status to another' (1967: 125). Garfinkel's case study is of a 19-year-old girl who had been born and brought up as a boy. Physically, she looked like a woman: she had ample breasts, a thin waist and clear complexion free of facial hair. In other words, Agnes had all the recognised female secondary sexual characteristics – together with a fully developed penis and scrotum. She appeared to be female and she lived her life as a female by a range of techniques that Garfinkel refers to as 'passing'.

Passing

Most of us are brought up with a very clear sense of our sexual and gender identity. As children we are socialised into the appropriate ways of behaving for our given identity. Agnes, in contrast, had to learn the appropriate ways of behaving for a young female adult. This learning process involved observing adult females and attempting to adopt their ways of behaving in an effort to 'pass' as a female, as Garfinkel explains:

> *The work of achieving and making secure their rights to live in the elected sex status while providing for the possibility of detection and ruin carried out within the socially structured conditions in which this work occurred I shall call 'passing'.* (Garfinkel, 1967: 118, italics in original)

Passing was not simply a matter of desire for Agnes. It was a necessity. What Agnes feared above all else was 'being noticed'; it was for this reason that the security of her identity was to be protected above all else. Garfinkel describes Agnes as a 'secret apprentice' and gives us a number of examples of such passing occasions:

o going to the beach without risking disclosure – Agnes wore tight-fitting underpants and a swimming costume with a skirt;
o sharing a room with another female – Agnes insisted that they respect each other's privacy and avoid nudity in front of each other.

These attempts to manage impressions are similar to the activity of the self with stigma in Goffman's analysis. Garfinkel discusses 'passing' in terms of 'management devices': 'attempts to come to terms with practical circumstances as a texture of relevancies over the continuing occasions of interpersonal transactions' (Garfinkel, 1967: 175).

One of the techniques Agnes used was 'anticipatory following': learning from people's questions or from situations by successfully analysing them in an effort to find clues to 'normal' ways of behaving. However, Agnes was forced to reveal the truth about her body and her upbringing to her boyfriend Bill. Agnes had been going out with Bill for some time and Bill wished to marry her. Although she was in love with Bill and told him this, she always had to refuse to have intercourse with him. At first she said she had an infection and then explained that she had a condition which prevented her from having sexual intercourse. Bill demanded to know more about 'the condition' and eventually Agnes had to tell him the truth.

Bill decided to continue with the relationship, but was very keen for Agnes to go ahead with the sex change operation that she had planned.

Both Bill and his mother (who did not know about Agnes's situation) became Agnes's instructors. Bill's mother taught Agnes how to cook, what clothes to wear, what styles to adopt and skills in home management. Bill taught Agnes details of how to behave in front of other men.

Activity

For many people 'passing' is seen as dishonest. One of the most important skills that we have is our ability to identify when a person has lied to us. How can you tell if a person is telling you a lie?

According to Harold Garfinkel passing is something that we all feel we have to do in our everyday lives. Identify some occasions in which you have attempted to 'pass', giving the impression that you had an identity which you feel was not really yours. Explain to yourself what you did and how you did it. How for example would a person under the age of 18 'pass' for an 18-year-old to gain entry to a public house or cinema?

Garfinkel attempts to generalise from Agnes's search for what she considered her true sexual identity in the following terms:

> (1) that the recognized rational accountability of practical actions is a member's practical accomplishment, and (2) that the success of that practical accomplishment consists in the work whereby a setting, in the same ways that it consists of a recognized and familiar organization of activities, masks from members' relevant notice members' practical ordering practices, and thereby leads the members to see a setting's features which include a setting's accounts, 'as determinate and independent objects'. (Garfinkel, 1967: 288)

What does Garfinkel mean by these comments?

o All aspects of our lives, including our identity or selves as people, are created by our own human agency – in other words, by our self.

o The success of any of our creations, including our creation of an identity for our self, involves us working to make the setting for our creations feel natural, and as such be treated by others as a fact.

Perhaps surprisingly, Agnes agreed that people who stood against 'normal' sexuality were in some way abnormal. It was possible for Agnes to think this way because she regarded herself as a natural female, except that she did not have a vagina. In Agnes's view the vagina should have been there all the time, while the penis was an accidental appendage. When Garfinkel asked her about male homosexuals or transvestites, Agnes would insist: 'I'm not like them', and Garfinkel reports that she found the comparison repulsive. As Agnes explained to Garfinkel: 'I *am* a female but the others would misunderstand if they knew how I was raised or what I have between my legs' (Garfinkel, 1967: 170).

Agnes had the sex change operation and went on to lead an active and sexually enjoyable life as a woman. None of the men that she made love with were aware of the history of Agnes's sexuality. Agnes observed other women; how they act and react in various situations, so as to fine-tune her own femininity. For Garfinkel, behaving as a man or as a woman is not simple or naturally given, it is a practical accomplishment by the human agent. In his view, 'normally sexed persons are cultural events' (Garfinkel, 1967: 181).

Activity

Harold Garfinkel raises important questions about gender; you might find it useful to answer the question: what does it mean to be a woman? Without a clear notion of what a 'woman' is it is not possible to have a theory of 'passing'.

Conversation analysis

According to ethnomethodologists (such as McNamee and Gergen, 1992; Shotter and Gergen, 1989), talk is a practical activity that we use to create and maintain our social selves: talk is one of the things that make us who we are as people. Talk does not take place in isolation, it is managed in an interactive way and is our central resource for constructing and maintaining social contexts. During the course of an interaction, it is the people who are present that determine the rules as to which people get to speak, and in what order.

Harvey Sacks, together with Gail Jefferson and Emanual Schegloff, developed Conversation Analysis upon the ethnomethodological assumption that Harold Garfinkel devised in the late 1960s. Sacks focused his analysis on the application of 'members' methods' to conversation, in order to identify the micro-practices of everyday language. Sacks assumed that words are not just descriptions, but are actions with practical consequences. The central features of conversation are:

o interactive reciprocity; and
o local management by persons.

These characteristics are seen in things like 'turn taking' in conversations (see Sacks et al., 1974). When there is a changeover in a conversation from one speaker to another, Sacks et al. (1974) referred to this as a **transition relevance place** (TRP). TRPs can be verbal or non-verbal and are operational in all conversations. Speakers draw upon TRPs to identify breaks in conversation and potential for their turn to speak. Talk is then an 'accomplished' activity, in other words it is interactionally managed. Speakers can select the appropriate TRP, which in turn is used to identify who will be the next speaker.

As Nofsinger (1991) explains:

Many of the conversational tendencies and orientations that we commonly attribute to participants' personalities or interpersonal relationships derive (at least in part) from the turn system. For example, other participants may listen to us not because they are interested or because we are fascinating, but because they have to. (1991: 89)

According to Cobb and Rifken (1991), the interactionally managed arrangements for conversation have a direct impact upon:

o who is to speak and when;
o the number of turns that a person can have in the conversation;
o the length time of each turn;
o the strength of the speaker's argument.

Activity: Lasch on self

(A)

Togetherness Both men and women have come to approach personal relations with a heightened appreciation of their emotional risks. Determined to manipulate the emotions of others while protecting themselves against emotional injury, both sexes cultivate a protective shallowness, a cynical detachment they do not altogether feel but which soon becomes habitual and in any case embitters personal relations merely through its repeated profession. At the same time, people demand from personal relations the richness and intensity of a religious experience. Although in some ways men and women have had to modify their demands on each other, especially in their ability to exact commitments of lifelong sexual fidelity, in other ways they demand more than ever. (Lasch, 1991: 194)

(B)

He: Shall we go to the movies tonight?
She: What's there?
He: Babe Darling in *Hearts Aflame*.
She: Oh, no, let's don't and say we did.
He: Alright, then to hell with it!
She: If that's the way you feel about it, let's go.
He: I don't want to go now.
She: Oh, come on now, let's go.
He: No, I only mentioned it because I thought you would like it.
She: Well, I would like it.
He: I doubt it . . .

The man begins by making a concession to the wife, hoping perhaps to reap some benefit. The woman is suspicious and begins attempting to make light of the concession, and the man immediately shifts his ground by assuming the role of one who has attempted to do a favour for another and encountered a surly response. The woman now attempts to take the pose of one who gives in to the other's wishes; it is well understood between them that this concession involves the right to criticize the program for the evening if anything goes wrong – and something probably will. The man sturdily holds his ground and refuses to go to the movies under such circumstances. The pattern of antagonisms beneath the surface is often less complex – less complex but not necessarily easier to deal with. (Lasch, 1977: 54)

Questions

(a) What do you understand by the term 'protective shallowness'?
(b) What does item (A) suggest is the nature of 'togetherness'?
(c) Outline *four* ways in which the notion of togetherness contained in item (A) differs from the way in which the idea of togetherness is used in everyday life.
(d) Outline the elements of the contribution to the sociology of the self contained in the items.

Summary

This chapter has looked at a number of contributions to social theory which take their starting point from an attempt to understand social action that, as I stated, is any action which has an intention behind it. Unlike the approaches that we addressed in the first two chapters (which are interested in looking at the whole society and conflicts between large groups of people), the action perspectives are primarily concerned with how and why individuals operate in their face to face interaction, within small groups of people. These approaches to theorising are often highly subjective. They raise issues about the nature of identity and what it means to be a person.

References

Ayer, A.J. (1956) *The Problem of Knowledge.* Penguin: London.

Berger, P. and Luckmann, T. (1967) *The Social Construction of Reality.* Penguin: Harmondsworth.

Blumer, H. (1962) 'Society as a symbolic interaction', in J.G. Manis and B.N. Meltzer (eds), *Symbolic Interaction: A Reader in Social Psychology.* Allyn & Bacon: Boston.

Cobb, S. and Rifken, J. (1991) 'Practice and paradox: deconstructing neutrality in mediation', *Law & Social Inquiry,* 16(1): 35–64.

Cooley, C.H. (1922) *Human Nature and the Social Order.* University of Chicago Press: Chicago.

Garfinkel, H. (1967) *Studies in Ethnomethodology.* Prentice-Hall: Englewood Cliffs, NJ.

Goffman, E. (1956) *The Presentation of Self in Everyday Life.* Edinburgh University Press: Edinburgh.

Goffman, E. (1959) *The Presentation of Self in Everyday Life.* Penguin: Harmondsworth.

Goffman, E. (1963a) *Stigma: Notes on the Management of Spoiled Identity.* J. Aronson: New York.

Goffman, E. (1963b) *Behavior in Public Places: Notes on the Social Organization of Gatherings.* Free Press: New York.

Goffman, E. (1968) *Asylums: Essays on the Social Situation of Mental Patients and Other Inmates.* Penguin: Harmondsworth.

Goffman, E. (1970) *Strategic Interaction.* Blackwell: Oxford.

Goffman, E. (1972) *Relations in Public: Microstudies of the Public Order.* Penguin: Harmondsworth.

Goffman, E. (1975) *Frame Analysis: An Essay on the Organization of Experience.* Penguin: Harmondsworth.

Goffman, E. (1981) *Forms of Talk.* Blackwell: Oxford.

Gouldner, A. (1971) *The Coming Crisis of Western Sociology.* Heinemann: London.

Gouldner, A. (1974) *For Sociology.* Penguin: Harmondsworth.

Hume, D. (1777) *Essays and Treatises on Several Subjects.* Thoemmer Press: Martin, TN.

Lasch, C. (1977) *Haven in a Heartless World: The Family Besieged.* Basic Books: New York.

Lasch, C. (1985) *The Minimal Self: Psychic Survival in Troubled Times.* Pan Books: London.

Lasch, C. (1991) *The Culture of Narcissism: American Life in an Age of Diminishing Expectations.* W.W. Norton: New York. First published, 1978.

MacIntyre, A. (1981) *After Virtue.* Duckworth: London.

McNamee, S. and Gergen, K.J. (eds) (1992) *Therapy as Social Construction.* Sage: London.

Mead, G.H. (1934) *Mind, Self, and Society,* ed. C.W. Morris. Chicago: University of Chicago Press.

Mead, G.H. (1967) *Mind, Self and Society: From the Standpoint of a Social Behaviorist.* Chicago: University of Chicago Press.

Nofsinger, R.E. (1991) *Everyday Conversations.* Sage: Newbury Park, CA.

Pfohl, S.J. (1985) *Images of Deviance and Social Control: A Sociological History.* McGraw-Hill: New York.

Rogers, M.F. (1981) 'Goffman on power, hierarchy, and status', in J. Ditton (ed.), *The View from Goffman*. Macmillan: London.

Sacks, H., Schegloff, E.A. and Jefferson, G. (1974) 'A simple systematics for the organization of turn-taking for conversation', *Language*, 50: 696–735.

Schegloff, E. and Sacks, H. (1973) 'Opening up closings', *Semiotica*, 7: 289–327.

Schegloff, E., Jefferson, G. and Sacks, H. (1977) 'The preference for self-correction in the organization of repair in conversation', *Language*, 53: 361–82.

Schutz, A. (1964) 'The problem of rationality in the social world', in *Collected Papers 2: Studies in Social Theory*. Martin Nijhoff: The Hague.

Schutz, A. (1972) *The Phenomenology of the Social World* (1932), trans. G. Walsh and F. Lehnert. Northwestern University Press: Evanston, IL.

Sennett, R. (1977) *The Fall of Public Man*. Faber & Faber: London.

Sennet, R. (1996) *Flesh and Stone: The Body and the City in Western Civilization*. Faber & Faber: London.

Shotter, J. and Gergen, K.J. (1989) *Texts of Identity*. Sage: London.

Taylor, C. (1989) *Sources of the Self: The Making of the Modern Identity*. Cambridge University Press: Cambridge.

Turner, J.H. (1991) *The Structure of Sociological Theory*. Wadsworth: Belmont, CA.

Wirth, L. (1923) 'Urbanism as a way of life', *American Journal of Sociology*, 44, 2.

Chapter contents

4

Feminist Approaches: Theorising Patriarchy and Oppression

By the end of this chapter you should:

o have a critical understanding of the concept of patriarchy;
o have a critical understanding of what it means to be a *woman*;
o be familiar with the 'three phases' of feminist theorising;
o have an understanding of liberal feminism, radical feminism, socialist feminism and standpoint epistemologies;

o be familiar with the argument of Michel Foucault in *The History of Sexuality* and understand its significance to understanding issues of gender and sexuality;
o have a critical understanding of postmodern feminists, notably Judith Butler;
o have a critical understanding of Camille Paglia, Naomi Wolf and Luce Irigaray.

The concept of patriarchy is widely used by feminists as both a description of the social position of women and as a theoretical explanation for the social position of women. The terms *sex* and *sexuality* are perhaps more problematical. 'Sex' is at the same time an activity, a classification of a person, a desire, a descriptor of anatomy, and a source of pleasure and fantasy. For most radical feminists 'sex' is treated as a 'given' and the notion of patriarchy has the status of a universal truth. The term 'patriarchy' was initially used in the social sciences by Max Weber (1978) to describe a form of household in which the eldest man dominated all other family members. The concept was developed by feminists to discuss the domination of women in all aspects of society but the family still had a key role to play as the central patriarchal institution.

Activity

Is it 'natural' for boys and girls to behave in particular ways? Make a list of these 'natural' ways of behaving. At the end of the chapter return to your list and reflect on the reasons why your views may have changed.

Search the Internet for 'Grrl', then look at the material on the sites and write a paragraph that summarises your findings.

No area of the social sciences is untouched by feminism. There is a huge feminist literature which covers a long period of time and which draws upon a range of social, political and philosophical traditions: radical feminism, socialist feminism, post-feminism, postmodern feminism. In addition, since the early 1990s much of this writing has become inaccessible to students because of the language that it is written in, for example the work of Camille Paglia and Luce Irigaray.

Although the concept of patriarchy was initially developed by Max Weber, the idea is found in historical documents such as Mary Astell's *A Serious Proposal to the Ladies* (1694) and Mary Wollstonecraft's *Vindication of the Rights of Woman* (1792). First we evaluate feminist research from the mid-twentieth century to the present: this includes Simone de Beauvoir's *The Second Sex* (1949), Betty Friedan's *The Feminine Mystique* (1963), Ann Oakley and Kate Millett and the developments in feminist thinking after 1970 and the ways in which feminist thought became more politicised with the emergence of the women's movement, radical feminism and socialist feminism. Later in the chapter we look at feminist thinking since 1990, including feminist thinkers who take as their starting point Foucault's work on sexuality. The concept of 'Grrl' emerged in the late 1990s on websites – such as Geekgrrl, Cybergrrl and Netchick – produced by and for young women who reject the older style of feminist rhetoric, enjoy their femininity and do not act like victims. The chapter concludes with an evaluation of post-feminist perspectives and postmodern feminism, from which the notion of 'Grrl' emerged.

Ann Oakley, in a range of books over many years, has demonstrated that gender roles are acquired via the process of socialisation rather than biologically determined. These roles vary considerably in different societies. Oakley (1981) argues that gender socialisation has four central elements:

o *Manipulation* – Parents encourage or discourage ways of behaving in their children on the basis of what they consider to be normal or abnormal behaviour for a male or female child.
o *Canalisation* – Parents direct their children's interests towards games and toys appropriate to their gender. Drawing upon his own experience, Stephen Pfohl (1992) talks about how he asked his parents if he could have a baby brother or sister. When they refused he asked if he could have a doll instead. Reluctantly, his parents agreed. While in his bedroom with the window open, Stephen heard his parents discussing the doll and their concerns about it. He then went downstairs and asked his parents to take the doll back to the shop and exchange it for a gun. His parents were pleased.
o *Verbal appellations* – This is the use of language to label children in a fashion that reinforces appropriate gender identification.
o *Different activities* – Girls are encouraged to participate in indoor activities that are often 'domestic' in nature, whilst boys are encouraged to participate in more outdoor activities.

Activity

Have a look at the advertisements screened during the breaks in children's television programmes. What products are targeted at girls and what products are targeted at boys? Do these representations have any significance in shaping our expectation of 'appropriate' gender behaviour?

The work of Ann Oakley established a sociology of gender built upon the universal conception of patriarchy as a form of domination, and some excellent books were to follow. For example, Sue Sharpe's classic study *Just Like a Girl* (1976) demonstrated the role that secondary school plays in girls' socialisation. She argues that the school curriculum was gender based; girls were discouraged from studying science. In Sharpe's study the girls' ambitions were children, husbands, jobs and careers – in that order.

It is through this gendered socialisation process that we develop our personality, our sense of self and our identity as female or male. Diverse cultures have diverse forms of socialising the people who live with those cultures. Hence my comments that gender roles vary considerably in different societies. The concept of **socialisation** assumes that although people may have biological drives they do not have instincts, because if people had fixed patterns of biologically determined behaviour this would prevent diverse processes of socialisation taking place. It would not be possible for people to form subcultures or adopt alternative lifestyles. It is this absence of biological instincts in humans that allows socialisation to take place.

Socialisation can be deliberate, as when we are given instruction, by parents or teachers, in the skills we need (for example language skills) or the roles we are expected to perform. Socialisation can also be unintentional, in which events or situations have a significant effect upon us that was never planned, although socialisation is thought to produce a degree of conformity. It should be noted that the child is active in the socialisation process: in other words the child has *agency* – the ability to think of himself or herself as a separate person and to act on that assumption.

Activity

Sex and Temperament in Three Primitive Societies (1935)

In 1935 anthropologist Margaret Mead published her ethnographic study of three societies on New Guinea: the Arapesh, Mundugumor and Tchambuli. She wanted to find out if the view of male and female temperament in Western society was 'universal'. Amongst the Arapesh, both males and females were found to be 'maternal' and the verb 'to bear a child' could apply to either a man or a

---

woman. The Mundugumor are characterised as aggressive by Mead: for them foreplay involved a great deal of scratching and biting. Finally, the Tchambuli had sex roles that were the opposite of the Western model in the 1930s. Women supported the family through work, whilst men spent a great deal of time finding ways of amusing and entertaining the women.

What do you think is the significance of the above passage?

Oakley, Sharpe and others assumed that the process of socialisation acted to fix a woman's identity: in other words that the concept *woman* had firm foundations, that it was an 'essential subject'. However, Rosalind Coward argues that patriarchy 'has a loose currency' (Coward, 1983: 270) because the use of the term 'patriarchal' for all facets of male control and control can make it difficult to understand the differences between various forms of control, which may be crucial to the understanding of relations between men and women. Coward also argues that the term 'patriarchy' does not do justice to the complexity of sexual divisions. As she explains:

> the term 'patriarchal' implies a model of power as interpersonal domination, a model where all men have forms of literal, legal and political power over all women. Yet many of the aspects of women's oppression are constructed diffusely, in representational practices, in forms of speech, in sexual practices. This oppression is not necessarily a result of the literal overpowering of a woman by a man. (Coward, 1983: 272)

In recent years, the category 'woman' has become problematic. What constitutes this category? It is not something that we can simply assume; this criticism came initially from 'black' feminists who were unable to develop any form of sisterhood with 'white' feminists. If there is no foundation, then the category is of little value to us. Later we look at Judith Butler's work: she argues that gender is 'performative' rather than fixed.

Activity

What does it mean to be a *woman*? Share your answer with fellow students and identify any similarities and differences between the responses of males and females.

Many radical feminists argue that women have a distinct epistemology and ontology: that they have knowledge that men could not possess, and think in ways that are different from the ways in which men think. As a man, how could I possibly discuss feminist analysis? Some justification is needed. I became interested in feminism through my reading of sociology, and reflections on experiences I had had with people of the 'opposite sex'. As I developed an interest in postmodernism I came to see forms of classification as tools that were often used to sustain social relationships and impose identities; although often people freely use the available classifications to *gender* themselves and others. At a personal level, rather than empowering me, I found patriarchy an arbitrary set of ideas, classificatory tools and practice that were completely irrelevant to the way I wanted to lead my life. The ironic thing was that although at an intellectual level it was clear to me that patriarchy had no substance or foundation, in everyday life patriarchy was constraining. Something that, in essence, did not exist but yet had an effect. As Naomi Wolf states: 'there is no "rock called gender" . . . it can change so that real mutuality – an equal gaze, equal vulnerability, equal desire – brings heterosexual men and women together' (Wolf, 1990: 152).

This would allow: 'an opportunity for a straight woman actively to pursue, grasp, savour, and consume the male body for her satisfaction, as much she is pursued, grasped, savoured, and consumed for his' (1990: 158).

In Wolf's opinion, patriarchy operates at the level of 'the gaze': if you are seen to break its rules, then you will be stared at in a disapproving fashion. Both men and women are made to feel vulnerable to judgement. And what of the people who stare? They are merely exercising their judgement without foundation or obligation to disapprove.

What is feminism?

In social theory, as in everyday life, we wrongly assume that people grasp familiar concepts in the same way as ourselves. Although feminism is not a unified perspective or set of ideas, there are some shared meanings and assumptions, in relation to what we understand by the concepts 'female' and 'male'. Textbooks historically outline three phases of feminist activism and theorising. First-wave feminists in the nineteenth and early twentieth centuries argued and campaigned for equality in the legal and political spheres. Second-wave feminism (of the 1970s) is built on the distinction identified by Simone de Beauvoir, between 'natural' sex and 'constructed'/cultural gender. The second wave is often associated with Betty Friedan's *The Feminine Mystique* (1965), Kate Millett's *Sexual Politics* (1970) and Germaine Greer's *The Female Eunuch* (1970). These writers wanted more than equal rights – they wanted to raise consciousness about a diverse range of issues in relation to identity and the gender hierarchy. In their view, all women shared a bond of oppressive patriarchy that was enforced by fathers, husbands and a range of other men. Christine Delphy argued that women were a social class, subjugated by compulsorily enforced reproductive heterosexuality.

Taken together, first- and second-wave feminists assumed that

- o females suffered discrimination because of their sex;
- o the social structure and culture were shaped by patriarchy, which was global, ahistorical and beyond the control of human agency;
- o patriarchy was experienced directly by all women;
- o male domination was found in personal and public aspects of a woman's life, from 'bodily integrity' (Petchesky, 1984), to unequal access to the professions and politics;
- o men denied women knowledge, through control of the processes of socialisation;
- o men were responsible for oppression and subordination, at both the institutional level and the level of ideas;
- o any or all of the above was often reinforced by violence.

Feminism's first and second waves took these assumptions as a direct and inevitable, biologically determined, division between 'feminine' and 'masculine'. This approach attempted to establish rigid divisions between 'male' and 'female'.

Radical feminism

Denise Thompson (2001) gives one of the fullest and clearest outlines of radical feminism. Thompson claims that to argue from a feminist standpoint is to take a 'political' stance that is beyond traditional politics and beyond the notion of gender as a 'social construction'. Feminism is a moral and social enterprise concerned with issues of 'value', good and evil, right and wrong, and creating a political framework for the human condition. This involves uncovering the social relations of power which are male supremacist in nature and invariably oppressive to all women. A key element of this domination is that the interests of men come to be seen as universal human interests. Only men are recognised as having the status of 'human', because the penis is 'the only symbol of "human" status allowed under conditions of male supremacy' (2001: 28–9). In Thompson's view this allows women to be denied the rights and dignities of being human. Hence for Thompson, 'sex is central to women's oppression', and the ideological construction of sex is around the penis. Women are complicit with this ideology in that they accept the second-class status that is accorded to them and eroticise their subordination by accepting heterosexual relations, feeling unfulfilled if they are without a man to structure their desire. Women subordinate themselves in the service of men: 'Men are nothing but their penises, women are nothing but objects to be used in its service' (Thompson, 2001: 41).

Thompson discusses the notion of *difference*. She argues that women may experience male domination differently, but she also makes clear that comparing the different experiences of women of colour or class is not in women's interests. Such comparisons: 'deflect attention away from the *real*

Mainstream

problem by disguising or ignoring the workings of male supremacy, or by reducing feminism to nothing but the trivial preoccupation of the privileged' (2001: 131, emphasis added). Second-wave radical feminism ascribed all forms of oppression to men and Thompson states that she wants to resurrect that argument. All forms of domination are rooted in masculinity; if we end male supremacy we have freedom for all:

> Imperialism, whether it takes the form of outright slavery, of the colonial dispossession of indigenous peoples, of the multinational control and exploitation of distant lands and their national economies, or of the forcible imposing of foreign cultures, requires the defining of subjugated populations as less than human . . . Hence imperialism requires dehumanisation. But so does masculinity in the sense that it is a 'human' status bought at someone else's expense. Domination already has a model of human beings who are not fully human – women. (2001: 139)

Men may seek to understand the feminist standpoint but they can never contribute to it. It is for this reason that Thompson (2001) refuses to discuss postmodern or poststructural contributions to feminism: 'To focus attention, even critically, on postmodernism would be to award it credibility as a feminist enterprise, when from a feminist standpoint it is merely another ruse of male supremacy' (2001: 2).

Thompson's book outlines three issues that have dominated second-wave feminist theorising since the 1970s.

The role of psychoanalysis in a feminist understanding of sexuality structured around the primary symbol of the phallus

Feminist critiques of psychoanalysis:

o   Psychoanalysis is ahistorical: it presents findings as timeless and universal when they are rooted in a specific period of time.
o   Psychoanalysis reinforces phallic authority, with notions such as penis envy, a girl's disillusionment with her clitoris and the view that she gives up her wish for a penis by wanting to have a baby.
o   Psychoanalysis does not have the tools to analyse the unconscious.
o   Psychoanalysis assumes that sexual events in childhood determine adult relationships.
o   Psychoanalysis is based upon biological determinist assumptions; sex drives must be controlled in order to have a stable identity.

Theorising about women of colour

Taking their point of departure from postmodern/poststructuralist critiques of universal principles, most notably that of Foucault, many radical feminists assume that white middle-class women are the norm for understanding women's oppression, which is often felt to be inappropriate for understanding the experiences of women of colour. Chris Beasley gives the following example:

> the rape of Australian Aboriginal women by Aboriginal men is not necessarily a subject appropriate for white feminists to discuss publicly and at a distance from the relevant Aboriginal communities in terms of men's brutal oppression of women . . . this kind of discussion reinstates whites as the interpreters of Aboriginal experience while evading the significance of the context of racism in generating violence. (Beasley, 1999: 109)

In 1996 Patricia Hill Collins, in a similar fashion to bell hooks, drew upon the thoughts, experiences, music and literature of black women to develop what she called a *black women's standpoint epistemology* which attempts to break down the images of black women that white feminists use to inform their racism. Collins is interested in the relationship between white feminism and the structures of power. This standpoint epistemology attempts to describe the subjugated knowledge of black women that has for so long been regarded as not real or valid intellectual knowledge.

Theorising about lesbians

Jill Johnston's *Lesbian Nation* (1973) argued very strongly for a form of political lesbianism that was based upon the separatist assumption that women who slept with men were 'sleeping with the enemy' and helping to maintain the hegemonic institution of heterosexuality, which was one of the central drivers of women's oppression.

Sylvia Walby: theorising patriarchy

Sylvia Walby (1989) argues that much feminist theorising is seriously flawed because it assumes that patriarchy has one sole foundation.

o Firestone (1974), who views reproduction as the basis of patriarchal relations;
o Delphy (1984), who views expropriation of women's labour by men in the home as the basis of patriarchal relations;
o Hartmann (1979), who similarly argues that patriarchal relations operate at the level of the expropriation of women's labour by men;
o Rich (1980), who views the institution of compulsory heterosexuality as the basis of patriarchal relations;
o Brownmiller (1976), who views male violence and especially rape as the basis of patriarchal relations.

In contrast, she argues that patriarchy needs to be conceptualised at different levels of abstraction; we need to recognise that it can take different forms and that it need not be a universalistic notion which is true in one form at all times and in all places. Drawing upon the processes that make up Giddens's theory of structuration, she attempts to construct a more flexible model of patriarchy which can be in either a 'public' or a 'private' form, and can be constructed out of six partially interdependent structures which have different levels of importance for different women at different times and places, rather than a simple universal base–superstructure model.

At its most abstract level patriarchy exists as a system of social relations, built upon the assumption that whenever a man comes into contact with a woman he will attempt to oppress her. The second level of patriarchy is organised around six patriarchal structures:

o   the patriarchal mode of production
o   patriarchal relations in paid work
o   patriarchal relations in the state
o   male violence
o   patriarchal relations in sexuality
o   patriarchal relations in cultural institutions, such as religion, the media and education

Patriarchy can take different forms and is dependent upon a range of structures. If one structure is challenged and becomes ineffective, another can easily replace it. Moreover, patriarchal relations are not simply *given*, they are created by individual people as a *medium* and an *outcome* of the practices that make up their everyday lives. Men draw upon the structures of patriarchy to empower themselves and make their social actions more likely to be effective. By doing so they reinforce these very structures. The structures of patriarchy are in constant flux as they are drawn upon by men, reinforced and recreated.

Walby's argument opens up the idea that all sociological notions of what constitutes 'femininity' and 'masculinity' are socially constructed. However, if this is true, not only can they be constructed differently, but they can be deconstructed out of existence. More importantly, our notions of male and female are also socially constructed. The politics of modernity allowed us to reject what Judith Butler (1993) called the 'biology-is-destiny formulation'. In other words, modernity allowed us to liberate ourselves culturally, socially and politically from our biology. The epistemological and ontological anchorage of feminism is based upon reading significance into natural anatomical sexual differences. This biologically determined view of masculinity and femininity is always unstated in feminist work, because it cannot be justified. Such concepts as *male–female* or *feminine–masculine* have currency only because people practise their masculinity and their femininity. They should not be used to categorise people but to describe activities that people *choose* to engage in. The categories 'male' and 'female' can only ever be what people choose to make of them. As a foundation for our theorising and research these concepts are irrelevant and redundant. As sociologists we have a tendency to identify, or invent, a set of categories, such as 'class', 'male', 'female', etc. which do not adequately define or explain, then we go out into the world and gather evidence which we arbitrarily fit into the categories, without attempting to justify our choice of categories.

Although Derrida had discussed going beyond binary divisions such as male–female, homosexuality–heterosexuality, etc., this view has also been suggested by a number of people less clearly associated with postmodernism, who work within lesbian and gay studies: Biddy Martin, Marjorie Garber, Diana Fuss, Julia Epstein, Kristina Straub and Judith Butler. As Janet Wolff notes, in the 1990s these writers: 'explored the instability of sexual identities and gender identities. This work goes beyond the anti-essentialist argument that gender is a social construct' (Wolff, 1995: 103).

What feminism needs is to engage in a much more thorough 'ethnography of the self' in which two key questions need to be asked:

o   What does it mean to be a woman?
o   How is the 'male' body eroticised?

Feminists have never got to grips with the implications of either question. They almost always view male sexual practice as a series of phallocentric, exploitative strategies, within structures of control and oppression. As Steven Seideman (1996) explains, feminists 'imagined male desire as revealing a logic of misogyny and domination' (1996: 10). Apart from the obvious oversight – that sex is pleasurable – the male body is not a particularly robust thing. Moreover, whilst involved in a sexual act, the body makes the man both psychologically and physically vulnerable. External genitalia are not well designed, either for comfort or convenience: they are very sensitive to the touch, and mishandling is painful. The external nature of his genitalia gives women a powerful role as spectator: critical comments and/or comparisons can be instantly humiliating. Internal genitalia are not so easily compared.

Socialist feminism

This feminist perspective brings together the central elements of the Marxian conception of power and the feminist conception of patriarchy. Zillah Eisenstein in *Capitalist Patriarchy and the Case for Socialist Feminism* (1981) argues forcefully for such a synthesis, in order to formulate the problem of woman as mother and worker, reproducer and producer. She argues that male supremacy and capitalism are the core relations determining the oppression of women. Socialist feminists are committed to understanding the system of power deriving from capitalist patriarchy. Eisenstein argues that such an understanding must 'emphasize the mutually reinforcing dialectical relationship between capitalist class structure and hierarchical sexual structuring' (Eisenstein, 1981: 5). The reasons for this position are that 'Power is dealt with in a dichotomous way by Socialist women and Radical Feminists: it is seen as deriving from either one's economic class position or one's sex' (1981: 6). Eisenstein attempts to replace this dichotomous thinking with a dialectical approach, not merely to add together the two elements, 'but to see them as interrelated through the sexual division of labour' (ibid.).

Eisenstein argues that the importance of Marxian analysis to the study of women's oppression is twofold:

o   It provides a class analysis necessary for the study of power.
o   It provides a method of analysis that is historical and dialectical.

Although Marx provides the tools for understanding all power relationships, claims Eisenstein, he was not sensitive to all power relationships. Eisenstein focuses on the Marxian notion of *alienation*, which she applies to women's oppression. '*Species beings*' she argues: 'are those beings who ultimately reach their human potential for creative labour, social consciousness and social living through the struggle against capitalist society and who fully internalise these capacities in communist society' (1981: 7).

Emancipation of our *human essence* provides the revolutionary potential, without which we would become happy slaves. Patriarchal relations inhibit the development of human essence. However, women are still potentially creative beings. It is this contradiction that provides women's revolutionary potential. But Eisenstein does provide the following warning:

> There is no reason to doubt, however, that in communist society (where all are to achieve species existence) life would still be structured by a sexual division of labour which would entail different life options for men and women which would necessitate continued alienation and isolation. Essence and existence would still not be one. Marx did not understand that the sexual division of labour in society organises non-creative and isolating work particularly for women. The destruction of capitalism and capitalist exploitation by itself does not insure existence, i.e. creative work, social community and a critical consciousness for women. (Eisenstein, 1981: 11)

For Eisenstein, exploitation is *economic* in nature and class based, whilst oppression is *non-economic* and rooted in alienation.

Eisenstein is highly critical of radical feminists because, she argues, they base their argument on the premise that men have power *as men* and that the world is organised into 'sexual spheres'. They do not link women's oppression and the economic class structure and are inclined to see the male hierarchical ordering of society as rooted in biology, rather than in the economy and/or history. In contrast, socialist feminism analyses power in terms of its class origins and its patriarchal roots. Capitalism and patriarchy are neither autonomous systems nor identical, they are mutually dependent: 'Oppression is inclusive of exploitation but reflects a more complex reality' (Eisenstein, 1981: 22–3).

This historical development of capitalist patriarchy can be dated from the mid-eighteenth century in England and the mid-nineteenth century in America: 'Capitalist patriarchy, by definition, breaks through the dichotomies of class and sex, private and public spheres, domestic and wage labour, family and economy, personal and political, and ideology and material conditions' (Eisenstein, 1981: 23).

Eisenstein argues that the Marxian understanding of the relations of production cannot be defined without an explicit connection to the relations that emerge from women's sexuality and the relations of reproduction: 'Capitalism uses patriarchy and patriarchy is defined by the needs of capital' (1981: 28). She argues in support of this view that:

o women stabilise patriarchal structures – the family, housewife, mother, etc. – by fulfilling these roles;
o women reproduce new workers for both the paid and unpaid labour force;
o women work in the labour force for less money than men;
o women stabilise the economy through their role as consumers.

Eisenstein concludes by arguing that if the other side of production is consumption, then the other side of capitalism is patriarchy.

Critics of socialist feminism might argue that what Eisenstein has done is simply to merge two theories which are inadequate at explaining women's oppression and from the synthesis produce an equally inadequate theory. The explanation of why women are the oppressed group and why men are not is still left unanswered in Eisenstein's analysis.

Third-wave feminism

As the chapter unfolds we shall see that third-wave feminism is characterised by a rich diversity. Naomi Wolf (1993) argues that second-wave feminism did not build upon its gains and also damaged the conception of feminism in the popular imagination. In contrast, Tamsin Wilton (1996) points out that many feminists have criticised lesbian sexual practices as sadomasochistic and argue that lesbians help to reproduce violent heterosexual practice. The end result has been to exclude lesbians from feminist groups. A number of third-wave feminists, notably Judith Butler, have been influenced by Michel Foucault and embrace postmodern theories that attempt to move away from the self as a unified subject. Butler quotes with approval Nietzsche's claim in *On the Genealogy of Morals* that 'there is no "being" behind doing, effecting, becoming; "the doer" is merely a fiction added to the deed – the deed is everything' (Butler, 1990: 25).

Michel Foucault, *The History of Sexuality*

Activity

The state gathers all types of information about individual people from the time and place of their birth to the cause of their death. Choose one of the types of information below and ask yourself why the state might be interested in gathering such information about people:

- how much money people earn;
- notifiable diseases, such as tuberculosis;
- how many people are in your house on the night of the census;
- (if we travel overseas) why we have passports.

By way of introduction to a number of the themes in Foucault's books, read the following passages from Angela Carter (1984) and Zygmunt Bauman (1988), and then attempt the questions.

With the aid of a French criminologist who dabbled in phrenology, she selected from the prisons of the great Russian cities women who had been found guilty of killing their husbands and whose bumps indicated the possibility of salvation. She established a community on the most scientific lines available and had female convicts build it for themselves out of the same kind of logic that persuaded the Mexican *federales* to have those they were about to shoot dig their own graves.

It was a *panopticon* she forced them to build, a hollow circle of cells shaped like a doughnut, the inward-facing wall of which was composed of grids of steel and, in the middle of the roofed, central courtyard, there was a round room surrounded by windows. In that room she'd sit all day and stare and stare and stare at her murderesses and they, in turn, sat all day and stared at her.

During the hours of darkness, the cells were lit up like so many small theatres in which each actor sat by herself in the trap of her visibility in those cells shaped like servings of *bab au rhum*. The Countess, in the observatory, sat in a swivelling chair whose speed she could regulate at will. Round and round she went, sometimes at a great rate, sometimes slowly, raking with her ice-blue eyes – she was of Prussian extraction – the tier of unfortunate women surrounding her. She varied her speeds so that the inmates were never able to guess beforehand at just what moment they would come under her surveillance.

By the standards of the time and place, the Countess conducted her regime along humanitarian, if autocratic lines. Her private prison with its unorthodox selectivity was not primarily intended as the domain of punishment but in the purest sense, was a penitentiary – it was a machine designed to promote penitence.

For the Countess P. had conceived the idea of a therapy of meditation. The women in the bare cells, in which was neither privacy nor dis-traction, cells formulated on the principle of those in a nunnery where all was visible to the eye of God, would live alone with the memory of their crime until they acknowledged, not their guilt – most of them had done that, already – but their *responsibility*. And she was sure that with responsibility would come remorse. (Angela Carter, *Nights at the Circus*, 1984: 210-11)

Panopticon may be compared to Parsons's laboriously erected model of the social system. What both works seek is nothing less than a model of well-balanced, equilibrated, cohesive human cohabitation, adaptable to changing tasks, capable of reproducing the conditions of its own existence, producing maximum output (however measured) and minimum waste. (Zygmunt Bauman, *Freedom*, 1988: 20)

1 The Panopticon was designed by the philosopher Jeremy Bentham, but it was never built. Bentham outlined a number of positive things that the Panopticon could offer: moral reform; the preservation of health; the invigoration of industry; a reduction in the public burden; lightening of the economy; and abolition of the Poor Laws. Outline some of the reasons that you can think of why the Panopticon was not built.

   In answer to this question you might consider whether the Panopticon was unnecessarily harsh, cruel or dehumanising.

2 Outline the reasons why the design of the Panopticon might be considered harsh and inhuman.

3 Think of an activity that you consider as abnormal or perverted. If, at some future date, you choose to involve yourself in this activity would you prefer to be seen doing this act or would you do it in secret, away from the public gaze? Outline the reasons for your answer and review them after you have read the section below on Michel Foucault.

Michel Foucault was born in Poitiers, France, in 1926 and died of AIDS, in Paris in 1984. His work became a major theoretical resource in the humanities and social sciences, from philosophy to gender studies and queer theory, and had a more general impact on the history of architecture, medicine, law and literature. A methodological reflection on how he wrote his books is presented in *The Archaeology of Knowledge* (Foucault, 1972). In 1946 he was admitted to the Ecole Normale Supérieure, the most prestigious higher education institution in France.

   From 1955 to 1958 Foucault taught philosophy at the University of Uppsala in Sweden, where he did the research for his first major book, *Madness and Civilization* (1971). He returned to France in 1960 to teach at Clermont-Ferrand and complete his Doctorate (1961) for *Madness and Civilization*, and do the research for *Birth of the Clinic*, published in 1989. In 1966 his history of systems of thought, *The Order of Things*, became a bestseller in France. Foucault responded to this by moving to Tunisia where he stayed until autumn 1968. Foucault missed the events of May 1968: however he listened to the 'night of the barricades' by telephone, which a friend had held next to a radio. Foucault returned to Paris to become head of the philosophy department of the newly created

University at Vincennes. He visited the United States often during the 1970s and early 1980s, regularly speaking at NYC and in California. Foucault was attracted to the gay lifestyle of LA, with its bathhouses and gay bars. During this period he published his two best-known books, *Discipline and Punish* (1977) and *The History of Sexuality*, Volume 1 (1990a). Finally, in late 1983 and early 1984, knowing that he was dying of AIDS, Foucault completed Volumes 2 and 3 of *The History of Sexuality*. Foucault died in hospital on 25 June 1984. The cause of Foucault's death was not released to the press, who reported that he had died of a brain infection.

In *The Passion of Michel Foucault* (1993) James Miller discusses at some length and in some detail the sexual orientation of Foucault. He argues that Foucault's life should be treated as one of his texts. Foucault, I believe, would have rejected the idea that knowing about a person's biographical experiences could inform a reading of their work. People make different readings, from different positions, and from this idea Foucault developed his notion of 'the death of the author', the idea that a text, once written, goes into the world and takes on a life of its own. No author can control how a text is read, how the reader will position the text in relation to themselves and their favoured ideologies. The issue of the personal identity of the author becomes a distraction when we should be addressing the discourses contained within the text.

In 'What is an author?' Foucault argued

> It does not seem necessary that the author function remain constant in form, complexity, and even in existence. I think that, as our society changes, at the very moment when it is in the process of changing, the author function will disappear. We would no longer hear the questions that have been rehashed for so long: Who really spoke? Is it really he and not someone else? With what authenticity or originality? And what part of his deepest self did he express in his discourse? Instead, there would be other questions, like these:
>
> What are the modes of existence of this discourse? Where has it been used, how can it circulate, and who can appropriate it for himself? What are the places in it where there is room for possible subjects? Who can assume these various subject functions? And behind all these questions, we would hear hardly anything but the stirring of indifference: What difference does it make who is speaking? (1986: 111–12)

Miller's argument – that Foucault's life should be treated as a text, which can be used to cast light on his work – is not without merit. Can knowing a person's biographical experiences inform a reader of their work? If Foucault had died of Alzheimer's disease rather than AIDS would this have made a difference to the tragedy of the death or give us less insight into his *History of Sexuality*? Has an understanding of what Foucault did in the privacy of his bedroom and with whom nothing to do with any of the papers he published during his career? Could Judith Butler's texts have been written by a Protestant wealthy white heterosexual male?

Foucault has been included in a chapter on 'Feminist Approaches' because he is the most influential theorist on matters concerning the body. He wrote about how the state attempted to manipulate, regulate and control all aspects of the body: in relation to gender, sexuality, madness, criminality and medical issues, to name but a few. All of this was motivated by a search for the causes of 'abnormality', searching for answers to the question of what makes some bodies sick or disobedient.

However, post-Foucault many people have questioned what a normal body is. Reshaping the body in an effort to reshape self and self-identity is now less likely to be viewed as abnormal. This is usually associated with the emergence of the postmodern condition, in which commonly held beliefs and certainties are questioned. There has been an explosion of interest in aerobics and the more aggressive forms of gym culture, such as piercing, cutting and sexual reallocation of the body – what we used to call 'the sex change'. Many people feel that their sexual identity is trapped in the wrong anatomical body. Nothing is fixed or stable. This has major implications for the sociology of gender.

The body is viewed as the 'visible carrier' of the self, something to be manipulated in an effort to improve self-image. Paul Komesaroff, in *Troubled Bodies* (1997), argues that the body is 'our source of meaning and meaning-creations', in that it is 'marked, inscribed, and made meaningful in relation to the culturally specific forms of intersubjectivity and language'. In this sense the body can play a key role in our self-defined identity, but are we still the same people when the body changes? In Franz Kafka's short story 'Metamorphosis' (published in 1915), Gregor Samsa maintained the same self even after he had been transformed into a giant insect. The same person but in a different body. Similarly, in Fay Weldon's *Life and Loves of a She Devil* (1983) Ruth, the she devil, still maintained the same self even though she built a new body for her self in the image of Mary Fisher, her husband's lover.

Other texts that have the influence of Foucault behind them include: Susan Leigh Foster, *Corporealities: Danger, Knowledge, Culture and Power* (1997) and Jennifer Terry and Jacqueline Urla, *Deviant Bodies* (1997).

In *The History of Sexuality*, as in his life, Foucault politicises sexuality and its role in the processes of self-formation. He shows how heterosexuality encodes and structures everyday life. In sharp contrast to Foucault, most of the theorists in the area of sexuality, including many feminist writers, assume that heterosexuality is a natural given. When heterosexuality is couched in naturalistic language it appears as a set of institutional constraints that cannot be challenged without going against 'nature'. In other words, heterosexual relations provide the foundation for understanding all other forms of sexuality, such as the butch/femme relationships that mirror the husband/wife relationship. Sexuality was viewed as something built upon a biological drive that was normal and essentially heterosexual in nature. With the emergence of postmodernism in the 1990s and the politics of difference, new forms of gay and lesbian identity were recognised which were not seen as derivations of the 'normal' heterosexual identity. In Foucault's work the 'social' and the 'sexual' become linked, through the notion of 'normal' behaviour.

Foucault's work on sexuality has to be seen as an account of how power became directly connected to the most intimate areas of the human body.

It should be seen in the context of his theories of power, exclusion and resistance.

Foucault analysed sexuality in terms of the development or emergence of 'discursive practices'. A **discourse** for Foucault is a body of statements that is both organised and systematic, and is in the form of a set of rules. These 'rules of discourse' first need to be identified by the researcher and then described in terms of what they allow to be said and what they prevent from being said. The rules also allow space for new statements to be legitimately made. Discourse is a system of representation that regulates meaning so that certain ways of thinking, speaking and behaving become 'natural'. Discourse is made up of statements, and one of the central purposes of the discourse is to establish relationships between statements so that we can make sense of what is being said to us. Discursive practices are used to present knowledge as 'true' and/or 'valid'. His analysis of discourse is *historical*, but it is a 'problem-centred' historical approach rather than a 'period-centred' approach. Foucault referred to this historical analysis of discourse as an 'archaeology' of knowledge, which he used to show the history of truth claims. Archaeology involves describing and analysing statements as they occur within the 'archive', which is 'the general system of the formation and transformation of statements' (Foucault, 1972: 130). For Foucault, a central concept in the history of any discourse was the 'will to power' – a term originally used by Nietzsche to demonstrate that powerful people were in a position to impose their views upon others as right, just and truthful. Foucault's position is one of Pyrrhonian scepticism: we cannot know anything, including the assumption that 'we cannot know anything'. For Foucault, there was no objective viewpoint from which one could analyse discourse or society.

o *Archaeology* is the appropriate methodology for analysing discourse.
o *Genealogy* refers to the tactics we use to describe local discourses or local knowledge.

The Order of Things

In *The Order of Things* (1969) Foucault identifies the arbitrary nature of systems of classification that users may believe to be both valid and 'natural'. He opens the book with an example from a Chinese encyclopaedia which divides animals into the following categories:

(a) belonging to the Emperor, (b) embalmed, (c) tame, (d) suckling pigs, (e) sirens, (f) fabulous, (g) stray dogs, (h) included in the present classification, (i) frenzied, (j) innumerable, (k) drawn with a very fine camelhair brush, (l) *et cetera*, (m) having just broken the water pitcher, (n) that from a long way off look like flies. (Foucault, 1969: xv)

For Foucault phases of history are organised around their own distinct 'episteme' or set of principles for categorising what we come into contact with. Epistemes generate 'orders of discourse' or 'discursive formations' which inform us on how we should construct our view of the world.

From the initial analysis of classification, in his later books Foucault develops his genealogical analysis to examine the history of how groups of ideas come to be associated with normal sexuality. One of the central themes of Foucault's work was how discursive power works on bodies, and this is seen most clearly in *The History of Sexuality*. Discursive formations allow us to allocate people to a network of categories, in other words to describe people as 'types': hetero/homo, normal/fairy, etc. In his discussion of discipline Foucault described the spreading notion of what constituted 'normal' through society as the 'carceral continuum'. All of us become self-regulated subjects, inscribed by institutions including the family, educational institutions and employers.

Foucault's work is important in understanding how aspects of sexuality became 'normal' and his work has a significant impact on theorising and politicising such diverse issues as the nature of 'the closet', why sexual intercourse is equated with closeness and intimacy and why the attainment of orgasm-via-penetration is regarded as the aim and measure of successful sex.

In the twentieth century 'the closet' was a key concept in our understanding of the gay lifestyle. The closet was a set of repressive social practices and strategies of censorship, which imposed a notion of 'normal' on all people, and which could generate feelings of guilt and self-loathing in private. The concept captured the need for secrecy and self-management of sexuality in the face of a social system that used the power of the state, medicine and criminal justice to enforce heterosexuality. Post-Foucault, people have successfully 'normalised' and 'routinised' their homosexuality in the eyes of others, who have then subjectively accepted them for what they are.

Sexual intercourse is widely regarded as the definitive sexual act which brings feelings of closeness and intimacy that one does not find with other sexual practices. However, interestingly, not all participants are able to explain why they are meant to feel this way. What lesbians and gay men do to each other is not 'real' sex because it is not 'real' intercourse. Post-Foucault, a number of feminists have argued that intercourse and in particular the attainment of orgasm-via-penetration as the only legitimate route to orgasm, have a central role to play in symbolising and enacting women's oppression: see Dworkin (1987), Jeffreys (1990) Ussher (1997), Irigaray (1985), Segal (1994) and MacKinnon (1987).

At an individual level the ability of a person to do what they wish is related to the notion of **subjectification**, which is concerned with:

o   how the person is trained into certain ways of behaving – the extent to which a person is the subject of power;
o   how the person understands their own capacities – the extent to which a person is subject to a body of ethics;

o how the person relates to others – the extent to which the person accepts the situation as true.

As Paul Patton explains:

> In this manner, the ways in which certain human capacities become identified and finalized within particular forms of subjectivity – the ways in which power creates subjects – may also become systems of domination. (Patton, 1998: 71)

The Enlightenment saw the development of biopower: new forms of control over the bodies of people (by the use of new disciplinary technology). Biopower can be viewed as the dark side of the Enlightenment. In the area of sexuality it manifests itself as: new scientific disciplines concerned with 'an anatomo-politics of the human body' and regulatory controls or a 'bio-politics of the population' (Foucault, 1990: 139). Foucault developed what he called a 'capillary' model of power in which he attempted to understand the 'relations of power' by looking at struggle and resistance.

o Struggles are not limited to any one place or any one time.
o Struggles are concerned with resisting the effects of power on bodies.
o Struggles are concerned with resisting the role of government in individual self-formation.
o Struggles are concerned with opening up and making clear how power is used in changing people.
o Struggles are concerned with the politics of self-definition and self-formation.
o Struggles are concerned with resisting the imposition of external standards of taste and decency.
o Political struggles are local and personal in nature.

There are a number of common themes running through Foucault's work on sexuality. His key concern was with how human beings become **subjected** – made into subjects within the modern world – by the dominating mechanisms of disciplinary technology. In addition, Foucault is concerned with how people become subjects of investigation for 'new' sciences such as psychiatry and psychology. All of this was motivated by a search for the causes of 'abnormality', for answers to the question: what makes some individuals perverted, sick or mischievous?

A central element for Foucault was **the state**, a political structure that emerged in the sixteenth century to look after the interests of 'the totality' – everybody within the community. The state gathered information about all forms of human activity: birth rates, death rates, unemployment, public health, epidemic diseases, crime and sexuality. All of these phenomena could be indicators of a serious threat to the community. A friend and colleague of Foucault, Paul Rabinow, in his introduction to *The Foucault*

Reader (Foucault, 1986) explains that within Foucault's work it is possible to identify what he calls three 'modes of objectification', in other words three organising principles used by Foucault to explain how individual human beings become subjects.

Dividing practices

This involves the exclusion of people who are viewed as a threat to the community. The most famous example of this is the forced withdrawal of lepers from the community into leper colonies during the Middle Ages. This exclusion did result in the eradication of leprosy from Europe, so it was believed that other threats to the community could be solved by similar exclusions. The poor were forced into workhouses. Criminals were placed in prison. The insane were excluded into mental hospitals, or 'ships of fools', which were said to be ships loaded with insane individuals which were pushed out to sea to find their sanity. Although the ships of fools may have been mythical, it is certainly true that the mad once played a recognised role within the local community, the village idiot for example, and that this role was taken away when they were locked up in secure institutions.

Foucault turns on its head the idea of progress in relation to the treatment of the mentally ill; the commonsense assumption that the more we progress the more we care is not true, in Foucault's eyes. The idea of dividing practices was fully outlined in *Discipline and Punish: The Birth of the Prison* (1977), which opens with two contrasting examples of punishment: the botched, messy and disturbing torture and execution of Damiens the regicide and Leon Faucher's 'rules for the house of young prisoners', which were drawn up only eighty years after Damiens's death.

What Foucault traces here is the decline and eventual disappearance of public spectacle in the punishment process, which many have perceived as a process of humanisation. The need to inflict pain on the body disappeared from penal repression, and options for readjustment, fines and confinement were considered more appropriate. However, the old 'truth–power' relation remained at the heart of the penal reform. The difference was that getting to the truth by the use of torture was no longer considered appropriate. With humanisation, crime became something which had to be eliminated by working on the 'soft fibres of the brain' (Foucault, 1977: 130): no longer was crime something which offended one individual or group. A criminal was one person against all – the whole social network. Bodies need to be trained in good habits to avoid criminality. As Foucault explains:

> Thus discipline produces subjected and practised bodies, 'docile' bodies. Discipline increases the forces of the body (in economic terms of utility) and diminishes these same forces (in political terms of obedience). In short, it dissociates power from the body; on the one hand, it turns it into an 'aptitude', a 'capacity', which it seeks to increase; on the other hand, it reverses the course of

the energy, the power that might result from it, and turns it into a relation of strict subjection. (Foucault, 1977: 138)

Disciplined bodies have four characteristics:

o Bodies know their appropriate geographical place.
o Bodies have an understanding of their appropriate activities.
o Bodies have an understanding of time.
o Bodies can control the various forces within them.

Foucault argues that from the beginning of the seventeenth century 'discipline' became similar in many respects to 'training': individuals were 'made' into something. In addition people were coerced not by pain, but by observation: 'each gaze would form a part of the overall functioning of power' (Foucault, 1977: 171).

The purpose of the gaze is not to repress, but to *normalise*. The power of the norm was disseminated through the standardised education delivered by the *écoles normales* (teacher training institutions). Normalisation may impose homogeneity, but it also allows us – as members of society – to categorise and measure people, place people in hierarchies on the basis of widely accepted rules. Individuality becomes institutionalised into a set of categories.

The *Panopticon*, developed by Jeremy Bentham in 1791, was a new architectural design for a prison that was the opposite of the dungeon. Where the dungeon kept the inmate out of sight, enclosed and hidden in the dark, the Panopticon stressed visibility; it was designed as a place where even the slightest movements could be observed and recorded. From a central observation tower, a supervisor could see into the cell of any inmate at any time. Panopticism was a key element in the 'disciplinary partitioning' of the abnormal from the normal – a space where the mad, the dangerous and the strange could be trapped by visibility and thereby induced into behaving in a way that was acceptable. The inmates were placed in a power situation where they never knew if they were being observed, so had to assume that they always were being observed. According to Foucault, power within the Panopticon was always *visible* and *unverifiable*: 'The Panopticon is a marvellous machine which, whatever use one may wish to put it to, produces homogenous effects of power' (1977: 202).

Scientific classification

The Enlightenment saw the emergence of a number of new sciences that were concerned with understanding the 'nature' of individuals. These new sciences defined what is 'normal' so that the 'abnormal' could be treated. The key tool was the **examination** (such as the examination you may receive from the doctor), which transformed visibility into power, classified people into cases and trapped them in a strait-jacket of documentation, which stated clearly if they were normal or not. Foucault refers to this as 'hierarchical observation': 'a mechanism that coerces by means of observation; an apparatus in which the techniques that make it possible to see induce effects of power and in which, conversely, the means of coercion make those on whom they are applied clearly visible' (Foucault, 1986: 189). If we take the case of psychiatry, the doctor has a notion of the 'normal' mind and classifies individuals into 'normal' or into a range of various diseased states. In Foucault's work, power relationships are based upon surveillance and need not be based upon physical punishment.

Subjectification

This relates to the process of self-formation, self-understanding and the way in which conformity is achieved by *problematising* activities and opening them up to observation and punishment. Foucault is concerned with what it means to be a self and how we as individuals are pressurised into creating our selves in a given fashion. Individuals define themselves as 'normal' in relation to a number of factors: sex, health, race and many more. This is primarily concerned with what Foucault was to call the 'power of the norm': all individual actions are now within 'a field of comparison' which both pressurises people and *normalises*. Normal people could legitimately regard themselves as members of a homogeneous social body – the society.

The History of Sexuality

In the first volume of *The History of Sexuality* Foucault explains that he wants to trace the origins of our 'restrained, mute, and hypocritical sexuality' (1990a: 3) in which silence about sexuality became the norm. Sex was placed into a 'discourse', supported by powerful mechanisms that functioned to control all forms of desire and pleasure. As suggested earlier in the chapter, discursive practices are rule-governed structures of intelligibility that both oblige people to behave in a given way and give consent to ways of behaving. From the eighteenth century onwards 'sex' became a 'police' matter, in other words it became regulated by public discourses, organised around canonical law, civil law and Christian pastoral support. The state took an active interest in the sexuality of the population. Potential deviations from 'normal sexuality' could have a detrimental impact upon the matrimonial relations and family organisation that were seen as important in maintaining the health and prosperity of the country. Legal sanctions were imposed upon minor forms of perversion and other types of sexual irregularity were redefined as mental illness. Foucault lists marrying a close relative, seducing a nun, engaging in sadism, deceiving one's wife and violating a cadaver:

> debauchery (extramarital relations), adultery, rape, spiritual or carnal incest, but also sodomy, or mutual 'caress'. As to the courts, they could condemn homosexuality as well as infidelity, marriage without consent, or bestiality. (Foucault, 1990a: 38)

In *The Use of Pleasure: The History of Sexuality Vol. 2* (1984) Foucault examines the manner in which sex and sexuality were 'problematised' by classical Greek and Latin doctors and philosophers, whose writings on how a person should conduct themselves sexually influenced later Christian ideas about the nature of sexual activity. The central concept in this volume is **the mode of subjection**: 'the way in which the individual establishes his relation to the rule and recognizes himself as obliged to put it into practice' (Foucault, 1992: 27).

A 'regimen' means rules on how one ought to behave. It is a sort of fiction insofar as it is used as a theory to condition which factual statements can be produced, and not the reverse. These rules covered areas as diverse as exercise, food, drink and sleep as well as sexual relations. What underpinned the regimen was the notion that such activities should be 'measured' and well managed because excesses were bad for the soul and the physical body. The misuse of sexual pleasure could lead to death. The regimen provided a guide on what to do in any given situation. Foucault provides the following example, from a letter by Diocles to King Antigonus:

> at winter solstice, which is the time when one is most susceptible to catarrh, sexual practice should not be restricted. During the time of the Pleiades ascent, a period in which bitter bile is dominant in the body, one must indulge in sexual acts with a good deal of moderation. One should even forgo them completely at summer solstice, when black bile takes over in the organism; and it is necessary to abstain from sexual activity, as well as from any vomiting, till the autumn equinox. (Foucault, 1992: 113–14)

One area that became problematised, argues Foucault, was the 'courting' of boys and young men by adult males. For Foucault these areas of sexual activity 'constituted the most active focus of reflection and elaboration; it was here that the problematization called for the most subtle forms of austerity' (Foucault, 1992: 253).

Many of these themes were taken up in *The Care of the Self: Vol. 3 of The History of Sexuality* (1984). Here Foucault draws upon the classical Greek text by Artemidorus, *The Interpretation of Dreams*. Artemidorus argues that nature had established the principle that there was a definite form of sexual act for each species, which was the one natural position. For humans the natural position was a man lying on top of a woman in a face-to-face position:

> All the other positions 'have been discovered by yielding to wantonness and licentiousness.' These unnatural relations always contain a portent of defective social relations (bad relationships, hostility) or a prediction of a worsening of one's economic situation (one is uncomfortable, financially 'embarrassed'). (Foucault, 1990b: 23)

In particular, Artemidorus disapproves of oral sex which, like many of the authors that Foucault reviews, he views as an 'awful act' and a 'moral wrong' because he believes it to be a 'wasteful discharge of semen', 'not in common with nature'. Other activities that Artemidorus disapproves of include: relations with gods, relations with animals, relations with corpses, relations with oneself and relations between women.

In the area of sexuality, just as in the areas of madness and illness, social and medical practices were used to define a pattern of what constituted 'normal'. A number of sexual practices were 'problematised' and subjected to a rigid set of 'epistemic' rules, discursive and punitive practices that together formed a 'disciplinary' model. **Subjectivation** operates in a quasi-judicial fashion. The person must conform to a rule or set of rules and to do otherwise is to run the risk of punishment. Sex was not *wrong*, but a person was expected to enjoy their pleasure 'as one ought'.

Critique of Foucault's work has revolved around the issue of whether Foucault overstated the extent to which people could be 'subjected', leaving them little scope for resistance. In addition, his emphasis on power in the processes of self-formation means that he ignored the global nature of power relations.

Critiques of Foucault

Many feminists have argued that Foucault's analysis is not a theory *for* women; his theorising has no distinctly female/feminist ontology or epistemology. A number of feminists, for example Sandra Lee Bartky (1988), have criticised Foucault because he does not place gender at the centre of his analysis and does not discuss the factors that impose gender on bodies. For many feminists, because Foucault has no interest in the sociopolitical significance of anatomical differences between men and women, this means that he reproduces the sexism found in most social theory and the forms of sexual dominance and sexual hierarchy found in the ancient cultures that he is critical of. In other words, Bartky is arguing that Foucault is wrong to reject the radical feminist argument that there is an unchanging essence to femininity.

Foucault's work made no contribution to a post-colonial discussion of gender relations; he had no interest in the racial origins of the bodies he theorises about. Terry Eagleton (1990) drawing upon the Gramscian notion of hegemony, argues that Foucault's theorising describes the forms of pressure that are brought to bear on bodies to conform sexually but because of his overemphasis on the self he provides no explanation of how to challenge what is essentially a class-based ideology. Foucault merely reproduces the power structures he seeks to sweep away.

Foucault's work provided the starting point for **queer theory**, which also draws upon a number of poststructuralist theories, such as those of Lacan and Derrida. What is queer theory? It is a collection of ideas and concepts, drawn from a range of disciplines which attempt to 'deconstruct' and undermine the power relations that maintain the idea that the binary sexual division between male and female is the only natural and legitimate basis for 'normal' sexuality.

Jacques Lacan's model of a decentred and unstable identity

For Lacan, the notion of identification is symbolic in nature as individuals are influenced by imaginary images that provide the individual with a base. Individuals have a view of themselves and their identity, but this view is influenced by a range of different concepts and ideas which are constantly changing. However, such mirror images exist within a complex symbolic web, which means that our identities are always unstable and in a process of continual change. However, it is important to stress that Foucault always distanced himself from psychoanalysis. As Joseph Bristow explains:

> in Foucault's view, Freud's inquiries into sexual maturation make perpetual appeals to the cultural laws that regulate the erotic identifications unconsciously achieved by individual subjects. Foucault stresses how the whole apparatus of the Freudian Oedipus and castration complexes, no matter how critical of earlier theories of sexual perversion and degeneration, assimilate prevailing assumptions about the indissociable link between sexuality and cultural prohibitions. (Bristow, 1997: 1980–1)

Jacques Derrida's notions of deconstruction and 'performativity'

Performatives/performativity: A concept derived from the philosophy of J.L. Austin (1911–1960); 'performative' denotes a form of words which in themselves perform an action and have a binding power, but which is not a promise; for example if a person says 'I give in' that is itself an act of giving in.

Deconstruction involves analysis and critique but has no firm outcome formulated in advance; in other words, the aim is to disassemble. Queer theorists, to dislocate categories such as masculine/feminine or male/female upon which patriarchy is based, use this notion of deconstruction. It involves making alterations to the foundations of our cultural practices. Performativity is one of the most influential concepts within queer theory. Performatives are when we do a *thing* with the use of words, such as marrying people. They generate a conventional procedure that participants agree to abide by. There are 'proper' ways of behaving for men and women, which are practices that are conventional and make use of appropriate words. Masculinity and femininity are such practices: they are neither true nor false, they simply exist and guide our behaviour in appropriate situations. However, all performatives can fail, and new social movements such as Outrage can make performatives in relation to sexuality fail.

Many lesbians and gays have questioned the notion of 'queer' and the identity that goes with it.

Judith Butler

In contrast to radical feminists and socialist feminists (who both argue that there is an unchanging nature or essence of the woman) and liberal feminists (who have the aim of making men and women the same in every possible respect), in *Gender Trouble* (1990) Judith Butler takes issue with the assumption that the notion of *woman* is a common identity. 'If one "is" a woman, that is surely not all one is' (Butler, 1990: 3). In other words, she is attempting to disrupt the notion of 'woman' as it is used in both everyday life and social analysis. Gender intersects with a range of other modalities that constitute our identity. According to Butler, what constitutes a gendered personhood needs to be described and explained, not simply assumed. Feminist analysis is in many cases built upon a notion that there is a 'truth' of sex that exists prior to personhood and automatically defines the gendered person. Butler also takes issue with the notion of universal patriarchy that underpins many feminist explanations of gender oppression. In Butler's analysis, 'being' of a particular gender is an effect, and what is needed is a genealogical investigation into the foundations and parameters of the gender ontology – a political and historical investigation into what it is that makes us accept the 'reality' of gender as a fact rather than as an arbitrary set of concepts.

The universal notion of 'woman' and the conceptions of gender and patriarchy that are associated with it are part of 'the heterosexual matrix', 'a grid of cultural intelligibility through which bodies, genders and desires are naturalized' (Butler, 1990: 151). This concept of the heterosexual matrix is built upon: Monique Wittig's notion of *heterosexual contact*; and Adrienne Rich's notion of *compulsory heterosexuality*.

Butler goes on to explain that 'a hegemonic discursive/epistemic model of gender intelligibility assumes that for bodies to cohere and make sense there must be a stable sex expressed through a stable gender (masculine expresses male, feminine expresses female) that is oppositionally and hierarchically defined through the compulsory practice of heterosexuality' (1990: 151). Butler's argument is that it is possible to deconstruct gender by the use of parody.

Marjorie Garber: *Vested Interests: Cross-Dressing and Cultural Anxiety*

What is gender? What is a man or a woman? Although it is easy to be amused by the sight of a person cross-dressing, Garber points out that according to Freud the laughter is in part the laughter of unease. One of the issues that Garber is interested in is the way 'in which clothing constructs (and deconstructs) gender and gender differences' (Garber, 1992: 3). The appeal of cross-dressing is found in its position as a symbol of the constructed nature of gender categories, and the power of cross-dressing is to be found in the way that the activity blurs the binarism of a simple division between male and female. As Garber explains:

> For me, therefore, one of the most important aspects of cross-dressing is the way in which it offers a challenge to easy notions of binarity, putting into question the categories of 'female' and 'male', whether they are considered essential or constructed, biological or cultural. (Garber, 1992: 10)

Garber outlines the history of dress from the sumptuary legislation of the sixteenth century, which laid down what men and women could and could not wear, and concludes that authority structures have always had anxieties about cross-dressing. Modern dress codes reflect economic, and patriotic or nationalistic motives, irrespective of the fashion at the time. School boards, the Academy, the army, the monarchy and so on have all had strict male and female dress codes because to allow cross-dressing may bring about a dissolution of all boundaries and highlight the arbitrary nature of law, custom and tradition. To reinforce this point, Garber draws upon Magnus Hirshfeld's groundbreaking study, *Die Transvestiten* (Transvestites) (1910).

One of the issues that Hirshfeld explores is the link between transvestism and the military. Military personnel had an 'intense love of uniform', they liked to dress up in them. For men military uniform was 'fancy dress', which involved a 'complicated interplay of male bonding, acknowledged and unacknowledged homosexual identity, carnivalized power relations, the erotics of same sex communities, and the apparent safety afforded by theatrical representation' (1992: 55–6). With its emphasis on *reading* and *being read*, self-enactment and analysing social practice from within, transvestism has the cultural effect of destabilising all boundaries within and between gender and sexuality: male/female; gay/ straight; sex/gender; such divisions are not only reversed, but 'denaturalised'. Garber quotes from a San Francisco guidebook that states:

> Cast aside stereotypes for your trip to San Francisco. Fathers now worry if a son's hair is too short, if his dress is too macho, or his muscles too well-developed, since these are the trademarks of the new breed of San Francisco gay man. (Garber, 1992: 148)

For Garber we are experiencing a 'category crisis' generated by the 'transvestite effect' and our inability to make sound definitional distinctions in the field of sex, sexuality and gender. This 'category crisis' is our central cultural anxiety.

Naomi Wolf

Naomi Wolf first became known with the publication of *The Beauty Myth* (1990). In this book Wolf recognises the economic, social and political advances that women have made since the 1970s. However, she argues, women do not feel as free as they should, given the victories they have won. Women are made to feel concerned about such things as body shape, hair and other aspects of their physical appearance. Wolf argues that there is a link between female liberation and female beauty:

> The more legal and material hindrances women have broken through, the more strictly and heavily and cruelly images of female beauty have come to weigh upon us . . . During the past decade, women breached the power structure; meanwhile, eating disorders rose exponentially and cosmetic surgery became the fastest-growing medical speciality . . . It is no accident that so many potentially powerful women feel this way. We are in the midst of a violent backlash against feminism. (Wolf, 1990: 10)

The beauty myth is a key element in this powerful backlash. The ideologies that constitute the myth operate at a psychological and ideological level. Ideas about what constitutes female beauty are used as political weapons to covertly control women, reinforcing the glass ceiling, excluding women from power, preventing them from exercising their hard-won rights and generating low self-esteem.

It is commonly assumed that notions of female beauty are ahistorical and, claims Wolf, that they operate 'objectively' and 'universally'. This is not true. According to Wolf, the ideologies of beauty are 'determined by politics' and are 'culturally imposed' by men. Such ideologies have no legitimate or biological justification. The myth is a 'social fiction that masqueraded as natural components of the feminine sphere' (1990: 15). The myth operates in a similar fashion to the Iron Maiden, an instrument of torture found in Germany during medieval times. This was a casket shaped and painted with the limbs and smiling face of an attractive young woman. The victim was placed inside the casket where she would die of starvation or by being stabbed by the metal spikes that held her in place. The present-day Iron Maiden is much more subtle: it is composed of 'emotional distance', politics, finance and sexual repression. It is used to impose ways of behaving upon women and is not simply about appearance. However, a key element of the Iron Maiden is the desire that women have to be thin, to lose a stone.

Wolf's argument about who controls the beauty myth is unclear. At various points she talks about 'the traditional elite' (p. 55), 'the elite of power structure' (p. 138), and the elite who maintain a 'caste system' (pp. 87 and 286). The working of these institutions is not explained or fully described. Moreover, the motive behind these institutions is also obscure. On page 282 Wolf appeals to women to reject the artificial nature of the myth by 'natural solidarity'. She seems to suggest that it is women who are to blame for the maintenance of the beauty myth. In other words, her argument that our conceptions of 'beauty' are built upon a false set of patriarchal representations imposed upon women by male-dominated institutions lacks theoretical complexity.

Drawing upon the work of Naomi Wolf, Efrat Tseelon (1995) has made use of Goffman's notion of stigma – notably 'abominations of the body' – to evaluate some of the key research findings on the beauty myth. She argues that a woman is more likely to be judged on the basis of her attractiveness, and more harshly rejected when thought to be deficient in it: 'the beauty system is naturalised by the ideology of sexual differences, and is made to feel essential to femininity' (Tseelon, 1995: 90). She suggests that according to the empirical evidence:

o   women perceive themselves to be heavier than they are;
o   women are more concerned about their body attractiveness than men;
o   women are more dissatisfied with some aspect of their appearance –
     and this includes not only mature women but children as young as six
     years of age;
o   for women body image has a significant effect upon psychological
     health, romantic relationships and femininity.

Feeling unattractive and/or obese can make a woman become *socially* unattractive. This means the withdrawal from a range of social situations because encounters with others are painful. Women are made to feel both dependent upon their attractiveness and insecure about it. For this reason they are much more likely to do dangerous things to improve their appearance, such as constant dieting and surgery.

Tseelon's analysis suggests that women are made to feel 'on-stage' and self-conscious about the impression of themselves they are giving. They are made to feel permanently insecure.

Her conclusion is that women are stigmatised by the very expectation to be beautiful. This becomes a woman's 'master status', which is independent of the real characteristics of the person herself.

Camille Paglia

> If civilization had been left in female hands, we would still be living in grass huts. (Paglia, 1990: 38)

Camille Paglia is often described as an 'anti-feminist' and she is certainly highly critical of feminism. Feminists are described as puritanical about sex, fascist in their thought processes, as having no knowledge of history and unable to be critical of 'trendy' French social theories. Paglia supports the feminist pursuit of political and legal equality, but regards academic feminism as a 'rickety house of cards' (Paglia, 1992: 84) with a simplistic view of patriarchy that does not recognise the positive contributions that a male-created world has given women.

Paglia's assumptions

In order to fully grasp Camille Paglia's argument the reader needs to be familiar with the concepts outlined below from three philosophers:

Marquis de Sade (1740–1814)

Sade is widely regarded as a monstrous transgressor who used his extremist vision to lead a truly scandalous life. In his novels, he theorised about the joys of inflicting pain. Sade assumed that both sexual deviation and criminal acts are natural. He used this assumption to justify extremely degrading sexual experiences, in which extreme violence and other cruelty was infliucted to attain sexual release. In the nineteenth century Richard von Krafft-Ebing took Sade's name to describe a form of sexual perversion involving the infliction of pain (*sadism*).

Thomas Hobbes (1588–1679)

Hobbes's philosophy as outlined in *The Leviathan* (1651) assumes that human nature is essential 'animal' and dominated by self-interest, which leads directly to an endless state of war between all individuals. In this state of nature life becomes 'solitary, poor, nasty, brutish, and short'. To avoid this condition, Hobbes argued that we should form a commonwealth, in which individuals place absolute sovereign power in the hands of a strong ruler. For Hobbes, this obedience to strong government is necessary in order to have control over our animal instincts, secure liberty and allow us to have respect for others.

Friedrich Neitzsche (1844–1900)

For Nietzsche morality, includes ideas of 'good' and 'evil' are imposed upon us by people who have the *will power*, the powerful

---

invent both god and religion to control the behaviour of others. Nietzsche's philosophy is a philosophy of 'becoming' in which the person should be free to lead their life as they wish and 'become' whatever they wish. Nietzsche allows us to think beyond the limits of moral obligation and what he would see as the fictitious demands of an imaginary god. For Nietzsche we should attempt to overcome external constraints on our behaviour by becoming *Übermensch* or 'Overman' (often referred to as 'Superman'), a person who attempts to rise up and overcome the imposition of morality and sanctions of others (the will to power) and prevent us from exercising our freedom.

As we shall see below Camille Paglia brings these three acts of philosophical ideas about morality, power, violence and human nature together to inform her analysis of gender issues.

In her first book, *Sexual Personae* (1990), Camille Paglia draws upon the work of Hobbes, Nietzsche and Sade in order to identify the character and origins of patriarchal civilisation. In contrast to Rousseau, for Paglia people are animals, they are part of nature and, in the words of Thomas Hobbes, their lives in a state of nature are nasty, brutish and short. Nature has a history for Paglia, which is a history of people attempting to control its power. Social organisation is an artificial creation, built as a defence against nature's power. Sexual power takes the form of Nietzsche's 'will to power' and this force is contained by Hobbesian social arrangements for strong government, as found in the Commonweal. As she later very forcefully explains: 'It is nature, not society, that is our greatest oppressor' (Paglia, 1992: 45). 'Society is not the enemy, as feminism ignorantly claims. Society is woman's protection against rape' (1992: 51).

Sex is not a matter of social convention, as feminists have mistakenly suggested; it is the interconnection of the social and nature: 'Sex is chthonian' (1990: 295), which Paglia describes as a 'pre-Christian form of the malevolent nature mother' (1990: 364). Meaning that sex is from the earth; sex is from the muck, muddle and danger that are found in nature. In a delicious Shakespearian phrase, which clearly shows her view that sex involves surrender to nature, Paglia argues that: 'Two people making love are the beast with two backs' (1990: 297). This danger is seen in the many 'daemonic' models of women found in mythology, such as the siren and the *femme fatale*. These women are depicted as 'vampires' whose ability to drain and paralyse men, by wielding nature's power, is a key element in all-female physiology. Such women are deadly to men and represent the fear that men still have of nature. All cultures contain within them the fear amongst men of the toothed vagina. As Paglia argues: 'Metaphorically, every vagina has secret teeth, for the male exists as less than when he entered . . . Physical and spiritual castration is the danger every man runs in intercourse with a woman' (1990: 13). The idea that the penis is power, she explains, is a lie that men tell themselves in order to overcome their fear of intercourse. The prostitute, in contrast to the feminist view, is not 'the victim of men but rather their conqueror, an outlaw who controls the sexual channel between nature and culture' (1992: 18).

According to Paglia, contemporary feminists have a naive and prudish view of sex. However, although she argues that women do not need legal protection from men she sees both sexual freedom and sexual liberation as modern feminist delusions: 'Society is our frail barrier against nature' (Paglia, 1990: 3). As she goes on to explain: 'Men, bonding together, invented culture as a defence against female nature' (1990: 9).

This invented patriarchal culture represented a shift from 'belly magic' – the magical power of nature as demonstrated in the biological functioning of the female body – to 'head magic', a male invention which stressed logic, and in particular the use and application of number. This was central to the creation of male civilisation and its attempt to control nature. It is with some irony that Paglia argues: 'The very language and logic modern women use to assail patriarchal culture were the invention of men' (1990: 9).

In sharp contrast to Naomi Wolf, Paglia argues that notions of 'beauty' allow us to categorise and conceptualise nature. Such conceptions allow us to feel that the daemonic nature of sex is under our control. This gives greater emphasis to what can be seen and undervalues the unseen danger-ous 'chthonian' nature of the female.

However, Paglia is at pains to explain that she is not a biological deter-minist. Her argument is that 'civilisation', as found in abstract law for example, marks our transition from barbarism to order. The issue here is that if people have the ability to liberate themselves from nature, as Paglia clearly believes that they do, then why does she claim that both sexual freedom and sexual liberation are modern feminist delusions? This delu-sion can be brought into reality by the same learning 'to behave as civilized beings' (Paglia, 1992: 67) that brought about patriarchy.

The relation between 'the social' and 'nature' implies that the social contains some form of agency, exercised by people, which acts as a constraint upon nature. Patriarchy is not the only form of liberation/ protection from nature, and not the only form of hierarchy. To make anatomical sexual differences significant is an act of human decision-making, not the inevitable outcome of the 'will to power'. If people choose to liberate themselves from nature they can do so in a variety of ways.

The modern world liberated people from childbirth as a consequence of intercourse. Winning that particular battle over nature does allow a form of 'recreational sex'. Paglia explains at great length that this is possible for homosexuals, but she denies that it is possible for heterosexuals – with no explanation.

Finally, although Paglia explains that she is not a biological determinist, at times her argument is clearly of this type. In a discussion of hormones, she argues: 'If you are in any doubt about the effect of hormones on emotion, libido, and aggression, have a chat with a transsexual, who must take hormones medically. He or she will set you straight' (Paglia, 1992: 186).

Joseph Bristow (1997) argues that Camille Paglia's arguments are based upon the assumption that people's achievements are rooted in energies that are naturally occurring within human nature. Rather than providing any sociological insight into why gender inequality persists, Paglia argues that men achieve success because of their anatomy.

Luce Irigaray

Another writer who looks at the relationship between nature and patriarchy is Luce Irigaray. In a book of essays, *Sexes and Genealogies* (1995), Irigaray argues that fathers and other men in positions of authority restrict female desire. This is said to be a matter of good health and of good virtue. The maternal function of women underlies the social order, and this is believed to be a woman's only 'order of desire'. Patriarchy is underpinned by a mythology of matricide which, argues Irigaray, is necessary for the foundation of the social order. She argues that we live in **sacrificial** societies. The use of sacrifice was traditionally one of the ways in which men attempted to control nature. Men have always had a need to kill, break and eat. Matricide is said by Irigaray to predate the murder of the father outlined by Freud in *Totem and Taboo* and signifies this sacrificial nature of patriarchy. The religion of sacrifice, she argues, including its social ceremonies, is almost universally performed by men, even though such activities 'serve as the basis and structure for the society' (Irigaray, 1995: 78).

This exclusion of women from the culture of sacrifice demonstrates that the hidden sacrifice of our society is the *extradition* of women – a ban on women's participation in the processes of social decision-making. Women are 'paralysed in and by cultural bonds that are not their own' (1995: 78). Moreover, women who attempt to fight this patriarchy will be eliminated because they cause trouble. Often it is claimed that women who try to disrupt the libidinal economy are mad, because they will not obey the phallic order. Creativity has, claims Irigaray, been forbidden to women for centuries – women are seen as mothers only. In addition, they are 'subjected to a normative heterosexuality' (1995: 20), which they must reject if they are to rediscover their genealogy. Women need to discover the history of their desires, and hence rediscover their identity and their desires free from the phallic order.

Je, Tu, Nous: Towards a Culture of Difference *(1982)*

In contrast to Paglia, Irigaray's analysis is built upon a very different set of assumptions about sex, patriarchy and nature. Irigaray argues that the area of sex is important for reproduction, culture and the preservation of life. As she explains: 'The issue . . . is one of whether our civilizations are still prepared to consider sex as pathological, a flaw, a residue of animality, or if they are finally mature enough to give it its human cultural status' (Irigaray, 1993: 36).

Women should come to accept that they have an identity that is different from that of men. Women can only enjoy any rights won by the women's movement if they find value in being a woman, and not just in motherhood. They must learn to both respect and enjoy female sexuality, outside of the male sexual parameters that are imposed upon women. Woman has to recognise that 'the geography of her pleasure is far more diversified, more multiple in its differences, more complex, more subtle, than is commonly imagined – in an imaginary rather too narrowly focused on sameness' (Irigaray, 1985: 28). To achieve this, centuries of socio-cultural values about what it means to be a woman need to be changed. Traditionally a woman's sexuality was defined, as a use value for a man, so there are layers of sexual oppression to overcome before a woman fully enjoy her needs and desires.

The biggest factor preventing this liberation of women's consciousness is the hold that patriarchy has on our civilisation. Patriarchal values appear to be both neutral and universal; however, these values involve the destruction of female genealogies. Patriarchy involves *one part of humanity having a hold over the other*, here the world of men over that of women' (Irigaray, 1993: 16, italics in the original). Both men and women are 'conditioned' (1993: 21) to feel that the father–son genealogy is superior to mother–daughter relationships – so much so that feminine becomes treated as simply non-masculine. We live in a between-men culture, seen most clearly in the use of grammar, where the appropriation of language by men has made 'feminine' syntactically secondary. Sexual justice cannot come about without changing the rules of language and the conceptions of truth and value that go with this: 'Man seems to have wanted, directly or indirectly, to give the universe his own gender as he wanted to give his own name to his children, his wife, his possessions' (1993: 31).

Irigaray goes on to explain that by the term 'possessions' she includes such diverse things as women's and children's bodies, natural space, living space, the economy of signs, images, social and religious representation. Women need to involve themselves in *parler-femme*, they must be involved in 'speaking as a woman', disrupting the discursive logic of male syntax.

What is 'the culture of difference?' The **culture of difference** is for Irigaray 'a respect for the non-hierarchical difference of the sexes: *he* means *he*, *she* means *she*. *He* and *she* cannot be reduced to complementary functions but correspond to different identities' (Irigaray, 1993: 48). The establishment of a culture of difference would involve a questioning of the categories upon which currently accepted discourses and truth are based. Women would contribute to the creation of culture on equal terms with men; therefore new rules and new subjective identities would be established.

Activity: do we still need feminism?

Read the passage below. Do you accept or reject the views expressed? Give some reasons for your answer.

I have come to the conclusion that the only people who have a vested interest in 'theorising patriarchy' are academic feminists, who need the concept to further their careers. We need to be suspicious of the concept of 'Woman'. This notion is itself an invention of patriarchy; it implies 'nature', 'the family', 'reproductive heterosexuality' and 'exclusivity'. Without the notion of 'woman' there could be no patriarchy. Feminism is no longer a project for female emancipation, it is a mere forum for sectional interests, and composed of individuals whose only interest in intellectual activity is securing their own employment. Feminism should be consigned to the waste bin of redundant ideas, not retained as a tool for social analysis. Source: Best (2001: 25)

Conclusions

There are rich and varied ways of theorising within feminism, but the starting point for this theorising is always the notion of patriarchy. The concept of 'Grrl' emerged in the late 1990s, and those who adopt this view argue that feminist analysis is based upon, and takes its foundation from, the very notions of gender and patriarchy that it claims it wants to dissolve. Conceptions of 'man' and 'woman' provide a naturalistic and seemingly unchallengeable gloss over a constructed set of patriarchal institutions and practices.

References

Astell, M. (1997) *A Serious Proposal to the Ladies*, parts 1 and 2 (1694). Pickering & Chatto: London.

Bartky, S.L. (1988) 'Foucault, femininity and the modernization of patriarchal power', in I. Diamond and L. Quinby (eds), *Feminism and Foucault: Reflections on Resistance*. Northeastern University Press: Boston.

Bauman, Z. (1988) *Freedom*. Open University Press: Buckingham.

Beasley, C. (1999) *What Is Feminism?* Sage: London.

Bentham, J. (1791) in *The Collected Works of Jeremy Bentham Vol. 6*. J.H. Burns, J.R.

Dinwiddy and F. Rosen (eds) (1984). Clarendon Press: Oxford.

Best, S. (2001) 'Just like a grrl: do we still need feminism?' *Social Science Teacher*, 30(1): 20–5.

Bristow, J. (1997) *Sexuality*. Routledge: London.

Brownmiller, S. (1976) *Against Our Will: Men, Women and Rape*. Random House: New York.

Butler, J. (1990) *Gender Trouble: Feminism and the Subversion of Identity*. Routledge: London.

Butler, J. (1993) *Bodies That Matter: On the Discursive Limits of 'Sex'*. Routledge: London.

Carter, A. (1984) *Nights at the Circus*. Picador: London.

Chodorow, N. (1978) *The Reproduction of Mothering: Psychoanalysis and the Sociology of Gender*. University of California Press: Berkeley.

Collins, P.H. (1986) 'Learning from the outside within: the sociological significance of black feminist thought', *Social Problems*, 33 (October): S14–S32.

Collins, P.H. (1996) *Black Feminist Thought: Knowledge, Consciousness, and the Politics of Empowerment*. Unwin Hyman: Boston.

Coward, R. (1983) *Patriarchal Precedents: Sexuality and Social Relations*. Routledge & Kegan Paul: London.

de Beauvoir, Simone (1974) *The Second Sex* (1949), trans. and ed. H. Parshley. Vintage: New York.

Delphy, C. (1984) 'The main enemy' in *Close to Home: A Materialist Analysis of Women's Oppression*, trans. and ed. Leonard. Hutchinson: London.

Derrida, J. (1991) *A Derrida Reader*, ed. P. Kamuf. Columbia University Press: New York.

Dworkin, A. (1987) *Pornography: Men Possessing Women*. Basic Books: New York.

Eagleton, T. (1990) *The Ideology of the Aesthetic*. Blackwell: Oxford.

Eisenstein, Z. (1981) *Capitalist Patriarchy and the Case for Socialist Feminism*. Monthly Review Press: New York.

Epstein, J. and Straub, K. (1997) *Body Guards: The Cultural Politics of Gender Ambiguity*. University Press of Kentucky: Lexington.

Firestone, S. (1974) *The Dialectic of Sex: The Case for Feminist Revolution*. Bantam Books: New York.

Foster, S.L. (1997) *Corporealities: Danger, Knowledge, Culture and Power*. Routledge: London.

Freud, S. (1960) *Totem and Taboo*, trans. A.A. Brill. Vintage Books: London.

Friedan, B. (1965) *The Feminine Mystique*. Penguin: Harmondsworth.

Foucault, M. (1969) *The Order of Things: An Archaeology of the Human Sciences* (1966), trans. A. Sheridan-Smith. Tavistock: London.

Foucault, M. (1970) *The Order of Things: An Archaeology of the Human Sciences*, trans. A.M. Sheridan Smith. Tavistock: London.

Foucault, M. (1971) *Madness and Civilization*, trans. R. Howard. Tavistock: London.

Foucault, M. (1972) *The Archaeology of Knowledge*, trans. A.M. Sheridan Smith. Tavistock: London.

Foucault, M. (1977) *Discipline and Punish: The Birth of the Prison*, trans. A. Sheridan-Smith. Penguin: London.

Foucault, M. (1986) 'What is an author?' (1969) in P. Rabinow (ed.), *The Foucault Reader*. Harmondsworth: Peregrine/Penguin. pp. 101–20.

Foucault, M. (1989) *The Birth of the Clinic: An Archaeology of Medical Perception*, trans. A.M. Sheridan Smith. Routledge: London.

Foucault, M. (1990a) *The History of Sexuality Vol. 1*, trans. R. Hurley. Penguin: London.

Foucault, M. (1990b) *The Care of the Self: Vol. 3 of The History of Sexuality*, trans. R. Hurley. Penguin: London. French original published 1984.

Foucault, M. (1992) *The Use of Pleasure: The History of Sexuality Vol. 2*, trans. R. Hurley. Penguin: London.

Fuss, D. (1991) *Inside/Out: Lesbian Theories, Gay Theories*. Routledge: London.

Garber, M. (1992) *Vested Interests: Cross-Dressing and Cultural Anxiety*. Routledge: London.

Garber, M. (1996) *Bisexuality and the Eroticism of Everyday Life*. Routledge: London.

Greer, G. (1970) *The Female Eunuch*. MacGibbon & Kee: London.

Hartmann, H. (1979) 'The unhappy marriage of Marxism and feminism: towards a more progressive union', in L. Sargent (ed.), *Women and Revolution: A Discussion of the Unhappy Marriage of Marxism and Feminism*. South End Press: Boston.

Hartsock, N. (1990) 'Foucault on power: a theory for women?' in L. Nicholson (ed.), *Feminism/Postmodernism*. Polity: Cambridge.

hooks, bell (1990) *Yearning: Race, Gender and Cultural Politics*. South End Press: Boston.

Irigaray, L. (1982) *Je, Tu, Nous: Towards a Culture of Difference*, trans. A. Martin. Routledge: London.

Irigaray, L. (1985) *This Sex Which Is Not One*, trans. C. Porter and C. Burke. Cornell University Press: Ithaca, NY.

Irigaray, L. (1993) *Je, Tu, Nous: Towards a Culture of Difference*, trans. A. Martin. Routledge: New York.

Irigaray, L. (1995) *Sexes and Genealogies*, trans. G.C. Gill. Cornell University Press: Ithaca, NY.

Jeffreys, S. (1990) *Anticlimax: A Feminist Perspective on the Sexual Revolution*. Spinifex Press: Melbourne.

Jeffreys, S. (1998) *The Spinster and Her Enemies: Feminism and Sexuality 1880–1930*. Spinifex Press: Melbourne.

Johnston, J. (1973) *Lesbian Nation: The Feminist Solution*. Simon & Schuster: New York.

Kafka, F. (1972) *Metamorphosis* (1915), ed. S. Corngold. Bantam Press: London.

Komesaroff, P. (1997) *Troubled Bodies: Critical Perspectives on Postmodernism, Medical Ethics, and the Body*. Duke University Press: Durham, NC.

Lacan, J. (1998) *The Four Fundamental Concepts of Psychoanalysis (The Seminar of Jacques Lacan, Book 11)*, ed. J.-A. Miller and trans. A. Sheridan. W.W. Norton & Company: New York.

Mackinnon, C. (1987) *Towards a Feminist Theory of the State*. Harvard University Press: Cambridge, MA.

MacKinnon, C.A. (2001) *Sex Equality*. Foundation Press: New York.

Martin, B. (1996) *Femininity Played Straight: The Significance of Being Lesbian*. Routledge: London.

Mead, M. (1935) *Sex and Temperament in Three Primitive Societies*. Mentor: New York.

Miller, J. (1993) *The Passion of Michel Foucault*. HarperCollins: London.

Millett, K. (1970) *Sexual Politics*. Hart-Davis: London.

Nietzsche, F. (1956) *On the Genealogy of Morals* (1877), Anchor Books: New York.

Oakley, A. (1972) *Sex, Gender and Society*. Maurice Temple Smith in association with New Society: London.

Oakley, A. (1981) *Subject Women*. Martin Robertson: Oxford.

Paglia, C. (1990) *Sexual Personae: Art and Decadence from Nefertiti to Emily Dickinson*. Penguin Books: London.

Paglia, C. (1992) *Sex, Art and American Culture*. Vintage Books: New York.

Patton, P. (1998) 'Foucault's subjects of power', in J. Moss (ed.), *The Later Foucault*. Sage: London. pp. 64–77.

Petchesky, R.P. (1984) *Abortion and Woman's Choice: The State, Sexuality, and Reproductive Freedom*. Northeastern University Press: Boston.

Pfohl, S. (1992) *Death at the Parasite Café*. Macmillan: Basingstoke.

Rich, A. (1980) 'Compulsory heterosexuality and lesbian existence', *Signs*, 5(4): 38–51.

Segal, L. (1994) *Straight Sex: Rethinking the Politics of Pleasure*. University of California Press: Berkeley.

Seidman, S. (1996) *Queer Theory/Sociology*. Blackwell: Oxford.

Sharpe, S. (1976) *Just Like a Girl*. Penguin: Harmondsworth.

Straub, K. (1992) *Sexual Suspects: Eighteenth-Century Players and Sexual Ideology*. Princeton University Press: Princeton, NJ.

Terry, J. and Urla, J. (1997) *Deviant Bodies: Critical Perspectives on Difference in Science and Popular Culture*. Indiana University Press: Bloomington and Indianapolis.

Thompson, D. (2001) *Radical Feminism Today*. Sage: London.

Tseelon, E. (1995) *The Masque of Femininity*. Sage: London.

Ussher, J. (1997) *Fantasies of Femininity: Reframing the Boundaries of Sex*. Rutgers University Press: Piscataway.

Walby, S. (1989) 'Flexibility and the changing sexual division of labour', in S. Wood (ed.), *The Transformation of Work*. Unwin Hyman: London.

Walby, S. (1990) *Theorizing Patriarchy*. Blackwell: Oxford.

Weber, M. (1978) *Economy and Society: An Outline of Interpretive Sociology* (1922), ed. G. Roth and C. Wittich; trans. E. Fischoff. University of California Press: Berkeley.

Weldon, F. (1983) *Life and Loves of a She Devil*. Cornet Books/Hodder & Stoughton: London.

Wilton, T. (1996) *Finger-Licking Good: The Ins and Outs of Lesbian Sex*. Routledge: London.

Wittig, M. (1992) *The Straight Mind and Other Essays*. Harvester Wheatsheaf: Hemel Hempstead.

Wolf, N. (1990) *The Beauty Myth: How Images of Beauty Are Used against Women*. Vintage/Random House: London.

Wolf, N. (1993) *Fire with Fire: The New Female Power and How it Will Change the 21st Century*. Chatto & Windus: London.

Wolff, J. (1995) *Resident Alien: Feminist Cultural Criticism*. Routledge: London.

Wollstonecraft, M. (1792) *Vindication of the Rights of Women*. Joseph Johnson: London.

Chapter contents

5

Anthony Giddens: Theorising Agency and Structure

By the end of this chapter you should:

- be familiar with the concepts of 'agency' and 'structure' in the work of Giddens, Bourdieu and Elias;
- have an understanding of the relationship between 'agency' and structure;

- have a critical understanding of Giddens's key concepts of structuration, modernity, time space distinctiation, globalisation, life politics, emancipatory politics, reflexive modernisation, risk society, trust and the third way;
- have an understanding of Elias and the notion of the civilising process.

In this chapter we look at the relationship between 'human agency' and structure in the work of Anthony Giddens. One of Giddens's central themes, even in his earliest work, was the move away from the 'dualism' of having individual person (human agent) on the one hand and the society or social structure on the other. Giddens aimed to bring together grand theories of how society worked with micro-theories of what motivated individual social action. He attempted this synthesis of theories by using a concept called 'structuration', in which individuals were in a constant process of creation and recreation of social life and social structure. Giddens was not the only theorist who tried to achieve such a synthesis. Pierre Bourdieu also attempted something similar.

At the end of the chapter we shall also have a look at the work of Norbert Elias, who also attempted to combine agency and structure by looking at internalised forms of compliance.

Giddens on the relationship between 'agency' and 'structure'

During her time as British Prime Minister, Margaret Thatcher once said that there was no such thing as society, just individuals and their families. This comment came as something of a surprise both to non-Weberian sociologists and non-sociologists alike. However, individual people cannot directly experience society, the social system and social structure. Such concepts are not in a form that can be directly experienced. Yet they appear to play a key role in our lives. Whatever unexpected event presents itself to us, the world still has a meaning because underneath the often unpredictable and unpleasant ebb and flow of events there is a 'structure' which is durable, permanent and can be held on to in a storm. We make use of such concepts as 'structure' as a coping device, because the world without a 'structure' would be a world in which things may happen without warning, a world without meaning. What we always have to keep in mind, however, is that concepts such as 'structure' exist merely at a conceptual level. Structure is a fiction: it has no existence beyond 'the conceptual'. In contrast, for Giddens in the 1980s, the person was often presented as the visible carrier of the structure. Whether or not we accept this notion, which is still commonly held by Marxists and feminists, all that we experience of the structure are the practices – the guided actions – of individual people. However, there is no reason to suggest that beneath or beyond the activities of the individual there is any durable or permanent structure that guides, programs and directs these activities.

Activity

According to Giddens: 'Structures must not be conceptualised as simply placing constraints upon human agency, but as enabling' (1976: 60).

Explain in your own words what Giddens meant by this statement. Do you agree with it?

For Giddens, human agency and structure are inextricably linked. Agency has three elements to it: the unconscious; the practical consciousness; and the discursive consciousness. To make the short journey from 'virtual existence' to 'no existence' would have profound implications for Giddens's conception of agency.

Strictly speaking, the agent for Giddens, because of its rule-forming and rule-following nature is the visible carrier of structure and should also have a virtual existence. The human agent as visible carrier of structure brings the structure out of its 'virtual' existence and manifests that structure in the situated activities that make up everyday life. So to argue that we have no structure is to have no human agent. What Giddens needs to address is the question, 'Do we choose the ideas which we hold in our heads?' Or does the structure impose ways of thinking and acting upon us, allowing only limited choice? In his later work Giddens got around this problem by not discussing 'structure' and by replacing agency with the undertheorised conception of 'self'.

Activity

Who are you? Are you a 'human agent' as Giddens describes? If your answer is yes, outline which resources you have made use of.

According to Anthony Giddens, one element of the self is the ability to make 'rules' and 'routines' which help you to feel comfortable and secure. Think of rules and routines that you make: do you make these rules for reasons of security or for other reasons? Your answers to this activity will allow you to evaluate Giddens's theory, by either saying that his theory is true in your experience or that it is not.

Look at a range of recent psychology textbooks such as Cardwell et al., *Psychology for 'A' level* (1996) and outline the arguments in favour of a 'biologically driven' notion of personality. Do you find the arguments more convincing than those of Giddens or less? Outline the reasons for your answer.

For Giddens in the 1980s structure exists as a memory trace, giving structure a status no different from a fictional account. When Giddens says that structure exists as a memory trace he draws upon that memory trace in order to make the statement. Are we to assume that Giddens's structure, memory and Giddens himself are all within the virtual existence? All we can be sure of is that Giddens is 'thinking'. He creates a world, and within that world he creates a structure; that structure creates agents, whose existence is dependent upon reproducing the rules which form the structure and their ability to recognise and follow such rules. The whole account is fictional – a delusive pretence. To say that structure has a virtual existence is to say something deliberately confusing.

Activity

Construct a list of reasons why you think people are reflexive. If you find a wide range of reasons, this can be used to evaluate the assumptions that Giddens makes about why people are reflexive.

Are people reflexive in order to enhance their opportunities to fulfil their desires? In Giddens's analysis, are individuals devoid of desire; apart from the security of the **'pure' relationship**? A 'pure relationship' is an intimate relationship based solely upon trust that cannot be underpinned by any guarantee, providing the individuals involved with meaning, stability and large tracts of relative security in day-to-day life. Share your answers with another student.

From emancipatory politics to life politics

Life politics represents a major epistemological and ontological shift in Giddens's work away from structures, rules and a self built upon a practical and discursive consciousness. Life politics is an activity that takes place against the backdrop of modernity as a 'juggernaut'. The Giddens phrase 'the juggernaut of modernity' clearly indicates the uncoupling of the human agent from any postmodern processes of structuration. Life politics is not rule governed. It is a politics without any fixed, clear, social referents. Within life politics, the 'social' that formed the very foundation of modernity is dissolving. Life politics is about multiple identities, ways of behaving and self-definition/self-creation, rather than sets of rules enclosed within institutions. The world is more fluid and chaotic than at any other point within modernity. Activists within the new social movements (NSMs) of life politics are not clearly defined groups or institutions, but are involved in a form of dialogue, to the extent that it is not easy for individuals outside the NSMs to see their sectional concerns. There is an eerie relationship between life politics and the postmodern. Before we explore these issues let us remind ourselves of the key concepts and debates in the area: emancipatory politics; life politics; self and structure.

Within the nation states, democracy is moving towards a 'dialogic democracy' that is similar in many respects to the 'pure relationship'. As Giddens explains:

> there is a close tie between the pure relationship and dialogic democracy. Dialogue, between individuals who approach one another as equals, is a transactional quality central to their mutuality. There are remarkable parallels between what a good relationship looks like, as developed in the literature of marital and sexual therapy, and formal mechanisms of political democracy. Both depend on the development of . . . a principle of autonomy. (Giddens, 1994b: 118–19)

In Giddens's view, we need to have a theory of democratisation which takes into account both everyday life and globalising systems. Towards this end Giddens develops his notion of 'dialogic democracy' which stands in opposition to all forms of fundamentalism and attempts to 'create active trust through an appreciation of the integrity of the other. Trust is a means of ordering social relations across time and space' (Giddens, 1994b: 116). We attempt to live with others in a relation of 'mutual tolerance'. As Giddens suggested above, our political relationships take on many of the characteristics of the 'pure' relationship.

All individuals strive for a 'pure' relationship, in Giddens's analysis; this is a relationship based solely upon trust, and cannot be underpinned by any guarantee. In previous ages, it was possible to trust an individual in an intimate relationship because of their family background or because of their professional background. This guarantee of trust can no longer be given in the 'new times' of 'high' modernity. In terms of politics, the significance of these developments is that within modernity we have moved from 'emancipatory politics' – which is itself a product of modernity – to 'life politics', the key factor pushing new social movements to campaign for a form of polity which is on the far side of modernity.

Emancipatory politics has two main elements:

o   an effort to break free from the shackles of the past;
o   overcoming illegitimate domination, which adversely affects the life chances of individuals.

> Life politics is a politics, not of life chances, but of life style. It concerns disputes and struggles about how (as individuals and as collective humanity) we should live in a world where what used to be fixed either by nature or tradition is now subject to human decisions. (Giddens, 1994b: 14–15)

Life politics emerges from emancipatory politics and is a politics of self-actualisation, in other words it 'concerns debates and contestations deriving from the reflexive project of the self' (Giddens, 1991: 215).

Self

Anthony Giddens discusses the notion of human agent under the concept of self-identity, and this is made up of three elements:

o   the unconscious – this is a concept derived from Freud to outline those elements of our self which we are not fully in control of, beyond our immediate intentions;
o   the practical consciousness – this is a concept derived from Harold Garfinkel to explain that human action is not pushed about, or determined by forces outside of the individual. Giddens also accepts, as suggested by Garfinkel, that individuals have the ability to establish rules and routines for themselves;
o   the discursive consciousness – a term imported from Alfred Schutz to suggest that individuals reflect upon their social actions to make sense of these actions.

As individuals, moderns need to maintain the body, because it is necessary for all forms of physical experiencing. Within modernity, the body became reflexively appropriated as a project. In other words, the body has become an object that we refashion and remodel to our own design and for our own reasons. The body, as the creation of the human agent, as a structure in itself, is ignored by Giddens. He fails to take into account that bodies are structures upon which individuals exercise intentional human agency, in a process of *bodily structuration*.

Agency and structure

For many sociologists structure is looked upon as a durable framework, rather like the metal girders within a concrete building. It constrains our behaviour, it is beyond our control and it is out of sight. In contrast, for Giddens structure is always both enabling and constraining; defined as rules and resources, it is the property of social systems and gives shape to social systems. Structures themselves are reproduced 'through the regularised conduct of knowledgeable agents' (Giddens, 1984: 199). 'Structure' helps the human agent to solve the problem of getting from one event to the next.

In *The Constitution of Society* (1984), Giddens's argument is rather complex, but contains the following points: Human agents make rules – rules form structures – rules are used by agents to deploy resources – resources help to form structures of domination – structures are outside of time and space: they have a *virtual* existence. Systems, on the other hand, depend upon the situated activities of human agents – rules and resources have to be organised as properties of social systems. The concept of the 'duality of structure' brings all these points together. What does Giddens mean by *rule*? In Giddens's 1984 book, rules are viewed as 'generalisable procedures', which apply in a range of contexts and allow for the 'methodical continuation of an established sequence'; they are 'applied in the enactment/reproduction of social practices'. Rules tend to come in sets, and agents tend to reproduce social life with such consistency that the rules take on an objective property. Hence, for the human agent social life is experienced as having a high level of facticity, in other words, people are believed to experience the world as a factual order, as 'real'. However, structures are outside of time and space, they have what Giddens refers to as a 'virtual existence'. What does this mean? It means that structures have no significance for individual human agents until they are made use of by the human agents. Social systems, which depend upon 'situated activities of human agents', do not have 'structures', but rather exhibit 'structural properties' found, for example, in the memory traces of social actors. These structural properties are key factors in orienting the conduct of knowledgeable human agents, most notably in terms of the deployment of both allocative and authoritative resources.

o   Allocative resources: raw materials, means of production and finished goods.
o   Authoritative resources: organisation of time and space, chances for self-development, organisation between people.

Structures are not external to individuals in Giddens's argument, as for example they are in functionalism or structuralism.

The problem for Giddens is bringing together rules and resources with the regular social practices created by the human agents. His solution is the 'duality of structure':

> The constitution of agents and structures are not two independently given phenomena, a dualism, but represent a duality. According to the notion of the duality of structure, the structural properties of social systems are both medium and outcome of the practices they recursively organise. (Giddens, 1984: 25)

For Giddens then, structure is defined as *rules* and *resources* and it is not possible to think of rules without also thinking of resources. Rules suggest 'methodical procedures' and relate to the 'constitution of meaning and to the sanctioning of modes of social conduct' (Giddens, 1984: 18). As such, rules allow us, as agents, to apply the right 'formula' or 'generalised procedure' in the right context and on the right occasion. This rule-making and rule-following ability is at the 'very core' of our knowledgeability, according to Giddens, and is what constitutes our practical consciousness, a key element of the self.

Most of the established critiques of Giddens's notion of agency and the relationship between agency and structure have little or no substance to them. Most of Giddens's critics are unwilling or unable to accept that structures have no life that is independent of the activities of the human agents. Sociology seems to be based upon the assumption that forces outside of the control of the human agent determine human behaviour. Giddens has attempted to move away from this traditional assumption of determination, and to redefine the relationship between agency and structure.

Margaret Archer (1988), for example, makes a number of criticisms about the nature of the relationship between agency and structure. First, she takes issue with Giddens's view that structure is both medium and outcome of the reproduction practices, because 'This involves an image of society as a continuous flow of conduct (not a series of acts) which changes or maintains a potentially malleable social world . . . "structuration" does not denote fixity, durability, or even a point reached in development. "Structuration" itself is ever a process and never a product' (Archer, 1988: 60). In contrast to Archer, we might suggest that because Giddens views the human agent as an entity which is constantly making and remaking rules, taking into account changes in circumstances because of both foreseen and unforeseen consequences, structure does not have a beginning and/or an end. Archer's critique is a little like asking: what does the wind do when it is not blowing? Or what does the 'flow' do when the river stops? Structures cannot be understood outside of the activity of human agents, which is a point we can raise against most of Archer's critiques.

Consider the following: in Giddens's work agents are both involved in producing recurrent social practices and at the same time generating new practices. Archer seems to assume that when agents are involved in recurrent social practices their behaviour is determined, while when they are involved in generating new practices their behaviour is voluntaristic. This is not the case. At times the individual agent follows rules, at other times the same agent will not. Why this happens is part of being a person. Readers should ask themselves why this is the case in their own personal experience. If there is a criticism to be made of Giddens here, it is concerned with his notion of the human agent. Choosing to avoid choice still involves evaluation. It is the criteria of this evaluation that Giddens leaves unexplored. His discussion of the motive/intentionality behind social action is limited to issues of *ontological security* – maintaining security from personal meaninglessness and dread in the modern world. As individuals we can choose to break routine if we wish, but the motives for doing so are not fully explained. Within life politics such a silence is unacceptable, as life politics is all about smashing the rules and routines of modernity.

For similar reasons, we can also dispel Archer's critique of the duality of structure, which she describes as something that 'oscillates between the two divergent images it bestrides'.

> Rather than transcending the voluntarism/determinism dichotomy, the two sides of the 'duality of structure' embody them respectively. They are simply clamped together in a conceptual vice. (Archer, 1990: 77–8)

A second line of critique that Archer develops is against Giddens's notion of structure. She asks: 'why should one accept this peculiar onto-logical status for structural properties in the first place?' (Archer, 1990: 78). My response would be that if we want to have a non-reified notion of structure, which genuinely has a relationship to the activity of people – not just a concept treated as a real thing – then we have to develop a conception of structure not wholly dissimilar to that outlined by Giddens. Archer's specific criticisms of Giddens's notion of structure are: First, 'Structural properties are integral to social constitution and reconstitution, but when do they throw their weight behind the one or the other?' (1990: 78). The answer would be that structural properties do not throw their weight about, because only people have agency, not structural properties. Structural properties only play a role when they are made use of by agents as a resource.

In addition, Archer argues that 'structural features logically pre-date the actions that transform them; and . . . that structural elaboration logically post-dates those actions. Yet recognition of both points is fundamental to any theory of structural elaboration as a process occurring over time' (1990: 83). My response here would be that time itself is a structure, constituted as it is by action; again the charge inherent in Archer's critique is part of the continuous flow of conduct which changes or maintains a potentially malleable social world. If Archer rejects Giddens's use of grammar, as an example of rules and resources, then she might consider time. It is clearly a human creation, agents manipulate it, and yet it has the ability to shape behaviour.

In 1995 Archer published another critique of Giddens, in which she described his structuration theory as elisionist in nature. Elisionism, she explains, is a theoretical orientation characterised by three distinct features. First, a denial of the separability of agency and structure, in other words they are mutually constituting. Secondly, that 'every aspect of "structure" is held to be activity-dependent in the present tense and equally open to transformation' (Archer, 1995: 60). In other words, any structural constraint is open for change by the human agent. Thirdly, that 'the conviction that causal efficacy of structure is dependent upon its evocation by agency' (ibid.). In other words, any effect that structures have upon human behaviour can only come about by human agents making it happen. Structures have no determining effect upon human behaviour that is independent of human agency.

The thrust of the 1995 critique is similar to the earlier ones. Archer asks 'why Giddens finds such virtue in his major premise about inseparability as contained in the notion of the "duality of structures"' (1995: 94). The central question, says Archer, 'is whether "duality" merely throws a blanket over the two constituents, "structure" and "agency" which only serves to prevent us from examining what is going on beneath it'. This is an interesting question, but the problem is that Archer regards the social world as 'a stratified reality where different properties, powers and problems pertain to the layered strata' (1995: 94). One would expect that for Archer nothing is 'going on' beneath the blanket, because individuals are simply pushed about by forces outside their control. Even the 'unintended consequences' of individuals' action she attempts to convince us have an influence upon us that is independent of human agency.

Archer points out that for Giddens 'structural properties' only exist if 'instantiated' in social practices by agents. In addition, agents carry 'structural properties' as memory traces that are passed between them in everyday life. Archer points out that 'there are other places, which generically could be called "the Library"' (1995: 98), which equally could be used as a source of structure in the way that Giddens describes. My view would be that libraries are merely a method for the transmission of memory traces by other means. In addition, one might ask, what use/value is a library which is not made use of (instantiated) by agents? The unused library is of little or no value, as readers of H.G. Wells's *The Time Machine* will no doubt testify.

Archer is critical of the 'virtual existence' of structure which is outside of time and space. Her criticisms are at the ontological level. First, there are elements of the theory that are described and yet are deemed, by Giddens, to be 'virtual'. Secondly, there are elements which are *'excluded because it [structure] cannot be conceived of as instantiated*, that is aspects of social reality which cannot be accommodated within the "social practices" of the agents' (Archer, 1995: 107, italics in original). The first point is dealt with by the fact that Giddens, as a human agent, has instantiated the rules and resources in the form of a written description. The second point is dealt with by explaining that anything that is outside of the knowledge of the agent, and/or anything for which the agent lacks the resources to bring about will remain, for that agent, uninstantiated. Archer makes use of William Sewell's paper on structure (1992) to develop her critique. She explains that for Sewell resources are not virtual because material things exist in time and space. Moreover, as Archer makes clear, 'this is so not just for allocative resources, but also for human ones, since human beings are embodied and like other material objects cannot be virtual' (Archer, 1995: 105). What Archer fails to consider is that bodies have to be instantiated by agents to be of any use to the agent in everyday life. If the agent does not maintain its body, the body will die, and go out of existence, perhaps surviving only as a memory trace.

John Thompson (1989) makes a number of informed critiques of the relationship between agency and structure in Giddens's work. He takes issue with Giddens's view of structure as constituted by rules and resources. First, there are ambiguities with the term *rule*. Thompson asks:

> Would 'That's a "butterfly"'', said to a child on its first excursion into the countryside, or 'Hold your toothbrush horizontally', uttered by a dentist to a patient whose dental hygiene was poor, be examples of the sort of rule that someone interested in social structure should be studying? (Thompson, 1989: 63)

My initial response would be yes, because rule making and rule following are part of the minutiae of everyday life. In addition, the individual who is having the rule imposed upon them could have acted otherwise. However, as Thompson rightly points out, Giddens views the sense of rule which is most relevant to our analysis of social life as that expressed by formulae such as a = n + n − 1. As Thompson explains: 'Analytically effective or not, this suggestion does little to clarify the precise character of the rules which could be said, on Giddens's account, to comprise social structure' (Thompson, 1989: 64). He goes on to explain that Giddens's idea of structural constraint 'cannot be readily reconciled with his proposal to conceive of structure in terms of rules and resources' (1989: 73). Giddens's outline of *rule* is clear enough; the issue is that Thompson seems unwilling to accept that structure can be formulated as an element of agency. This issue is also raised by Derek Layder, who argues that Giddens's attempt to overcome the dualism between agency and structure, by introducing the conception of the 'duality of structure', raises a number of problems about how structure can be formulated by agency. In Giddens's view, action and structure both have their origin in social practices. For Layder, however, the 'old' problem of the dualism of action on the one hand and 'objective' social structure, which is independent of individual action, is not tackled, but replaced by a new issue with a new solution. Layder makes his position very clear in the following way:

> society has more or less objective components, and . . . these influence activity in both an internal and external way. In this sense, there is a case to be made that Giddens underplays the objective force of structural constraints insofar as he suggests that they only exist in the reasons and motivations of actors. (Layder, 1995: 145)

In support of this view Layder gives the example of procedures for the employment of university lecturers. In developing her own similar critique Archer gives the example of the Highway Code. Both of these have been designed by people and can be changed by people. However, in terms of the big picture, Giddens is attempting to show that the 'old' notion of a social structure that was said to be independent of the activity of individual actors was never a valid proposition. Social structures could only ever have their origins in social action; there could be no other source. Where else could any human creation come from other than human beings?

Layder returns to one of the issues raised by Archer: that of Giddens's overemphasis on individual freedom of action, what Archer termed 'hyperactivity'. In response to this Giddens has suggested that individuals' 'transformative capacities' at least partly depend upon circumstances, and that individuals have a tendency to reproduce the structures that are already there. As Layder points out: 'this is a far cry from the idea that the routines and patterns of social relations are being transformed in the process' (Layder, 1995: 145). I do not believe that Layder is taking into account choice. Individuals like routine, it gives a feeling of ontological security; bringing about change is unsettling and few people would wish to bring about change as an end in itself. However, this does not mean that the transformative capacity is lost simply because individuals choose not to make use of it at any one moment in time. Individuals are always capable of bringing about great change in the social structure. Let us return to Archer's point about 'hyperactivity'; she argues:

> it follows that if structural properties are inherently transformative then actors generically enjoy very high degrees of freedom – at any time they could have acted otherwise, intervening for change or for maintenance. Hence the counter-factual image of hyperactivity in which actors explore and exploit their generous degrees of freedom. Hence too the outcomes must be correspondingly variegated; society is not just 'potentially malleable', it becomes highly volatile if the possibility of change is recognised as inherent in every circumstance of social reproduction. (Archer, 1990: 63)

Eastern Europe has seen such an outburst of hyperactivity by agency and as such the innate volatility of society, with highly variegated outcomes. Lots of different people were involved in a range of different forms of protest which have had a number of different outcomes. The collapse of communism in Eastern Europe has not produced one model of democratic outcome, but a rich variety of outcomes. Some entail little more than drawing a border and a polite name change; others involve death camps, nationalism and NATO bombardment. Has the 'transformative capacity' of human agency no role to play in this?

Ian Craib (1992) has also developed a critique of the relationship between agency and structure in the writings of Anthony Giddens. According to Craib, what Giddens has to say about social organisation is little more than a precondition of social organisation and Giddens leaves us with nothing to say about the operation of social organisation at all. In addition, in Giddens's work: 'agency presupposes structure and structure presupposes agency' (Craib, 1992: 148) and 'the analysis itself depends upon a prior and implicit conception of social structure that Giddens's theory cannot recognise' (1992: 149).

Craib is asking a question about the origin of the structure in rules, then criticising Giddens for how the structure operates in everyday life. The origin and operation of structure are two separate issues. The structure can constrain behaviour but at the same time human agents create the structure. This seems to produce the paradox that individuals constrain their own behaviour, a situation not unlike the final episode of *The Prisoner*. Individuals following rules, which often take the form of routines, give the human agent a feeling of security. To break a rule, or transform a rule, is to risk losing such security. The agent has to decide on the costs and benefits of their actions: this is part of being a person. The structure is a flow, not a static object. When you join the flow, as an agent, you have to negotiate the rules imposed by others. Here the agent is dependent upon their limited knowledgeability. This is the prior social structure. However, I do not believe that Giddens would be taken seriously if he argued that the social structure was recreated from scratch every day.

Giddens's notion of agent, which many sociologists believe operates well under conditions of modernity, is clearly inadequate for the postmodernity generated by life politics: hence the change of name from 'agency' to 'self'. The practical consciousness and the discursive consciousness are together rule generating, rule recognising and rule following. However, life politics takes place in a world so free of rules and rule-governed intention that even the construction of the self, as Giddens describes it, is now inadequate. A self has to create itself in a world which is often beyond its own recognition, gesture, ritual, ceremonial, language, class, birth status, codes of ethics, morality and all other rule-governed, security. For Giddens self-identity is rule governed, rule forming and rule following; life politics is about pushing modernity beyond such rules. In this process of de-structuration the self has a virtual existence outside of the obviously increasingly chaotic situated activities of both human agents and institutions.

Giddens's critique of postmodernism

Most theorists of postmodernity view the postmodern condition as the absence of any foundation for reliable knowledge, which makes it impossible to have any systematic understanding of social action, or to be engaged in any form of social engineering. However, as Giddens points out, from this perspective: 'To speak of post-modernity as superseding modernity appears to invoke that very thing which is declared (now) to be impossible: giving some coherence to history and pinpointing our place in it' (Giddens, 1990: 47).

For Anthony Giddens, instead of looking for postmodernity we need to take a closer look at modernity itself, which he argues has been poorly grasped in sociology. Modernity is becoming more radicalised and universal. Modernity is attempting to develop a greater understanding of itself, and for individuals life has a much more uncertain feel about it because we have to live through this radicalisation of modernity, in which the traditions which gave us comfort are swept away. A self-reflexivity is now questioning modernity, turning its critical rationality upon itself in a way that never happened in the past. The postmodern condition, for Giddens, would involve a radical transformation of the present institutional dimensions of modernity: capitalism, industrialism, military power and surveillance, towards a new social order.

This postmodern condition would be institutionally complex, global, and a post-scarcity system, in which the goods needed for life are readily available to everyone. The postmodern will also be capitalist, where the market will merely indicate choice, not be a source of deprivation. The politics will be life politics, and polyarchic in nature; this means that power will be widely shared and individual people will be free to choose from a rich variety of lifestyles. However, it is also possible that the post-modern could be a dark, dangerous and unpleasant place, characterised by the growth of totalitarian power, collapse of economic growth mechanisms, ecological decay and nuclear conflict or large-scale warfare. These are the high-consequence risks of the current dimensions of modernity; and, in Giddens's eyes, at the moment modernity is still with us.

Life politics, social movements and the far side of modernity

For Anthony Giddens, within modernity all nation states have a tendency towards polyarchy, which is the most advanced form of pluralism – a condition within a community in which power is widely shared amongst a multiplicity of groups and organisations, all of whom have their own sectional interests. Polyarchy includes a set of authoritative rules assigned in response to the citizens' wishes. This is necessary for the democratic process to work. These rules guarantee our civil and political rights.

Modern states are shaped by political/social movements that operate with all four of the dimensions of modernity that Giddens outlines.

In Giddens's analysis the modern world has four characteristics:

o   capitalism
o   industrialism
o   centralised administrative power – which makes use of surveillance
o   centralised control of military power.

In his analysis, social movements have a key role to play in the transition from 'modernity' to 'postmodernity'. However, unlike most of the writers who consider its nature, Giddens views postmodernity as a form of 'uto-pian realism' that has institutional dimensions that have been changed by the activities of social movements. Not only do social movements have opportunities to exercise countervailing powers within society, their activities have moved the 'overall trajectory of development of modernity' (Giddens, 1992: 59) towards a 'radical democratisation' within which all people have greater opportunities to exercise power in society. Giddens provides us with a 'conceptual map' in which social movements are placed within the four dimensions of modernity, and are actively engaged in forms of struggle with the institutions that operate there. Social movements attempt to enhance the citizenship rights of individuals within each dimension, and bring about significant change.

In the 1990s Giddens argued that NSMs had important democratic qualities; they 'open up spaces for public dialogue in respect of the issues with which they are concerned' (Giddens, 1994b: 17). NSMs give people opportunities to discuss issues which were undiscussed by traditional political parties; including such issues as how people live their lives and the choices they make about any activity they choose to be involved in. Giddens refers to this as **dialogic democracy**; which is an attempt by people to talk to each other in an effort to create active trust with others in an effort to further what Giddens calls **life politics**, the politics of self-actualisation or self-creation. However, Giddens argues that NSMs cannot be viewed as 'socialist' in nature. In contrast to the class-based issues of socialism, NSMs 'have a deep involvement . . . with the arenas of emotional democracy in personal life' (Giddens, 1994b: 121).

> New forms of social movement mark an attempt at a collective reappropriation of institutionally repressed areas of life. Recent religious movements have to be numbered among these, although of course there is great variability in the sects and cults that have developed. But several other new social movements are particularly important and mark sustained reactions to basic institutional dimensions of modern social life. Although – and in some part because – it addresses questions which antedate the impact of modernity, the feminist movement is one major example. In its early phase, the movement was pre-eminently concerned with securing equal political and social rights between women and men. In its current stage, however, it addresses elemental features of existence and creates pressures towards social transformations of a radical nature. The ecological and peace movements are also part of this new sensibility of late modernity, as are some kinds of movements for human rights. Such movements, internally diverse as they are, effectively challenge some of the basic presuppositions and organising principles which fuel modernity's juggernaut. (Giddens, 1991: 208–9)

> New social movements cannot readily be claimed for socialism. While the aspirations of some such movements stand close to socialist ideals, their objectives are disparate and sometimes actively opposed to one another. With the possible exception of some sections of the green movement, the new social movements are not 'totalizing' in the way socialism is (or was), promising a new 'stage' of social development beyond the existing order. Some versions of feminist thought, for example, are as radical as anything that went under the name of socialism. Yet they don't envisage seizing control of the future in the way the more ambitious versions of socialism have done. (Giddens, 1994b: 3)

Why are individual selves reflexive in modernity?

To be reflexive is to have a **life narrative**; to choose a character, mould our personal identity and decide upon the moral and rational organising principles that we might use to make sense of the reservoir of subjective experience. This narrative is what we use to authenticate our selves as a self. Individuals, then, have to create and constantly recreate themselves, choosing from lifestyle resources to develop and monitor their chosen life narrative. It is surprising, if Giddens accepts this notion of the life narrative, that he includes any notion of the unconscious within his concept of self, not only because of its biologically driven Freudian undertones, but also because of the suggestion that many actions are outside of the control of the agent.

In Giddens's analysis, however, individuals have become reflexive in order to compensate for the breaking down of the basic security system of customs and traditions within local communities, brought about by the advancement of modernity. This is a situation that individuals may find existentially troubling, because this protective framework gave psychological support and without it individuals may feel the ontological insecurity of personal meaninglessness and dread. As Giddens makes clear in *The Transformation of Intimacy* (1992):

> The self today is for everyone a reflexive project – a more or less continuous interrogation of past, present and future. It is a project carried on amid a profusion of reflexive resources: therapy and self help manuals of all kinds, television programmes and magazine articles. (Giddens, 1992: 30)

For Giddens, individuals are reflexive for reasons of basic security: they change in order to gain an enhanced sense of ontological security. Other than security, individuals have no active decisions to take. This is a rather limited view of human agency. On the far side of modernity people engaged in life politics are reflexive for a variety of possible reasons.

People are reflexive in order to enhance their opportunities to fulfil their desire. In Giddens's analysis, individuals are devoid of desire; apart from the security of the 'pure' relationship. Any other relationships he dismisses as 'plastic sexuality'. What Giddens fails to take into account are the risks that individuals are prepared to encounter in order to engage in 'plastic sexuality', and the motives and intentions that people have, clearly other than security, for finding opportunities for individual bodies to touch, taste and explore other bodies. Consider for one moment the legal problems faced by such diverse groups as transsexuals, gay men and women, bisexuals, transvestites and paedophiles.

In the late 1990s Giddens, in collaboration with Ulrich Beck, developed the notion of the **risk society**, which draws upon his notion of the shift from emancipatory politics to life politics with late modernity.

Risk

For Ulrich Beck risks are 'social constructs which are strategically defined, covered up or dramatised in the public sphere with the help of scientific material supplied for the purpose' (Beck, 1996a: 4). A central concept within Beck's conception of risk is the notion of 'individualisation' in which people are engaged in a constant process of constructing the key aspects of their biography largely free from the constraining certainties of early modernity.

According to Deborah Lupton (1999) 'risk' is never static: it constantly has to be reconstructed and negotiated within the networks of interaction and meaning that people inhabit. She argues that since the publication of Beck's *The Risk Society* the theorising of risk has generated the following insights:

o   Risk has become an increasingly pervasive concept of human existence in Western societies.
o   Risk is a central aspect of human subjectivity.
o   Risk is seen as something that can be managed through human intervention.
o   Risk is associated with notions of choice, responsibility and blame. (Lupton, 1999: 25)

Ulrich Beck, therefore, argues that modernity is breaking free from the contours of classical industrial society and we are in the midst of a transition from an industrial society to a risk society. This means that we are moving from a social situation in which political conflicts and divisions were defined by a logic of the distribution of 'goods' to a social situation in which conflicts are becoming defined by the distribution of 'bads' – in other words the distribution of hazards and risks.

The risk society is not a class society, as both rich and poor are subject to ecological risks. In place of the class vs. class division of the industrial society, the risk society places sector in conflict with sector, with some sectors becoming 'risk winners', for example chemicals, biotechnology and the nuclear industry, while others may become 'risk losers', for example the food industry, tourism and fisheries. The risk society is global and knows no national boundaries – for example the effects of Chernobyl – although in practice the poor, most notably in the third world, are more likely to be adversely affected.

Beck's analyses are based upon a three-stage historical periodisation of pre-industrial, industrial and risk societies. Each of these three types of society contains risk and hazards, but there are qualitative differences between them in terms of the types of risk encountered. In pre-industrial societies, risks were not man made; they were 'natural', for example crop-destroying weather. In modern industrial societies, there are industrially produced hazards. However, the insurance principle provides some support in the form of accountability and compensation. The risk society is a society in which:

1   'risks' become the axial principle of social organisation. Coping with risk is becoming an essential element in the way we organise our society;

2 'risks' take on a form that is incalculable, uncompensatable, unlimited and unaccountable.

In such societies compensation is impossible because we are facing irreparable damage in which accountability is limited for ecological catastrophes because of the difficulty of enforcing the 'polluter pays' principle.

So the world is no longer so clearly defined in terms of modernity and tradition in the way that Durkheim, Weber and Tönnies described at the turn of the last century. Today we live in a form of reflexive modernisation.

Reflexive modernisation

In Giddens's analysis risk society is not postmodernism; rather, modernity is increasingly becoming an essentially post-traditional and post-nature form of social order, which brings with it the threat of personal meaninglessness. The self has to become *reflexive*, in other words as individuals we have to make a variety of lifestyle choices in an effort to avoid the new forms of risk that we must live with in the modern world. This has to be understood as the self-organisation and self-monitoring of life narratives. As individuals we should feel free from structures. Moreover, an underlying element is that, as a social form, modernity begins to reflect upon itself. Modernity has, as Giddens explains, an intrinsic reflexivity at an institutional level. We have overcome the dogma of tradition, but this does not mean that tradition has no place in the modern world; just that traditions need to be justified before they are acceptable to individuals. This brings with it new problems, as Giddens explains: 'the reflexivity of modernity actually undermines the certainty of knowledge, even in the core domains of natural science' (Giddens, 1994a: 294).

There is a significant shift in trust relations because of this notion of reflexivity. Trust is no longer a matter of individual people interacting with each other face to face; trust is now much more likely to make use of expert systems. I trust that the fund manager who looks after my endowment mortgage will generate sufficient money to pay for the cost of my home in twenty-five years' time. As we all know, however, people make mistakes.

According to Giddens, in traditional cultures the risk environment was dominated by the hazards of the physical world. Infant mortality was high, the death of women in childbirth was high, life expectancy was low, and rates of chronic illness and infectious disease were high. In the modern world, however, we have a new risk profile which has its origins not in nature, but in the 'outcome of socially organised knowledge'; a manufactured uncertainty. By **manufactured uncertainty**, Giddens means uncertainties created by people which have no real precedents, or a volatile character that cannot be easily calculated, for example over global warming or nuclear power. Individuals may find this situation **existentially troubling**. Giddens's discussion is similar in a number of important respects to the discussion of risk in the work of Ulrich Beck.

Reflexive modernisation is made up of two processes: *individualisation* and *globalisation*.

What is individualisation?

A key element in any fully developed modernity is the single person, cut loose from previously supportive social forms such as social class or fixed gender roles. According to Beck, this is a 'new mode of societalization' involving a redefinition of the relationship between the individual and society. On the one hand, Beck outlines an abstract or 'ahistorical model of individualization' which has three components:

o the *liberating dimension* or disembedding, which involves the breaking down of socially and historically prescribed commitments;
o the *disenchantment dimension* or loss of traditional security, which involves the breaking down of 'practical knowledge, faith and guiding norms' (Beck, 1992: 128);
o the *control/reintegration dimension* or re-embedding, which involves the creation of new forms of social commitment.

In Beck's view, individualisation 'means that each person's biography is removed from given determinations and placed in his or her hands . . . biographies become *self-reflexive*, socially prescribed biography is transformed into biography that is self-produced and continues to be produced' (Beck, 1992: 135).

This is perhaps nowhere more clearly seen than in the area of sexuality. With the development of industrial society, the heterosexual married couple became the only legitimate form of sexuality. However, the foundations upon which this legitimacy is based are going through a process of dissolution, allowing individuals the opportunity to make lifestyle choices to a degree unheard of in previous generations. The gender relationship within industrial society is said by Beck to be feudal in nature. However, marriage can no longer be seen as a forum in which women can be subjected to coercive or pressurised sex. Individuals will either leave the relationship, or make alternative arrangements. Sex outside marriage has been subject to various moral and legal sanctions. Moreover, although there exists a legal hostility to recreational adultery, homosexuality and transsexuality, the legitimacy of this hostility cannot be defended. According to Annette Lawson (1988), over the past generation women have experienced a sexual revolution. Women have come to prioritise sexual pleasure; there has developed what Ferguson (1989) calls a **sexual consumerism**. Women are much less likely to be virgins at marriage, are more likely to have had more sexual partners than their parents' or grandparents' generations, are as likely to have committed adultery as men and as with almost as many partners, which they are more likely to describe as 'one night stands' or 'casual'. In 1953 Alfred Kinsey found that 26 per cent of women were having a sexual relationship outside their marriage. Shere Hite, in her report on *Love, Passion and Emotional Violence* (1991), found that of women who had been married for five years or more, the figure was 70 per cent, although most of these women reported that they still believed in monogamy. Most women do not begin affairs because they fall in love, as Shere Hite explains:

> The majority of women having affairs say they feel alienated, emotionally closed out, or harassed in their marriages; for 60 percent, having an affair is a way of enjoying oneself, reassessing one's identity, having one person to appreciate you in a way that another doesn't. (Hite, 1991: 396)

Moreover, 21 per cent of women gave inadequate, poor or lack of sex with their husbands as their main reason for starting affairs, and women who were virgins at the time of their marriage found affairs appealing as a form of sexual experimentation.

In a similar fashion, changes have taken place in the ways in which individuals choose to define and redefine themselves in relation to individuals of the same sex. In terms of homosexuality, up until 1861 sodomy was still punishable by execution: in that year the death penalty was replaced by a prison term of between ten years and life. However, the 1885 Criminal Law Amendment Act widened the range of sexual activities defined as offences, by introducing the catch-all phrase 'gross indecency' which criminalised such activities as men masturbating each other, any form of contact between male genitalia, or for two men to kiss in public. Perhaps surprisingly, even given the changes to the law in 1967 which decriminalised such activities between consenting adults in private, in 1990 almost 5,000 gay men were convicted for consenting homosexual relations. Sexual relationships between females is less criminalised: this may well be based upon the legal prejudice that women have little interest in or desire for sex. In a similar fashion, men who are penetrated are free from prosecution, because they are assumed to be passive, playing a female role.

In addition, the law does not recognise transsexuality, and only a man and a woman can marry. Any transition from female to male or male to female has no legal standing, and post-operative transsexuals are unable to marry or take up the rights of their new gender within the social security system.

What is globalisation?

Globalisation is the process by which the whole world is becoming a single place, economically, politically and culturally. It appears to enhance choice for the individual by giving a person the opportunity, for example, to sample fifteen different cuisines in any one week – although each may well have been fashioned to suit a distinctly Western taste, and is presented to a global population via the mass media from a distinctly Western gaze. This global homogenisation can sweep aside local or national cultural identity; this is not without risks. As Roland Robertson makes clear:

> The fact and perception of ever-increasing inter-dependence at the global level, the rising concern about the fate of the world as a whole and of the human species (particularly because of the threats of ecological degradation, nuclear disaster and AIDS), and the *colonization* of local by global life (not least, via the mass media) facilitate massive processes of relativation of cultures, doctrines, ideologies and cognitive frames of reference. (Robertson, 1992: 87)

Both of these tendencies intrude deeply into the reflexive project of self. For Ulrich Beck, *reflexive* means 'self-confrontation' rather than reflection. Individuals are expected 'to live with a broad variety of different, mutually contradictory, global and personal risks' (Beck, 1994: 7), which means that we as individuals have to recognise the unpredictability of the modern world. In order to cope with these 'risky opportunities', the self becomes fragmented into a number of 'contradictory discourses' of the self. This type of modernity, as a social form has been brought about by the success of capitalism, which has made industrial society much more radicalised: it is this which Beck terms the risk society. The risk society has just one developmental dynamic, which Beck refers to as a 'conflict dynamic'.

In 1998 Beck published an essay on the politics of the risk society in which he argued that the script of modernity had to be rewritten, redefined and reinvented. The risk society begins where nature and tradition end, argues Beck. In classical modernity our concern was with what nature could do to us; in the reflexive modernity of risk societies the concern is with what we have done to nature. The risks that we experience are caused by unforeseen consequences of our expanding knowledge applied by experts to the processes of modernisation that were initially designed to reduce the risk from nature. Hence Beck defines risk as a *man-made hybrid*. These unforeseen consequences of attempts to control nature have severely damaged traditional certainties that we had in science and politics. Scientists have no more knowledge of the consequences of their research than lay people, yet more than ever they are expected to reflect upon possible consequences:

> Now manufactured uncertainty means that risk has become an inescapable part of our lives and everybody is facing unknown and barely calculable risks. Risk becomes another word for 'nobody knows'. We no longer choose to take risks; we have them thrust upon us. We are living on a ledge – in a random risk society, from which nobody can escape. Our society has become riddled with random risks. (Beck, 1998: 12)

Politics becomes dominated by 'risk conflicts' that appear as *'forms of organised irresponsibility'* (Beck, 1998: 15, italics added). Beck ends his 1998 piece by appealing for a second Enlightenment in which we recognise the self-inflicted dangers of industrial civilisation.

In the same volume Giddens also published a piece that takes up many of the themes contained in Beck's article. Giddens defines a risk society as: 'a society where we increasingly live on a high technological frontier which absolutely no one completely understands and which generates a diversity of possible futures' (Giddens, 1998c: 25). In support of this view Giddens draws upon the case of Nick Leeson. Nick Leeson worked for Barings Bank in the Far East and was accused of losing 1.3 billion dollars on risky investments, which resulted in the financial collapse of the bank. He was sentenced to six years for forgery and cheating. He was operating in complex and often barbaric futures markets, on the frontier of modern technology that contained structures that even the participants did not fully understand. This is a world which is becoming increasing familiar to us, at the end of tradition and at the end of nature

Anthony Giddens has a clear but limited notion of the self. The concept of agency that he develops is a very shallow and unambitious one. For Giddens, we as individuals are reflexive and construct our own personal life narrative in order to enhance feelings of security and avoid the feelings of dread or personal meaninglessness that are common in the modern world. However, I have suggested that individuals are reflexive for a variety of reasons: to create a personality; to enhance life chances in the class structure; to avoid prejudice; to fulfil their desires, attract partners and enhance opportunities to participate in *plastic sexuality*. Giddens needs to look beyond security if he wishes to say anything meaningful about agency in postmodernity.

It might be suggested that the notion of **self-identity** is a rather shallow concept that never does more than glance beneath the surface of the self as agent. Issues about inner human dignity, personality, how we solve issues of right and wrong and why some activities are defined as satisfying are beyond the scope of identity; but are some of the key issues for a life politics.

Pierre Bourdieu

Bourdieu uses three key concepts to explain the nature of social life: **practice**, **habitus** and **field**. Bourdieu takes his starting point from Marx's eighth thesis on Feuerbach:

> Social life is essentially *practical*. All mysteries which mislead theory to mysticism find their rational solution in human practice and in the comprehension of this practice. (Marx, 1969/1845)

Bourdieu attempts to construct a model of social practices that are made up of processes which are partly conscious and partly not. Practices often act as signifiers of taste that people draw upon in an effort to make a distinction between themselves and others. People invest in certain practices in an effort to gain a reward. Bourdieu rejects dualisms such as agency and structure and views practice as both a medium and an outcome of agent's living in a structure. As individuals we acquire habits, either knowingly or unknowingly, from a structural context. We use these practices to live out our everyday lives. In a similar fashion to Giddens, Bourdieu argues that practices are not random, and also like Giddens he views practices as a *practical accomplishment*, yet we experience practice as having a rule-like quality. Once we have learned a practice, we usually do not reflect upon it: instead we have a habitual response to most practice. Practice both enables and constrains us in our everyday life, including what we think and feel about things as well as our actions. **Habitus** is a set of dispositions that bring about a unity between the personal histories of people within a community. As Bourdieu explains, it is 'an acquired system of generative schemes objectively adjusted to the particular conditions in which it is constituted' (Bourdieu, 1977: 95).

People who live in the same area are more likely to share the same **social field**, to share the same habitus and engage in similar practices. In other words:

habitus + field = practice

However, socialisation into a particular habitus does not mean that there will be no conflict within the field. People will have their own interpretation of the habitus and their own ideas about the appropriate practice to follow.

Habitus is also a constructed system of structuring qualities that are found in the 'active aspect' of practice. Although it has no specific design or rule that it must follow, by its nature 'practice' has a structuring quality and generates regular and durable social relations, including our ideas of what is 'reasonable' and what is 'common sense'; we internalise the habitus as a second nature. These social relations are cognitive and motivational, but 'arbitrary' in that there is no natural or inevitable form that they should take; but at the same time habitus makes our actions mutually intelligible. Our perceptions of the world, including its economic relations, family relations and the division of labour, are shaped by the habitus. In other words, the habitus is constituted by practice and at the same time our future practice is shaped by the habitus. Bourdieu explains the significance of this:

> The *habitus* contains the solution to the paradoxes of objective meaning without subjective intention. It is the source of these strings of 'moves' that are objectively organised as strategies without being the product of a genuine strategic intention. (Bourdieu, 1990: 62)

There is a link between taste and class habitus. Lifestyle choices – such as leisure patterns and taste, the type of holiday we go on, the sports we play, the music we enjoy, the food we eat and the books we read – reflect the class we belong to. The activity of people in higher class positions confines access of lower-class people to certain forms of less desirable lifestyle and taste choices. Bourdieu identifies three broad class/taste groupings:

o the legitimate – classical music, broadsheet newspapers, non-fiction books, Tuscany;
o middlebrow – *Inspector Morse*, *Daily Mail*, skiing;
o popular – TV soaps, tabloid (red top) newspapers, commercial music, Loret De Mar, Spain.

For people to successfully engage in practice they have to work within an identifiable habitus; people feel an obligation to share in the lifestyle, tastes and dispositions of a particular social group. However, people also have to improvise beyond its specifies rules and conventions. The habitus structures but does not determine choice of practice. This raises the question: does Bourdieu fully overcome the dualism of agency and structure?

Norbert Elias

An interesting contrast with Giddens's theory of structuration is that of Norbert Elias on the civilising process. In a similar fashion to Giddens, Elias argues that in the social sciences we usually find a conceptual separation of 'structure' and 'agency'. This is found in such phrases as 'the structure of sport in Britain changed between 1850 and 1950', a statement built upon the assumption that 'structure' is a 'thing' that is somehow separate from the people involved in sport. Elias viewed theorising in this way as dichotomic, reifying, actionless and changeless – as *Zustandsreduktion*, a German term that means the conceptual reduction of observable processes to steady states.

Norbert Elias attempts to bring together 'agency' and 'structure' with his concept of the 'figuration'. For Elias, 'figuration' refers to a web of interdependent people who are bonded to each other on several levels and in diverse ways. Within a figuration relationships are open, processual and intrinsically 'other-directed' in character towards the people who help to comprise the figuration. Figurations are then made up of the actions of a plurality of interdependent people who mesh to form an interwoven structure which has a number of emergent properties such as the social actions that underpin power ratios, axes of tension, class and stratification systems, sports, wars and economic crises. Power is a fundamental property of any figuration, unlike the Marxian conception of power that is built upon the ownership of the means of production. For Elias it has a many-sided character. He explains that power

> is a structural characteristic . . . of *all* human relationships . . . We depend on others; others depend on us. Insofar as we are more dependent on others than

they are on us, they have power over us, whether we have become dependent on them by their use of naked force or by our need to be loved, our need for money, healing, status, a career, or simply for excitement.

Also in contrast to the Marxian conception of the independent state, Elias views the state as an inter-societal 'attack-and-defense' or 'survival' unit, in constant competition with other states. The 'attack-and-defense' or 'survival' elements are some of the central preconditions for the emergence of the state.

Within states there is a struggle for control over industrial, financial and educational institutions – and, in less developed state-societies, over religious institutions too. The struggle for control of the state forms one of the principal ongoing features of the dynamics of all state-societies and shapes the key characteristics of all states, notably:

o the 'division of labour', which Elias views in less economistic terms than Marxian writers, as the structure of 'interdependency chains' between people. This affects the degree of 'democratisation' within the state, and the reciprocal controls within and between groups and the position of groups within the overall system of interdependence;
o the degree of effective stability state centralisation has produced in the face of various destabilising forces from within and from without;
o the form taken by the state – is it 'capitalist' or 'socialist' – and the degree to which it influences the nature of other institutions;
o the degree to which the economy is integrated into an inter-societal framework;
o the balance of power between constituent groups.

Elias believes we have to take into account 'the immanent dynamics of figurations', the ongoing process of struggle and change. This dynamic process is shaped by the structure of social figurations that at the same time transforms them. In the long term, change within figuration has an unintended or unplanned feel, because it is the product of many intentional and unintentional actions of the interdependent groups and individuals that make up the figuration.

However, although such change is unplanned, it still has a determinable structure. Since the Middle Ages European societies have been going through a unilinear, progressive and irreversible 'civilizing process'. The central elements of this process are:

o state-formation, with increasing political and administrative centralisation, which has brought about greater 'pacification' of the population;
o monopolisation by the state as the only body that has the right to use force and impose taxes;
o a lengthening of interdependency chains;
o greater 'functional democratization' – an equalising of the balance of power between social classes;

o the imposition and refinement of manners and social standards;
o an increase in the social pressure on people to exercise self-control over sexuality, aggression and emotions in public and private;
o change of personality, a greater emphasis on conscience ('superego') as a regulator of behaviour.

Elias developed the theory of the civilising process in *What is Sociology?* where he claimed it was possible to measure the stage of development that a society has reached by drawing upon the concept of 'the triad of basic controls'. These are:

o the society's control over 'extra-human nexuses of events', or in other words 'natural events';
o the society's control over inter-human connections, that is, over 'social life';
o the extent to which individual members have learned to exercise self-control.

In *Quest for Excitement: Sport and Leisure in the Civilizing Process* (1986) Eric Dunning argues that:

> Scientific and technological developments correspond to the first of these basic controls; the development of social organization to the second; and the civilizing process to the third. According to Elias, the three are interdependent both in their development and in their functioning at any given stage. However, he warns against 'the mechanistic idea that the interdependence of the three types of control is to be understood in terms of parallel increases in all three'.

The people in pre-industrial time enjoyed a number of pastimes – such as cock fighting, bull and bear baiting, burning cats alive in baskets, prize fighting, watching public executions – which reflected 'the violent tenor of life' in Europe during the Middle Ages and which continued until well into 'modern' times. People in the medieval era had a comparatively high 'threshold of repugnance' with regard to witnessing and engaging in violent acts which, as Elias has shown, is characteristic of people in a society that stands at an earlier stage in a 'civilizing process' than Western society.

By contrast with its folk antecedents, modern rugby exemplifies a game form that is civilised in at least four senses that were lacking in the ancestral forms. It is typical in this respect of modern combat sports more generally. Modern rugby is civilised by:

1 a complex set of formally instituted written rules which demand strict control over the use of physical force and which prohibit it in certain forms, for example 'stiff-arm' tackling and 'hacking', that is kicking an opposing player off his feet;
2 clearly defined intra-game sanctions, that is 'penalties', which can be brought to bear on offenders and, as the ultimate sanction for

serious and persistent rule violation, the possibility of exclusion from the game;

3 the institutionalisation of a specific role that stands, as it were, 'outside' and 'above' the game and whose task is to control it, that is that of 'referee';

4 a nationally centralised rule-making and rule-enforcing body, the Rugby Football Union.

This civilisation of rugby football occurred as part of a continuous social process. Two significant moments in it were: (a) the institution, at Rugby School in 1845, of the first written rules. These attempted, among other things, to place restrictions on the use of hacking and other forms of physical force, and to prohibit altogether the use of 'navvies' (the iron-tipped boots which had formed a socially valued part of the game at Rugby and some of the other mid-nineteenth-century public schools); and (b) the formation in 1871 of the Rugby Football Union. The Rugby Union was formed partly as a result of a public controversy over what was perceived as the excessive violence of the game. One of its first acts was to place, for the first time, a total ban on hacking. What happened at each of these moments was that the standards for controlling violence in the game advanced in two senses: first, it was demanded that players should exercise a stricter and more comprehensive measure of self-control over the use of physical force; and secondly, an attempt was made to secure compliance with this demand by means of externally imposed sanctions.

To speak of rugby as having undergone a 'civilising process' is not to deny the fact that, relative to most other sports, it remains a rough game. Features such as the 'ruck' provide the opportunity for kicking and 'raking' players who are lying on the ground. The scrum offers opportunities for illegitimate violence such as punching, eye gouging and biting. Given the close packing of players that the scrum involves, it is difficult for the referee to control the interaction.

Research activity: why do people fall in love?

Context: This question is very open because the meaning of the term 'love' is generally thought to be highly introspective or subjective. However, Anthony Giddens argues in *The Transformation of Intimacy* (1992) that people resolve their feeling of meaninglessness and dread by looking for a 'pure' relationship: a love relationship that is based solely upon 'trust'. When individuals find such a relationship, their lives are full of meaning. However, if our trust is broken for any reason, then our feelings of meaninglessness and dread return with greater strength. In addition, we must not confuse the 'pure' relationship with 'plastic sexuality' – the term Giddens uses to describe the pleasure we can gain from having a short-term sexual relationship with another person. Our research should allow us to test Giddens's theory that people fall in love to maintain their sense of security and reduce feelings of meaninglessness and dread.

Method: Ask people about their love relationships. Why were they attracted to another person? Ask how they knew that they were 'in love' and how this differed from the feelings they had during periods that they were out of love.

Evaluation: This should consider the motives and feelings that people shared with you and a comparison with the findings that Giddens presents. You may want to reflect upon the methodological problems involved in collecting this information. Were people willing to share such intimate feelings with you? Were they aware of their motives and intentions? Would people be willing to give you information about their experiences of 'plastic sexuality'?

Activity

Find out what Giddens has had to say about the issue of culture and globalisation by looking at http://www.lse.ac.uk/Giddens

---

Conclusion

According to Giddens, in the modern world traditions are either disappearing or at least need to be justified. Individuals have to overcome feelings of meaninglessness and dread. In addition, they have to overcome feelings of manufactured uncertainty generated by people in their attempt to control nature. People attempt to overcome such problems/feelings by generating rules and routines, to provide a degree of certainty in their lives. In particular they attempt to form a 'pure relationship', this is a love relationship that is built solely upon trust and has no additional foundation or guarantee.

References

Archer, M. (1988) *Culture and Agency: The Place of Culture in Social Theory*. Cambridge University Press: Cambridge.

Archer, M. (1990) 'Human agency and social structure: a critique of Giddens', in J. Clark, C. Modgil and S. Modgil (eds), *Anthony Giddens: Consensus and Controversy*. Falmer: London.

Archer, M. (1995) *Realist Social Theory: The Morphogenetic Approach*. Cambridge University Press: Cambridge.

Beck, U. (1992) *The Risk Society*. Sage: London.

Beck, U. (1994) 'The reinvention of politics: towards a theory of reflexive modernisation', in U. Beck, A. Giddens and S. Lash (eds), *Reflexive Modernization: Politics, Tradition and Aesthetics in the Modern Social Order*. Polity: Cambridge.

Beck, U. (1998) 'Politics of risk society', in J. Franklin (ed.), *The Politics of the Risk Society*. Polity: Cambridge.

Bourdieu, P. (1977) *An Outline of a Theory of Practice*. Cambridge University Press: Cambridge.

Bourdieu P. (1990) *The Logic of Practice*, trans. R. Nice. Polity: Cambridge.

Cardwell, M., Clark, L. and Meldrum, C. (2000) *Psychology for A Level*. Collins Educational: London.

Craib, I. (1992) *Anthony Giddens*. Routledge: London.

Dunning, E. (1986) *Question for Excitement: Sport and Leisure in the Civilizing Process*. Basil Blackwell: Oxford.

Elias, N. (1978) *What is Sociology?* Hutchinson: London.

Ferguson, M. (1989) *Der Aquariussameuzwering: Persoonlijke en Maatschappelijke Transformatie in de Tachiger Jaren*. Ankh-Hermes: Deventer.

Giddens, A. (1976) *New Rules of Sociological Method*. Hutchinson: London.

Giddens, A. (1981) *A Contemporary Critique of Historical Materialism Vol. 1: Power, Property and the State*. University of California Press: Berkeley and Los Angeles.

Giddens, A. (1984) *The Constitution of Society*. Polity: Cambridge.

Giddens, A. (1985) *The Nation State and Violence: Volume Two of A Contemporary Critique of Historical Materialism*. Polity: Cambridge.

Giddens, A. (1990) *The Consequences of Modernity*. Polity: Cambridge.

Giddens, A. (1991) *Modernity and Self Identity*. Polity: Cambridge.

Giddens, A. (1992) *The Transformation of Intimacy*. Polity: Cambridge.

Giddens, A. (1994a) *Reflexive Modernisation*. Polity: Cambridge.

Giddens, A. (1994b) *Beyond Left and Right*. Polity: Cambridge.

Giddens, A. (1998a) *The Third Way*. Polity: Cambridge.

Giddens, A. (1998b) 'After the left's paralysis', *New Statesman and Society*, 1 May.

Giddens, A. (1998c) 'Risk society: the context of British politics', in J. Franklin (ed.), *The Politics of the Risk Society*. Polity: Cambridge.

Hite, S. (1991) *The Hite Report on Love, Passion and Emotional Violence*. Optima: San Francisco.

Hutton, W. and Giddens, A. (2000) *On the Edge: Living with Global Capitalism*. Jonathan Cape: London.

Lawson, A. (1988) *Adultery: An Analysis of Love and Betrayal*. Blackwell: Oxford.

Layder, D. (1995) *Understanding Social Theory*. Sage: London.

Lupton, D. (1999) *Risk*. Routledge: London.

Marx, K. (1969) 'Theses on Feuerbach' (1945), in K. Marx and F. Engels, *Selected Works Vol. 1*, trans. W. Lough. Progress Publishers: Moscow.

Robertson, R. (1992) *Globalization*. Sage: London.

Thompson, J.B. (1989) 'The theory of structuration', in D. Held and J.B. Thompson (eds), *Social Theory of Modern Societies: Anthony Giddens and his Critics*. Cambridge University Press: Cambridge.

Chapter contents

6

Postmodernism: Theorising Fragmentation and Uncertainty

By the end of this chapter you should:

- have a critical understanding of the notions of postmodernism and postmodernity;
- appreciate the significance of Nietzsche to postmodern theorising;
- be familiar with the key postmodern writers: Lyotard, Bauman, Baudrillard, Vattimo, Deleuze and Guattari, Rorty, and Fish;
- be aware of some of the central critiques of postmodernism: Sokal, Habermas, Giddens, Philo, Kellner.

Friedrich Nietzsche

Friedrich Nietzsche (1844–1900) invented many of the central ideas and concepts which postmodernism raises about the foundations of society. In particular, Nietzsche's anti-foundationalist ideas, built upon the assumption that 'God is dead', together with his refusal to privilege his own position, have influenced most of the postmodern writers that we shall review in this chapter. According to Anthony Giddens: 'Nietzsche offers a refuge for those who have lost their modernist illusions without relapsing into complete cynicism or apathy' (Giddens, 1995: 261).

Nietzsche attempted to undermine the foundations of truth, morality, science, identity and religion. Truth, in Nietzsche's view, was nothing more than a mobile host of metaphors and illusions, and in the last analysis the 'will to truth' is a manifestation of 'the will to power'. In other words, for Nietzsche, truth like everything else is a function of power. Nietzsche's 'project' was to undermine the foundation of all systems of belief; an intellectual process that he called the transvaluation of all values, in which the *will to truth* would be seen for what it is, the social theorist attempting to impose their will or prejudices upon others, whilst presenting their ideas as truth.

Above all, Nietzsche argued that all people attempted to impose their thoughts, ideas and morality on others, by all possible means including danger, pain, lies and deception, which he termed the 'will to power'. When people say morals are necessary what they mean is 'I don't like how you are behaving', hence for Nietzsche the police are always necessary to impose morality.

A philosopher recuperates his strength in a way quite his own . . . he does it, for instance, with nihilism. The belief that there is no such thing as truth, the nihilistic belief, is a tremendous relaxation for one who, as a warrior of knowledge, is unremittingly struggling with a host of hateful truths. For truth is ugly. (Nietzsche, 1967: §598)

In *Beyond Good and Evil* Nietzsche makes a distinction between **master morality** and **servant morality**, and argues that the traditional ideals of Christian morality are based upon self-deception, as they were built upon the will to power. The concept of the **slave morality** was taken up by Nietzsche in his later works such as *The Antichrist, Curse on Christianity* (1888), where he argues that Christianity is a religion for weak and unhealthy people and that its central ideas, such as compassion for the less fortunate, have undermined Western culture, in that people are made to feel guilt for attempting to fulfil their desires.

In *Thus Spake Zarathustra* (1888) Zarathustra informs the people that God is dead and that with an understanding of the eternal return we need no longer be seduced by notions of good and evil or threats of hell and hopes of paradise. The theory of the eternal return suggests that we are all going to live our identical lives over and over again, down to the smallest details, because time is an ever-repeating cycle: 'Everything goeth, everything returneth; eternally rolleth the wheel of existence. Everything dieth, everything blossometh forth again; eternally runneth on the year of existence' (Nietzsche, 1999: 153).

Moreover, because we have no soul that lives after the body is dead and no recollection of living our lives over and over again – escape is impossible. However, the concept of the eternal return is Zarathustra's gift to humankind. Armed with the knowledge of the eternal return a person can become the ***Übermensch*** (the overman/superman, people such as Caesar, Napoleon, Goethe, Dostoevsky and Thucydides): they can undertake a process of self-overcoming, liberate themselves from the arbitrary constraints of truth and morality imposed upon them and can become whatever they desire and achieve satisfaction with themselves. For Nietzsche, you are what you do, in other words the person is constituted by *practice*, hence there is no 'being' behind doing, effecting, becoming; 'the doer' is merely a fiction added to the deed – the deed is everything. The *Übermensch* is a person with qualities beyond those of an ordinary person. As described by Nietzsche, the *Übermensch* was a self-created person who was emotionally 'tougher' than most people, because of having created a personality drawn from many contradictory dimensions.

Activity

Would you like to live in a world where morally anything goes? Outline two lists: one of arguments in favour of living in such a morally free world, and one of arguments against living in such a world. Complete the following chart.

I would like to live in a morally free world because . . .	I would not like to live in a morally free world because . . .
1	1
2	2
3	3

The postmodern approach to ethics does not reject the moral concerns that individuals in the modern world have. However, it rejects the coercive response to ethical issues by any central authority. The simple division between the 'right way' and the 'wrong way' becomes subject to forms of evaluation that allow actions to be viewed as 'right' in one way or 'wrong' in another. Bauman (1997) makes a division between the 'economically pleasing', 'aesthetically pleasing' and 'morally proper'. The modern world became secular as individuals lost belief in religious dogma. Their lives became fragmented to the degree that any unitary vision provided by a religion could never be satisfactory in explaining aspects of an individual's life.

Outline, in a short paragraph, why a world with no moral code might be a place of great cruelty. Discuss your findings with another sociology student.

At this point, should the state attempt to create a comprehensive moral code and impose it upon individuals?

Activity

1 Do you feel sympathy, and other forms of emotional attachment, for people who are weaker than you? Suggest some reasons for your answer.
2 In your view, does this provide a sound foundation for a theory of 'rights'?

I will critically outline the contribution of a range of postmodern writers: Lyotard, Rorty, Bauman, Deleuze, Vattimo and Baudrillard, and will attempt to show that their theorising has a postmodern feel to it. However, beneath the postmodern gloss there is a coherent set of modernist assumptions which in many cases lack the sophistication of a writer such as Durkheim. Finally, by way of a summary, I will extrapolate from these writers a set of characteristics or feeling states that an individual might well experience in the postmodern condition. This will allow readers to reflect on whether people do experience the uncertainty that postmodern writers suggest.

Activity: what is postmodernism?

Nigel Wheale (1995) outlines what he calls a lexicon of postmodern techniques – a list of key terms that you would expect to find in postmodern texts. He suggests that:

> An all-purpose postmodern item might be constructed like this: it uses eclecticism to generate parody and irony; its style may owe something to schlock, kitsch or camp taste. It may be partly allegorical, certainly self-reflexive and contain some kind of list. It will not be realistic. (Wheale, 1995: 42)

Wheale goes on to explain the terms in the sentences below. Read the sentences and rewrite the quote from Wheale, using your own words.

Explanation of key terms

o *allegory*: the idea that any item can have covert or secret meanings other than the obvious meaning.
o *camp*: the culture of a minority clique or group, usually built upon a closet or private language. It can be a key source of identity for the individuals involved.
o *eclecticism*: a picking and mixing of styles and themes.
o *irony*: postmodern items are said to be ironic because they are not based upon any moral code or other foundation separate from the item itself.
o *kitsch*: 'bad taste', combined with bragging. People gloat about the things they have or the things they give but are unaware of the bad taste of the items.
o *lists*: postmodern items usually contain lists of paraphernalia or other things from which a choice can be made.
o *parody*: a copy of an original, often in a satirical fashion.
o *schlock*: nonsensical or frivolous things.
o *simulacrum*: first used by Baudrillard (1983) to explain that media products are constantly reproduced to the point where they take on a meaning mainly by reference to earlier versions of similar media products, hence they have a pace and reason of their own. It is not possible to distinguish between the 'real' and the 'representation': we live in a world of 'hyperreality', where media representations give an experience of the world which feels realler than real.
o *realism*: the opposite of the postmodern way.

'Gloss' and 'disclaimers' in the writings of Jean-François Lyotard

Postmodernism is said to be both historically and conceptually different from modernism or theories rooted in modernity. It is a rupture with the past, a fundamental departure from 'modernity'. Theories firmly established in modernity are said to include Durkheim's sociology, Marxism, functionalism, feminism and other 'grand narratives'. Narratives are 'stories' which provide people with values. In addition, narratives give explanations; identify causes and chains of events. When we read a narrative, we can anticipate how the events will unfold within that narrative. Grand narratives are 'big theories' which strive to spell out movements of history, as well as giving us advice on how people lead their lives, what to think and how to think it. As Lyotard says in *The Postmodern Explained to Children*:

> These narratives aren't myths in the sense that fables would be (not even the Christian narrative). Of course, like myths, they have the goal of legitimating social and political institutions and practices, laws, ethics ways of thinking. (Lyotard, 1992: 29)

When Jean-François Lyotard (1924–1998) died in April 1998 his obituary in *The Times* suggested that he was one of the people who 'unleashed' postmodernism on the unsuspecting modern world. Lyotard embraced uncertainty and rejected all grand theories (grand narratives) such as Marxism or feminism as 'totalitarian'. Lyotard's writings are often described as 'episodic' or 'drifting', which makes a coherent summary difficult. In this section we shall look at what Lyotard had to say in his key texts and evaluate his contribution to postmodern thought.

For Lyotard modernity is a mode of thought that is concerned with organising time and mastering nature. Contained within all grand narratives of modern ways of thinking is the idea of a 'universal history of humanity'. Nevertheless, in the modern world 'grand narratives' compete with each other, for example the Marxian and the capitalist. All such narratives are concerned with emancipation and the creation of a community of subjects, and have 'freedom' as their end point. Having read Lyotard one would think that grand narratives contain the notion of purity, and that those who do not accept the grand narrative are impure and must be dealt with accordingly. This may be by the use of new academic programmes: clearly defining how one can and cannot address others, the semiotic strait-jacket of political correctness, the mental hospital, or the gulag. If modern ways of thinking are about anything they are about the definition and treatment of the 'other'. Lyotard backs away from such a critique. He does not have the will to see his analysis to its obvious postmodernist conclusion.

Although he talks about 'incredulity' towards grand narratives and a 'war' on 'totality', through a re-examination of the Enlightenment, Lyotard was not a postmodernist; his analysis is in many respects a debate within parameters set by Freud, Marx and Saussure. Lyotard's analysis adopts the modernist distinction between 'facts' and 'signs' and 'nature' and the 'social'. Many of his later books have a postmodern gloss, but they all contain a modernist disclaimer, to distance Lyotard from the consequences of his postmodern gloss.

The postmodern gloss

In *Philosophy and Painting in the Age of Their Experimentation: Contribution to an Idea of Postmodernity* (1984a) Lyotard argues that:

> philosophy heads not towards the unity of meaning or the unity of being, not towards transcendence, but towards multiplicity and the incommensurability of works. A philosophical task doubtless exists, which is to reflect according to opacity. (Lyotard, 1984a: 193)

The modernist disclaimer

In *The Postmodern Condition* (1984), after Lyotard has signalled the breaking up of grand narratives, he explains:

> This breaking up of the grand Narratives leads to what some authors analyse in terms of the dissolution of the social bond and the disintegration of social aggregates into a mass of individual atoms thrown into the absurdity of Brownian motion. Nothing of the kind is happening. (Lyotard, 1984: 15)

What is the role and purpose of the narrative for Lyotard?

Narratives are made up of 'statements', which are in themselves 'moves' within a 'framework' of 'generally applicable rules' (Lyotard, 1984: 26). The narrative has three purposes:

o It bestows legitimacy upon institutions, which Lyotard refers to as the function of myth (1984: 20). People learn the culture of a society in the form of 'little stories'; when the stories are repeated this allows the community to feel it has permanence and legitimacy.
o The narrative represents positive or negative models, which Lyotard refers to as creation of the successful or unsuccessful hero (1984: 20).
o Individuals are integrated into established institutions: Lyotard refers to this as the creation of legends and tales (1984: 20). Narratives enable the self-identification of a culture and help to maintain self-identity of a people who share the culture.

As Lyotard makes clear: 'What is transmitted through these narratives is the set of pragmatic rules that constitutes the social bond' (1984: 21).

The narrative defines a community's relationship to itself and its environment. Moreover, the narration 'betokens a theoretical identity between each of the narrative's occurrences' (1984: 22). I believe this means that the narrative contains within itself the pragmatic rules of when and why it should appear. Each time the narrative is drawn upon, this suggests something about the appropriateness of the narrative's use, role and purpose in holding together the social bond. Narratives have to be put into 'play' (1984: 23) within institutions by people. The narrative in this way defines what is right and what is appropriate within a culture. At the same time, the narrator has a need for collective approval; the narrator must be seen to be competent.

So narratives permit a society in which they are told to fix the limits of its basis for competence and to evaluate according to those limits what actions are carried out or what actions can be carried out. In an effort to distance himself from modernist ways of thinking, Lyotard outlines what he calls a non-universalised pragmatics for the transmission of narratives. He is keen to point out that this does not mean a set of pre-existing categories. Instead the pragmatic of the narrative is 'intrinsic to them' (Lyotard, 1984: 20): for example a narrative may have a fixed formula. In addition, the narrator has no other claim to capability for telling the story than having heard the story before. The narrator is an agent, and his or her role presupposes a social relationship in which one person is telling the story and the others are cast in the role of listeners. These narrator–listener relationships, and the ability to recognise and follow the narrative structure, pre-date the telling of the narrative, despite Lyotard's claim that he does not intend a set of pre-existing categories. It is for this reason that I suggest that Lyotard's notion of narrative presupposes a social relationship in which narration can take place.

For Lyotard, postmodernity is about mourning the destruction of meaning because 'knowledge is no longer principally narrative' (1984: 26). This may well mean that Lyotard mourns the destruction of the social relationship in which grand narration takes place – modernity. Nevertheless, the social is still in a narrative form, albeit little narratives rather than grand narratives. The narrative function remains the same.

The notion of the language game, a key element in narration, is more fully developed by Lyotard in *The Différend*.

Lyotard, *The Différend: Phrases in Dispute* (1988)

According to Lyotard, people make language for their own ends. A 'differend' describes a case in which there is a conflict between two parties that cannot be resolved because both sides have a legitimate case, but they speak in different idioms. Because there has been a decline in universalist discourses, such situations are more problematical than ever.

Taking his starting point from Ludwig Wittgenstein's *Philosophical Investigations* (1953), Lyotard describes the decline in universalist doctrines as the decline in the acceptance of terms which would once have been used to resolve differends – for example reality, subject, community and finality. Universality cannot be based upon sensations such as impressions, affect or taste. It is not possible to avoid conflicts, and such conflicts are much more intense because there is no 'universal genre of discourse to regulate' (Lyotard, 1988: xi) such conflicts. As Lyotard explains:

> A case of differend between two parties takes place when the 'regulation' of the conflict that opposes them is done in the idiom of one of the parties while the wrong suffered by the parties is not signified in that idiom . . . The differend is signalled by [the] inability to prove. The one who lodges a complaint is heard, but the one who is a victim, and who is perhaps the same one, is reduced to silence. (Lyotard, 1988: 9–10)

The purpose of *The Différend: Phrases in Dispute* is to 'examine cases of differend and to find rules for the heterogeneous genres of discourse that bring about these cases' (Lyotard, 1988: xii).

Any phrase is constituted by a set of rules which Lyotard labels as the **phrase regimens**; these include reasoning, knowing, describing, recounting, questioning, showing, ordering, prescriptiveness, evaluation, interrogativity, etc. It is important, claims Lyotard, to distinguish between different phrase regimens as this limits the competence of people to comment on only one form of phrase. The links between phrase regimens cannot have relevance. The impertinence may be opportune within a genre of discourse. In addition, Lyotard discusses **genres of discourse** which supply rules for linking together heterogeneous phrases. Genres of discourse always provide the framework for phrases and determine what is at stake in linking phrases. These include: 'the prescriptive', 'the cognitive', 'the appraisal' and 'the phrase of the Idea', all of which make some appeal to authority. The only exception to this is 'vengeance', which makes no appeal to authority; such as statements about the time. These rules help us to attain certain goals: to know, to teach, to be just, to seduce, to justify, to evaluate, to rouse emotion. In particular, 'reality' is found within three families of phrases – cognitive phrases, nominations and ostensives. However, genres of discourse merely shift the differend from the point of phrase regimens to that of ends.

According to Lyotard, 'validation' is a genre of discourse, not a phrase regimen. No phrase can be validated from inside its own regimen, and a descriptive can be validated cognitively only by recourse to an 'ostensive'. A 'prescriptive' is validated juridically or politically by a 'normative' – comments which start with the statement *it is the norm that* . . . – or ethically, by reference to a feeling state that *things ought to be.*

A cognitive phrase, such as 'This wall is white' can be validated by a descriptive phrase such as 'It was declared that the wall is white'. A conjunction verifies a referent. With a cognitive phrase a conjunction is required which takes the form of a conjunction of knowledge. Judgements outside of the area of cognition are not based upon an appeal to knowledge but refer to moral, aesthetic appeals or make some other appeal to the imagination or intuition. It is not possible to make statements about such positions in relation to the 'truth' content or 'falsehood' of such statements.

One of the central issues here is that authority is exercised at the level of the normative phrase. Acceptance of the norm transforms a prescription into a law. This is the notion of the 'metalanguage', which performs the important function for authority of building a connection between heterogeneous phrases, allowing some and forbidding others. The problem with any metalanguage is that the addresser can also play the role of addressee: what is acceptable is acceptable only according to the view of one party. As Lyotard suggests: 'Ethics prohibits dialogue' (1988: 111).

In Lyotard's view, it is by following an order, by doing it, that a new norm is created. However, as he points out in his discussion of Auschwitz, the Nazis made laws without reference to anyone except themselves. The reason for this was because the 'absence of an addressee is also the absence of a witness' (Lyotard, 1988: 102). The notion of *we* vanished at Auschwitz. For Lyotard, Auschwitz designates: 'the conjunction of two unconjugateable phrases: a norm without an addressee, a death sentence without legitimacy' (1988: 103). This is a universalising logic which states that 'what is foreign to the people gives rise to a policing by extermination' (1988: 106). Clearly, Lyotard rejects 'terror' as something which is without morality and accepts 'justice' as something which is moral.

In Lyotard's view a differend can be brought to a satisfactory conclusion for all parties by the imposition of a narrative. The key narrative function is the imposition of a space of internal peace, which involves the pushing aside of pertinent meaning to the edge of a community and hence ending disputes. This is known as a 'regimentation in principle' (Lyotard, 1988: 153), by which a community assures itself of meaning. The narrative constitutes the culture of the community. The universalisation of the community reduces conflict within the community.

Both phrase regimens and genres of discourse are used to neutralise differends within narratives. This is because the narrative has a privileged place, because it has an affinity with the people. Lyotard gives the example of the narrative '*Love one another*' (1988: 159, italics in original). This statement has authority that can be extended to all narratives, although it may take on a more secular or worldly form, such as 'republican brotherhood' or 'communist solidarity'. The narrative has then a universal and moral character that applies to all people within a community.

Critique of Lyotard

One of the problems with *The Différend* (1988) is Lyotard's Manichaean worldview – his belief that the world can be clearly divided between good and evil forces: the Postmodernists against the Fascists. However, Lyotard ends up committing the same sin that he accuses the modernists of committing. He argues in favour of universalist metalanguage because it can guarantee freedom and liberty, whilst at the same time condemning universalist metalanguage because it cannot guarantee freedom and liberty, leading in the last analysis to Auschwitz. This would suggest that there is nothing in itself inherently wrong with universalist metalanguage, and oddly enough, Lyotard draws upon a number of ethical phrases to create the norm that Fascism is wrong. Lyotard has an unstated universalist moral code, which draws upon ideas of what it means to be 'human' and how the human should be treated.

As we saw above, Lyotard argues that the breaking up of grand narrative does not lead to the dissolution of the social bond. In addition, he suggests that 'language games are the minimum relation required for society to exist' (1984: 15). This statement, however, presupposes that a 'social' relationship exists before the 'language game' can take place. As Lyotard makes clear, we as individuals are 'nodal points' (ibid.) in the framework of social relationships. There is then an unstated notion of the social that is universalist in nature. Lyotard never embraced uncertainty. The narrative structure, with its pre-existing social relationship, is this unstated and universal notion of the social that allows Lyotard to have an answer to the question 'How is society possible?' This is seen most clearly in his 'Philosophy and painting in the age of experimentation' (1984a), where he discusses the concept of 'structure'. In place of 'structure' or 'system' Lyotard refers to a 'game' relationship between an addresser and an addressee on a stage that has no 'off-stage' component. Each component of the stage is an 'instance' or 'episode' and our ability to speak to each other can switch from one episode to another. When the addresser speaks to the addressee they present 'micrologics' – tiny universes that are envious of other 'micrologics'. This is said by Lyotard to reject the 'concrete universal', but it does not because such 'games' presuppose a pre-existing 'social' relationship. The notion of 'game' is yet another gloss. In short, Lyotard's work is 'modernist' in nature, because of its essential, but often valid, appeal to a universalist notion of the social.

Activity: what does the word 'social' mean?

Contemplate for a few moments what you consider to be the difference between the following lists of terms, and then attempt the question below:

Term	Definition	Term	Definition
Justice		Social justice	
Democracy		Social democracy	
Welfare		Social welfare	
Security		Social security	
Care		Social care	
Work		Social work	

What do you understand by the term 'social'? Write a short paragraph in which you outline your ideas.

Richard Rorty

Richard Rorty is one of the world's most persuasive contemporary post-modern philosophers. He has looked at a number of issues which socio-logists have concerned themselves with, notably the nature of solidarity – where Rorty attempts to answer the age-old sociological question 'How is society possible?' In addition he has investigated the nature and foundations of knowledge, and rejected the traditional conceptions of 'the self'. Rorty endeavours to create a theory of morality/solidarity in a situation of loss of certainty in people's lives. He discredits traditional philosophy, replacing its well-established but misguided foundations with concepts and constructs that are more postmodern in nature. In *Contingency, Irony and Solidarity* (1989) Rorty argues that it is possible to develop a theory which treats both our individual need for self-creation and our collective need for human solidarity as equally convincing and yet at the same time distinct. Rorty defines his key terms as **liberal**: 'people who think that cruelty is the worst thing we do' (1989: xv) and **ironist** as: 'the sort of person who faces up to the contingency of his or her own central beliefs and desires'. The 'ironist' is an individual who is aware that their core convictions and aspirations are related to the circumstances that they choose to place themselves in. Another key concept is **vocabulary**, which is primarily concerned with giving indications of possible future outcomes, such as 'What shall I be?' and 'What can I become?' The 'liberal ironist' is a person who wishes to end the suffering and humiliation of other human beings. The central idea of a liberal society is that in terms of words and persuasion 'anything goes'.

In Rorty's view, human solidarity is something that we as people have to accomplish; it is not simply 'given'. In other words, solidarity is created not discovered. A key element of this accomplishment is our ability to see 'others' not as strange people whom we can marginalise, but as fellow human beings, who can feel pain. The task of bringing about a change in our perception of 'the other' is not one for theory, but a task for ethno-graphers, docudrama makers and especially novelists. What works of fiction can do is to show us the kind of cruelty we are able to inflict upon other humans and at the same give us an opportunity to redefine our-selves. Books can encourage us to become less diabolical and Rorty divides them into two types:

o   books which encourage us to comprehend the consequences of routines, customs and institutions for others;
o   books that encourage us to see the consequences of our own personal peculiarities for others.

The result of this is that for Rorty 'doing philosophy' is like having a conversation: often-imaginary conversations with dead authors. Both 'truth' and 'solidarity' emerge from such conversations. By reading stories, such as the ones mentioned above, we investigate different vocabularies and reconstruct both society and ourselves.

At the end of the eighteenth century, intellectuals across Europe started to accept the notion that 'truth' was something to be created rather than discovered. This was highly significant for politics because it meant that humans were capable of creating new forms of society.

Rorty is not suggesting that there is no truth. In contrast, he is suggesting that truth is a property that all true statements share; and that it is the name we give to statements that can be justified as good in relation to our beliefs. In the latter case, we may not be in a position to prove that the time is 3.30p.m.; however, we can say that we believe that clocks can be used to tell the time and trust that others will share our interpretation that the clock hands can be read as saying that it is 3.30 p.m.

Rorty makes a distinction between the statements 'The world is out there' and 'The truth is out there'. The first suggests that the world is a 'thing' that exists independently of human thought. The world was created without the use of the mental processes of human beings. In contrast, the latter statement, that 'The truth is out there', is not acceptable, because individual people create the truth. The truth is built up of sentences, constructed by people and used to describe and explain the world. These sentences can be either true or false, but they are only there in time and space because we place them there. Truth is a property of any sentence. As Rorty explains: 'only sentences can be true, and . . . human beings make truths by making languages in which to phrase sentences' (1989: 9).

We can spell out Rorty's argument as follows:

o   Truth is a characteristic of sentences.
o   Sentences can exist only if vocabularies exist first.
o   Vocabularies are created by human beings.
o   It follows that human beings create truths.

Rorty argues that there is no pre-linguistic truth embedded within a pre-linguistic consciousness that could act as a criterion for judging the validity of any truth statements. Truth is found within our final voca-bulary. To create a new vocabulary, we need to have a detailed knowledge of past writers. This will give us an insight into forms of intellectual life that are different from our own. Truth in these circumstances becomes a matter of classification: taking an expression or idea from our reading and conversations and reviewing it in the context of other expressions or ideas that we might be willing to make our own. Rather than the traditional view of truth – attempting to find a match between an idea and some 'given' external reality over which we have no control – in Rorty's view 'truth' and 'meaning' are one and the same.

The human self is also created by vocabulary, which is a set of words that people make use of to defend their actions, beliefs and how they organise their lives. The traditional view of the self was that we had a 'core self' which held beliefs and desires. These were expressed by the self if and when the self thought it appropriate to do so. The views as expressed by the self could be criticised on the grounds that they did not agree with reality. Rorty's argument is that the core self is a network of beliefs and desires; and, just like truth, statements are human creations dependent upon sentences and in the last analysis upon vocabulary; so is the self. The self is made and it is a linguistic entity. In getting to know ourselves, we come to accept that we cannot discover a 'true' self but we can create a self. In dealing with the situations that individual selves find themselves in, we have to create a new language upon which our self will be built.

The ironist has serious doubts about their chosen vocabulary, and is often impressed by rival vocabularies. For the ironist we can revise our own moral identity by revising our vocabulary, but nothing can act as a critique of our chosen vocabulary except an alternative vocabulary and there is nothing beyond vocabularies. Hence, the ironist spends a great deal of time reflecting on whether they have chosen the wrong vocabulary and reading books in an effort to experience alternative vocabularies.

There is always more than one vocabulary and liberal societies are bound together by common vocabularies and common hopes. This suggests that the liberal society always has great potential for conflict. Therefore, in liberal societies, we have a need for persuasion rather than force; reform rather than revolution; open rather than closed meetings. In other words, the liberal society 'is one which has no purpose except freedom' (Rorty, 1989: 60). As Rorty states:

> If we take care of freedom, truth can take care of itself. If we are ironic enough about our final vocabularies, and curious enough about everyone else's, we do not have to worry about whether we are in direct contact with moral reality, or whether we are blinded by ideology, or whether we are being weakly 'relativistic'. (1989: 176–7)

Traditionally, the need for 'human solidarity' has been seen as a component of the 'core self' of all individuals. But Rorty rejects the notion of a 'core self': people are what is socialised into them, and this does not include any inner freedom, biologically driven desire or built-in human nature for solidarity. All we share with others is the ability to feel pain. In Rorty's view solidarity is, in the first instance, built upon **we-intentions**. A 'we-intention' is a sentence drawn from our vocabulary that starts with the phrase: 'We all want . . .' rather than 'I want . . .'. Hence we feel our strongest sense of solidarity with people who are thought of as 'one of us', people who are viewed as 'local' rather than as members of the human race. Whom we choose to define as 'local' is a matter for our 'final vocabulary'. Solidarity is about breaking down these divisions, making 'they' into 'we', viewing 'others' as people who can feel pain and humiliation, the same as we do. 'We-intentions' as the foundation of a moral obligation allow us to develop ethical considerations within a sense of solidarity and because of an attraction we have as individuals to another individual. Finally, 'we-intentions' allow us to develop our own personal self-creation as an ethical process.

This means that for Rorty, in contrast to Marxists, solidarity is produced in the course of history and political progress is brought about by the 'accidental coincidence' of a private obsession with a public need. Rorty then attempts to produce a form of postmodern politics which is without a 'certainist discourse' and without absolute foundations, such as the Marxian mode of production, and in which people have a full and fair chance to achieve their potential. There will be a willingness to listen, as this will be a world of political liberals and philosophical ironists.

One of the consequences of Rorty's attempt to construct a postmodern ethics built, as it currently stands, upon an anti-foundationalism, is that morality becomes a matter of personal taste. To do otherwise is to argue from a position that assumes a universally valid foundation for all morality, which would be outside of an individual's vocabulary. One might ask if Rorty's theory of truth/solidarity/morality can be built upon the foundation of personal taste. In Rorty's view liberal democracy is 'good' and Fascism is bad, yet his anti-foundationalism prevents him from discussing this. But how do people justify acts of cruelty to themselves? What is so attractive in humiliating and hurting others? Concentration camp guards are people; they too can feel pain and humiliation; they too can read Nabakov and Orwell; they too have families that they love and care for – yet they choose a vocabulary of cruelty and humiliation. What Rorty does is to make all vocabularies of equal validity and for this reason we might wonder why a person could or should become an ironist. In a world where nothing can be wrong, why search for what is right?

Zygmunt Bauman

When the kids had killed the man,
I had to break up the band.
David Bowie, 'Ziggy Stardust'

Here I outline the continuity of modernist assumptions in the English-language writings of Zygmunt Bauman (1925–present) from the 1970s through to the end of the 1990s. Bauman's work on morality is found to be yet another illustration of the agency–structure debate which has dominated sociological theorising throughout the twentieth century. He attempts to locate and describe the relationship between the external relations in the world (the structure, or the social) and the internal condition of the person (the nature of agency). Bauman's work is built upon a modernist concept of the social, of the self as a person type, his notion of a postmodern ethics is oppressive and could be used as a justification for cruelty. The postmodern Bauman never existed: it is a myth created by people such as the editors of the *Theory, Culture & Society Festschrift*. I will end by giving an indication of what an amoral postmodern self should look like.

No area of either academic life or popular culture is untouched by the influence of postmodern ideas and yet there is confusion about the nature of postmodernism. What is it? For many people, Zygmunt Bauman is the person who has provided the most effective response to this question. Taking as my starting point Bauman's postmodern ethics, the opinion developed here is rather different: that Bauman speaks from a moral position that he cannot acknowledge.

Bauman's work on ethics in a postmodern world draws heavily upon the work of Emmanuel Levinas. Understanding 'the Other', understanding their suffering and powerlessness even when the Other is a stranger, is central to his conception of intersubjectivity. We have a responsibility for the Other, and a duty to respect the difference of the Other. In contrast to what he terms the 'philosophy of subjectivity' – the strong emphasis on self – which underpins most modern philosophy and to Descartes's *cogito ergo sum* (I think, therefore I am), Levinas offers the Hebrew phrase *Hineni* (Here I am). Our relationship with 'the Other' may not be one of equality, but it should be such that we attend to their suffering. Levinas terms this **the ethical relation**. Responsibility for the Other is what underpins the pursuit of justice.

In *Alone Again: Ethics after Certainty* (1994) Bauman opens his discussion by contrasting the views and life experience of Leon Shestov who believed that 'In each of our neighbours we fear a wolf' with Knud Logstrup who believed that 'It is a characteristic of human life that we mutually trust each other' (1994: 1). He accounts for the difference in views between the two philosophers by comparing their very different life experiences in two very different societies: 'Their generalizations contradicted each other, but so did the lives they generalized from. And this seems to apply to all of us' (1994: 2).

This comment, on the surface, is a rather obvious statement; however, it contains Bauman's notion of the 'social' (first developed in his Ph.D. thesis) and an inclination of how the 'social' operates on the individual human agent.

From this point Bauman goes on to outline his theory of morality:

> morality means *being-for* (not merely being-aside or even being-with) the Other. To take a moral stance means to assume responsibility for the Other; to act on the assumption that the well-being of the Other is a precious thing calling for my effort to preserve and enhance it, that whatever I do or do not do affects it, and that if I have not done it, it might not have been done at all, and that even if others do or can do it this does not cancel my responsibility for doing it myself . . . And this being-for is unconditional. (Bauman, 1994: 18–19)

These ideas are more fully developed in *Life in Fragments* (1995) in which Bauman repeats the above comment:

> We are, so to speak, ineluctably – *existentially* – moral beings: that is, we are faced with the challenge of the Other, which is the challenge of responsibility for the Other, a condition of *being-for*. (1995: 1)

The difference between *being-with* and *being-for* the Other is about our level of commitment, about our emotional engagement with the Other. This involves regarding the Other not as a type or a category but as a unique person. It means:

o   rejecting indifference towards the Other;
o   rejecting stereotyped certainty about the Other;
o   viewing the Other in a fashion that is free from sentiment.

It is in relation to the Other that we make our choice between good and evil. Moreover, as Bauman clearly explains, *being-for* the Other is in the last analysis a power relationship because it involves being responsible for the Other:

> I am responsible for defining the needs of the Other; for what is good, and what is evil for the Other. If I love her and thus desire her happiness, it is my responsibility to decide what would make her truly happy. If I admire her and wish her perfection, it is my responsibility to decide what her perfect form would be like. If I respect her and want to preserve and enhance her freedom, it is again my responsibility to spell out what her genuine autonomy would consist of. (Bauman, 1995: 65)

What Bauman is doing has a great deal in common with the approach of Durkheim and Giddens. Far from being a postmodernist, Bauman is a collaborator with all the key modernist assumptions contained within his social theory. He claims to have found a natural moral faculty within the human being. But how are such moral judgements possible? The answer is through our human faculty – our human agency. The problem with the natural moral faculty is that it is questionable if 'nature' has any 'morality'. It is when Bauman talks about the source of morality that his convictions appear on the scene. Bauman attempts to give morality a basis, but morality itself is regarded as something universal and 'given'. It is treated as 'that which has always been', which justifies the actions of a person in the eyes of 'the Other'. Suffering is something that must be done away with. What is the aim of Bauman's conception of morality? To shame the person into obedience? To make us believe in our own virtue? Or discover our conscience? To find our soul? At the same time Bauman attempts to cast the postmodern self as the wicked but happy 'Other'. As we shall see in our discussion of his 'postmodern ethics', for Bauman morality is a mode of biological fact. Fundamentally, Bauman provides what he calls a 'natural', hence beyond critique or emancipation, discussion of what causes us to desire our own domination.

One of the many problems with Bauman's theory of morality is that what is fair to one may not be fair to another. There is always the risk that morality can be little more than an apology for cruelty. Whenever a person raises the issue of morality, they have 'the Other' in mind and the idea in their head of 'the Other' behaving in a way which is unacceptable. The appeal to morality allows one to impose one's will on the Other with justification. In this sense Bauman is no different from the Nazis he so strongly condemns in *Modernity and the Holocaust* (1989).

Whatever else postmodernism is about, it is about saying goodbye to morality and about losing the ability to be appalled by acts of cruelty. In contrast, Bauman's postmodern ethics is about providing a justification for action against the behaviour of others. We do not like the behaviour of the Other; it breaks our moral code, so we take action. To act is to impose our will on the Other and this may mean acting in a way that makes use of the methods that cruel people use. Moral codes not only harbour their own kind of purity, they necessarily provide justifications for cruelty.

The creation of a postmodernist

In his contribution to the *Theory, Culture & Society Festschrift* of Bauman's work, Stefan Morawski commented:

> Richard Kilminster suggested to me that I should possibly focus on the Polish track. A reasonable idea – in line with the famous saying of Goethe: '*Wer den Dichter will verstehen, muss in Dichters Lande gehen*' (who wants to understand the poet, must go to the poet's homeland). There are compelling elements of Zygmunt's biography which bear on his scholarly achievements. (Morawski, 1998: 29)

The image of Bauman that Richard Kilminster and Ian Varcoe (1998) present is a myth, the sole purpose of which is to inflate Bauman's post-modernist representation of himself in his own work. The *Festschrift* presents an image of Bauman as a free-floating individual, general socio-logist, independent thinker and postmodernist, expelled from both his homeland and his chair by a harsh and oppressive communist regime. On becoming an intellectual refugee Bauman is said to have moved from Tel Aviv to Leeds – a home for intellectual refugees. However, this is a created biography. Bauman was an intellectual tourist. He had spent a considerable time in England prior to his expulsion from Poland in 1968, first as a research student at the LSE under the supervision of Robert McKenzie, from the mid- to the late 1950s, and then as a lecturer at the University of Manchester in the early 1960s.

In Bauman's writings at this time, which are often confused, he attempts to make clear his relationship to modernity, Marxism, human agency and the Communist Party. Far from a postmodern narrating of uncertainty, the modernist assumptions he developed in these works are still to be found in Bauman's current writings. The only difference is that his writings now have a surface postmodern gloss. People who are impressed by Bauman's work see this surface shine and confuse it with depth. It is not.

Bauman is unable to abandon specific key Enlightenment assumptions. I argue that Bauman's sociology is constructed around several modernist inventions: the social, the self, categorisation, person types and the biological origin of morality built upon the animal pity we sense when we see human suffering. Bauman uses these modernist assumptions to conceal his (arguably) inadequate notions of the self as agent and solidarity.

Bauman as modernist

1972

What are the modernist assumptions within the writings of Zygmunt Bauman? To answer this question we need to take a close look at his writing career, starting with his 1972 text, *Between Class and Elite: The Evolution of the British Labour Movement. A Sociological Study*. Bauman explains that his study is 'sociological in character. Its primary task is to grasp general social laws and trends, while the presentation of a chronology of historical events falls into a subsidiary place' (1972: 230).

What is the sociological content of Bauman's 1972 text? Bauman views the social as something which is over and above the individual human agent and which shapes the agent and the actions of the agent. The social is described as a 'superstructure sui generis' (1972: 141). In addition the social evolves in a similar fashion to the evolution that we find in modern Marxian or functionalist sociologies 'determined not just by the contemporary cultural climate but by the material characteristics of an evolving environment' (1972: 34). Bauman also takes up the notion of person types and undervalues the role of the human agent. Consider the following examples: 'The personal characteristics which designated the man who possessed them as a potential leader of a workers' organisation were determined by the social milieu in whose terrain the organisation was to function' (1972: 54) and 'The widely differing cultural backgrounds and diverse origins of the masses of factory workers made them plastic, receptive and ready to accept conceptions and structures from without' (1972: 29).

Bauman concludes his study as follows:

> What seems to be significant is the fact that nothing important happens in human history unless the two analytically separable deterministic chains of 'situation' and its 'ideological assessment' meet, i.e. unless an available ideology renders a privately or collectively experienced situation intelligible to the actors and does it in a way which makes the ideologically reshaped aims of the actors feasible. The relation is dialectical and not deterministic, since the compatibility of a situation with an ideology within reach happens to be an after-effect of this ideology as it was operative at an earlier phase; at least to the same extent the selection of an ideology from those which are available is a function of the form taken by the situation. (Bauman, 1972: 327)

The human agent can only choose what to believe from within a narrow range of given ideologies. This undervaluing of the human agent is a theme that is found in all of Bauman's texts, even those that are presented with a postmodern gloss.

1973

In *Culture as Praxis* (1973) Bauman makes clear the concept of **person types** that plays an important but hidden role in his latter texts:

> Using the term 'culture' with the indefinite article makes sense only if supported by an implicit assumption that nothing universal can be a cultural phenomenon; there are, to be sure, numerous universal features of social and cultural systems, but they do not, by definition, belong to the field denoted by the word 'culture' . . . and would have been better referred to some psycho-biological, proto-cultural phenomena. (1973: 22)

> The only idea of universally compatible with the differential concept of culture is the universal presence of some sort of a culture in the human species (exactly as in the case of Saussurean language); but what is meant in the above statement is rather a universal feature of human beings, not of culture itself. (1973: 23)

Bauman further develops his modernist notion of structure, writing that 'social structure is a hard core of the social organisation . . . the lasting, time-spanning, little changing skeleton of the social practice' (1973: 107). This builds on his earlier notion that 'the social' is a 'superstructure sui generis' (1972: 141).

Bauman's descriptors of structure (1973)

o   'structure is limiting'
o   structure = communication
o   structure = rules
o   rules = patterns
o   'structure is not directly accessible to sensory experience. Neither is it derivable directly from processing the experiential data'
o   'Universals are generative rules, found in all areas of social life, which cannot be seen but which "govern" human praxis' (Bauman, 1973: 63–4, 80)

This modernist notion of structure is supplemented by Bauman's discussion of culture as reality. For him, 'ordering human environment and patterning human relations is one of its universally admitted functions' (1973: 100).

What is the role of the human agent in this structure? According to Bauman, forces outside of its control shape the person: 'universals may be established on the level of factors operative in shaping both "epistemic beings" and "praxis actors", i.e. both human individuals and networks of their relationships' (1973: 79–80).

Bauman also gives a full and clear outline of 'uncertainty', which he describes as by no means a subjective phenomenon' (1973: 66).

1976

For Bauman in 1976 there is a distinction between 'being', which he claims is an attribute of nature, and 'becoming' which is described as a 'human way of being-in-the-world' (Bauman, 1976a: 34). Bauman also makes a distinction between 'reality' and 'possible reality'. Drawing upon rationality to bring about a change from the current objective reality to an alternative objective reality Bauman described as 'the human modality' (1976a: 35). In other words, rationality is the resource that the agent draws upon to make a difference in the world. The human is essentially rational.

For Bauman, 'reality' is to be approached sociologically as an 'object'. The social, or as he terms it 'the social background', should be seen 'as an objectified artefact of human thinking' (1976a: 37).

In his 1976 work Bauman (1976a) describes the social as an 'impersonal structure', which contains a 'civil society' made up of a 'network of economic dependencies' and 'a web of communication'. The social has a game-like quality that takes the form of a structure beyond the control of the individual human agent:

> The activity of meaning-negotiating never takes off from a zero-point; in each case the cards have already been distributed and the hands are not even, while the rules of the game itself are hardly open to negotiation by the current players. (1976a: 40)

The 'game', and the social as a game, is a common theme in Bauman's work well into the 1990s. In the 1976(a) text there is a discussion of morality within the Soviet system, where Bauman make use of his notion of 'game'. As he explains, Soviet morality 'frowns upon shy mutterings about the individual's right to disobedience, for non-compliance with the rules of the game is a social sin and puts the sinner outside the community' (1976a: 91).

In a similar fashion, in his discussion of planning in the Soviet Union Bauman argues that: 'The forced labour conditions imposed upon Soviet industry made the workers' performance essentially independent of the game of material rewards' (1976a: 94–5).

In summary a 'game' is contained with 'the social' and has a number of characteristics:

o   It binds and controls people.
o   It restricts choice.
o   It directs thought.
o   It exists independently of the historical epoch.
o   It is objective.
o   It is concrete.

Bauman's conception of 'the social' in 1976

o   It is a codified domain.

o   It is free of subjective human traits – objective and impersonal.

o   It is an objective civil society.

o   It is a network of economic dependencies.

o   It is web of communication.

o   It is rule governed.

o   The human agent is rational within it.

o   The human agent is rule following rather than rule making.

o   The social has a game-like structure, with the rules outside of the control of the human agent.

o   The behaviour of the human agent is at least partly determined by economic factors.

o   Debates between systems of thought take place independently of the human agent.

It is little wonder that Bauman describes the human agent as 'the abandoned individual' (1976b: 48).

This 1976(b) text also returns the reader to the notion of uncertainty, which also is a key theme in Bauman's later texts. He outlines several 'objects' which are privately owned and which 'control access to the means of existence' (1976b: 92). They include tools of production, new materials and access to merchandising. The 'supreme uncertainty' is said to be 'terror'. As Bauman explains: 'Whoever controls these objects, therefore, holds in his hands paramount foci of uncertainty' (ibid.). Terror is said to be 'in the situation of individuals, the paramount determinant of conduct, deflating all the other traditional factors' (1976b: 95).

1978

Bauman's *Hermeneutics and Social Science: Approaches to Understanding* (1978) is about the response of social science to hermeneutics. Here Bauman uses the opportunity to outline what he understands by the nature of understanding:

> Understanding as such can be achieved only by 'universalising' anew the Spirit hidden in the endless variety of human cultural creation. (1978: 28)

Bauman assumes that essential subjective human action can be understood objectively – the psyche can not only be described but its motivation can be classified and understood. This world is a reality for Bauman because it is built upon a biological morality. The 1978 text make only passing reference to morality; however, it does look at some length at the 'stock of knowledge', information which is needed for social action to take place: 'Perhaps parts of the stock are elements of "natural endowment" of a human agent, Kant-like; perhaps other parts are societally-induced and sedimented from initial stages of socialization' (1978: 183).

Bauman also introduces the notion of classification into 'types':

> 'Types' are an indispensable element of the stock of knowledge. Our impressions are not analysable if chaotic, they are thinkable only if they are from the start organized into objects and events which belong to classes, each with its distinctive features and clues facilitating their recognition. Types have a lasting quality; an important feature of the natural attitude is the 'and so forth' generalization, implying that things will continue to be what they are at the moment, and that, consequently, I will be able to repeat in the future the same operations that I have committed on things in the past. All this I accept uncritically . . . (1978: 183)

In the light of this comment, we need to read very carefully the comments about 'structure' in Bauman's 1991 book, *Modernity and Ambivalence*, for example, when Bauman argues that structure is 'a normal aspect of linguistic practice. It arises from one of the main functions of language: that of naming and classifying . . . To classify . . . is to give the world a *structure*: to manipulate its probabilities; to make some events more likely than some others; to behave as if events were not random, or to limit or eliminate randomness of events . . . Language strives to sustain the order and to deny or suppress randomness and contingency' (1991: 186). The natural attitude is real, the natural endowment is real, and these factors shape our experience of the world and divide up the world into distinct categories that organise experience and form the basis of all ontology.

It is important not to underestimate the role of 'nature' in Bauman's analysis; nature is 'the realm of unfreedom', it is 'the ultimate limit of human action' (Bauman, 1976a: 2). As Bauman makes explicit in *Towards a Critical Sociology: An Essay on Commonsense and Emancipation*. '"Nature" is a cultural concept. It stands for that irremovable component of human experience which defies human will and sets unencroachable limits to human action' (1976b: 2). This may sound innocent enough; however, Bauman continues by saying: 'it is Nature, the hostess, who sets the rules of the game, and who defines this freedom' (1976b: 4). What is important here is that Bauman identifies the origin of **the rules of the game**, which play such a crucial role in all his later works. Finally, he gives us a clear account of the relationship between human action and nature: 'Nature supplies not just the boundaries of reasonable action and thought: it supplies reason itself. All valid knowledge is a reflection of nature' (1976b: 5).

Bauman as postmodernist

Bauman starts his postmodern analysis with what he considers to be the uncertain and/or unfamiliar and traces it back to what he considers to be both certain and familiar. However, all people have the ability to 'suspend the natural attitude' and treat anything and everything as uncertain and unfamiliar. Most of us seem to regard the world as a fairly ordered place, until something comes along to make us think otherwise. What Bauman simply does is to 'suspend the natural attitude' about everything, and pass this off as postmodernism. Moreover, Bauman reimposes 'the natural attitude' on the ground where he felt most comfortable, his own moral conviction about the attitude we should have towards the Other.

For the moment let us look in the window, at the consumer gloss. For Zygmunt Bauman, 'the postmodern' is not only about disregarding the 'totality' in our theorising, but also about the creation of a distinct epoch of history, detached from the past. For Bauman, modernity is a social totality which is Parsons-like in nature and murderous in the bureaucratic rationality of its intent:

> a 'principally co-ordinated' and enclosed totality (a) with a degree of cohesiveness, (b) equilibrated or marked by an overwhelming tendency to equilibration, (c) unified by an internally coherent value syndrome and a core authority able to promote and enforce it and (d) defining its elements in terms of the function they perform in that process of equilibration or the reproduction of the equilibrated state. (Bauman, 1992: 189)

For Bauman modernity is essentially bureaucratic in nature, and this is dangerous in the extreme. The Holocaust was a direct consequence of the Prussianised Weberian bureaucracy:

> in Weber's exposition of modern bureaucracy, rational spirit, principle of efficiency, scientific mentality, relegation of values to the realm of subjectivity etc. no mechanism was recorded that was capable of excluding the possibility of Nazi excesses . . . moreover there was nothing in Weber's ideal types that would necessitate the description of the activities of the Nazi state as *excesses*. For example, no horror perpetuated by the German medical profession or German technocrats was inconsistent with the view that values are inherently subjective and that science is intrinsically instrumental and value free. (Bauman, 1989: 10, italics added)

> *I propose to treat the Holocaust as a rare, yet significant and reliable, test of the hidden possibilities of modern society* . . . Modern civilisation was not the Holocaust's *sufficient* condition; it was, however, most certainly its *necessary* condition. Without it the Holocaust would be unthinkable. It was the rational world of modern civilisation that made the Holocaust thinkable. The Nazi mass murder of the European Jewry was not only the technological achievement of an industrial society, but also the organisational achievement of a bureaucratic society . . . bureaucratic rationality is at its most dazzling once we realise the extent to which *the very idea of the* Endlosung *was an outcome of the bureaucratic culture* . . . At no point of its long and tortuous execution did the Holocaust come in conflict with the principles of rationality. The 'Final Solution' did not clash at any stage with the rational pursuit of efficient, optimal goal implementation. On the contrary, *it arose out of a genuine rational concern, and it was generated by bureaucracy true to its form and purpose.* (Bauman 1989: 12, 13, 15 and 17, italics added)

Guenther Roth, the distinguished Weberian scholar, has said of these views that he cannot agree with one sentence. 'Weber was a liberal, loved the constitution and approved of the working class's voting rights (and thus, presumably, could not be called in conjunction with a thing so abominable as the Holocaust)' (cited in Bauman, 1989: 10).

Bauman sees the modern social system as a self-regulating and self-balancing system, with its own shared values, attitudes, beliefs and mechanisms of self-reproduction. All human agents and institutions have a role and function to perform under the clear direction of a single rational legal authority which sets targets that cannot be reached and are often undesirable. Such progress, in the eyes of the central authority, is essential for maintaining solidarity. The human agent within this form of modernity is a cultural dope characterised by 'universality', 'homogeneity', and pushed about by forces outside of their control. In contrast:

> Postmodernity is modernity coming of age: modernity looking at itself at a distance rather than from inside, making a full inventory of its gains and losses, psychoanalysing itself, discovering the intentions it never before spelled out, finding them mutually cancelling and incongruous. Postmodernity is modernity coming to terms with its own impossibility; a self monitoring modernity that consciously discards what it was once unconsciously doing. (Bauman, 1991: 272)

In other words, postmodernity is a 'modernity conscious of its true nature' (Bauman, 1992: 187). A form of modernity that is self-critical, self-denigrating and self-dismantling. The most visible characteristics of this 'modernity for itself' are 'institutionalized pluralism, variety, contingency and ambivalence' (ibid.). Bauman is particularly concerned with the issue of 'ambivalence' and has devoted a book to this. Ambivalence is characterised by action that takes place within a habitat where one would expect individual human agents to have to choose between many rival and contradictory meanings: a situation where action is not determined by factors outside of human control. In a postmodern politics, this ambivalence becomes the main dimension of inequality, as access to knowledge is the key to freedom and enhanced social standing. Postmodernity has its own distinctive features which are self-contained and self-reproducing, constructed within a cognitive space which is very different from that of modernity.

The nature of postmodernity is described, by Bauman, as a pattern generated by human agents from their own random movements which may emerge for a short time before continuing with its constant renewal; a form of sociality rather than society that is both undetermined and undetermining, and contains no notion of progress in the modern sense of the word. In contrast to Giddens's conception of modernity, Bauman argues that postmodernity: '"unbinds" time, weakens the constraining impact of the past and effectively prevents colonization of the future' (1992: 190).

In Bauman's postmodern analysis, one would expect the focus to be upon the self-constituting human agent, which operates within the postmodern habitat. The concept of **habitat** is explained by Bauman as a 'complex system', a term derived from mathematics which suggests, first, that the system is unpredictable and, secondly, that forces outside of the control of the human agents do not control it that operate with it. There are no goal-setting, managing or coordinating institutions within the complex system, this makes constraint fall to an absolute minimum. Therefore, the human agents or any other element cannot be discussed by reference to its functionality or dysfunctionality; and no one agency can determine the activity of any other agent. Although Bauman explains that 'the postmodern eye (that is, the modern eye liberated from modern fears and inhibitions) views difference with zest and glee: difference is beautiful and no less good for that' (1991: 255).

In a similar fashion to a range of other writers, in Bauman's work the term 'postmodern' suggests a radical or 'experiential' break with the past. Whereas for Jean-François Lyotard, the postmodern condition is a situation in which individuals have lost faith in what he calls 'grand narratives', belief systems that were once accepted and that gave us a feeling of security, for Bauman postmodernity is characterised by a rejection of rationality in all its forms. We feel as if the 'social' is dissolving. The bonds of rational legal authority, which once held communities together, no longer have the same force. As a social formation postmodernity has no foundations, no shared culture to give us a feeling of security, no grand theory to help us explain or understand the situation we are in. The self is isolated in the postmodern condition without logic, rationality or morality to guide it. The postmodern condition is a world without certainty. However, everyone is said to have a need for both meaning and predictability in their lives and relationships.

Meanings generate a basis for predictability in our social relationships; but in the postmodern condition there is no legitimate order to provide such a foundation. Postmodern meanings take the form of kitsch, camp and above all the simulacrum (see 1991: 332).

What is a modern person?

Individual people have knowledge of their own existence, and a belief that they are the authors of their own actions. We can say that the self is an 'agent'. In other words, people feel that they are responsible for their actions. In addition individual people have an identity, a feeling of being part of a wider group, of being part of a number of wider associations, yet at the same time, a feeling of being unique. People who do not believe that they are themselves are thought to be suffering from some form of mental illness, such as Capgras Syndrome – a condition where an individual believes that either themselves or those close to them have been taken over by hostile agents.

The modern identity

The modern identity had two key elements:

o   to be like the other people within a group and
o   a common categorising of outward phenomena, such as race or the clothes people wear

In summary, a modern person is an agent, a unique individual with an identity. The modern sociological analysis of these issues was based upon the search for 'person types'.

In the postmodern condition notions of self, agency and identity should have changed. For the postmodernist there is no unitary self. Our analyses should involve very different conceptual strategies to cope with the plural and unstable constitution of the postmodern self. As Foucault made clear, before the end of the eighteenth century the self as we know it did not exist and with the coming of the end of modernity the self will be 'erased, like a face drawn in sand at the edge of the sea' (cited in Ashley, 1997: 20). Many postmodern writers have recoiled from this startling conclusion of the death of the self.

According to Zygmunt Bauman (1996), in the postmodern world identity is becoming reconstructed and redefined, beyond these two key elements. Bauman agrees with Foucault that identity was a modern innovation. In the modern world, the problem was how to construct and maintain our identity in an effort to secure our place in the world and avoid uncertainty. This was because in the modern world the avoidance of uncertainty was seen as an individual problem, although support was always available from various professionals such as teachers and coun-sellors. Modern people view the city as a desert, a place in which name and identity are not fixed or given. The modern city is a place of nothingness that people had to find their way through. For this reason modern people would construct an identity not out of choice but out of necessity. With-out our pilgrimage to a secure identity we may become lost in the desert. In the first instance, on our journey we need a place to walk to. This is our life project, which ideally should be established early in life and be used to make sense of the various uncertainties, fragments and divisions of experience that make up the post-traditional world. By creating a fixed and secure identity we attempt to make the world more ordered and more predictable for ourselves.

In contrast, in the postmodern world the problem of identity is one of *avoiding* a fixed identity and keeping our options open, avoiding long-term commitments, consistency and devotion. In place of a life project estab-lished as early as possible, that we loyally keep to, postmodern people choose to have a series of short projects that are not fixed. The world has the feel of being in a continuous present. It is no longer agreeable to pilgrims. In place of the pilgrim, a number of other lifestyles emerge: the stroller, the vagabond, the tourist and the player. These lifestyles are not new to the postmodern world, but whereas in previous times marginal people in marginal situations adopted such lifestyles, they are now common to the majority of people in many situations.

These four successors to the pilgrim are postmodern life strategies:

o   The **stroller** or the *flâneur*. According to Bauman this became 'the central symbolic figure of the modern city' (Bauman, 1996: 26). This identity type looks at the surface meaning of things in the metropolitan environment: there is no deeper meaning underneath the surface of anything. The shopping mall is the place where we are most likely to see the *flâneur* in the postmodern world.

o   The **vagabond**. This identity type is continually 'the stranger'; in a similar fashion to the pilgrim this person is perpetually on the move, but their movements have no preceding itinerary. In the modern and pre-modern world the vagabond was unable to settle down in any one place because they were always unsettled: 'The settled were many, the vagabonds few. Postmodernity reversed the ratio . . . Now the vagabond is a vagabond not because of the reluctance or difficulty of settling down, but because of the scarcity of settled places' (Bauman, 1996: 29). The world is becoming increasingly uncertain and unsettled.

o   The **tourist**. The tourist moves purposefully away from home in search of a new experience. In the postmodern world we are losing the need for a home, but have a greater taste for the new experience. Home may offer security, but it has the numbing boredom of a prison.

o   The **player**. For the player life is a game. Nothing is serious, nothing is controllable and nothing is predictable. Life is a series of 'moves' in a game that can be skilled, perceptive and deceptive. The point of the game is to 'stay ahead' and to embrace the game itself.

Life then is developing a rather shallow feel; it is fragmented and discontinuous in nature.

Wagner (1994) also outlines the notion of self in the postmodern condition. He argues that modernity gave individuals scope to construct their own identities but in the postmodern condition a superabundance of material products, cultural orientations and consumer practices has led to a very wide range of identity constructions. In addition, the 'enterprise culture' led directly to the 'enterprise self' – and to a significant increase in individual autonomy:

> Rather than resting on a secure place in a stable social order, individuals are asked to engage themselves actively in shaping their lives and social positions in a constantly moving social context. Such a shift must increase uncertainties and even anxieties' (Wagner, 1994: 165)

Modernism was a form of social organisation that attempted to refashion and control the irrational forces of nature in the interests of satisfying human need or human desire. Relationships between people were almost always rational and logical. Legal codes were put together on the basis of 'due process' of law and policed by rational organisations using bureaucratic methods. Within modernity, life had a secure and logical feel. Postmodernity is the form of society we are left with when the process of modernisation is complete. Human behaviour has little or no direct dealing with nature: we live in an artificial or manufactured environment. In the postmodern condition, the world has an abandoned, relative and unprotected feel for the individual human agent. Even sex and food, which for thousands of years were the pleasurable building blocks of life, are now amongst the numerous sources of danger. Lacking the protection of class and communal togetherness, lacking racial and gender identities, individuals are left to experience isolation and detachment, having to create their own bonds of solidarity, selfhood and rectitude. This is the postmodern predicament; for individuals *anything goes*: morally, spiritually and communally. For many of us, life is in fragments and we experience everyday life as an open space of moral, political and personal dilemmas.

Although his labels of tourist etc. seem postmodern, what Bauman is attempting to do is to identify 'person types'. This is exactly the same as the modernist practice of labelling people as homosexual, delinquent, hyperactive, nymphomaniac, etc. Such categories of self/identity are pre-fashioned and action limiting. Identities are given, formed by historical factors outside the control of the individual. This is most clearly stated when Bauman discusses life as having a 'game'-like structure. The self, in Bauman's analysis has an inherent property, like the 'thing' in Durkheim's analysis. In Bauman's work there is no deconstruction of the self or identity, no attempt to reflect on the possibility of the obvious terminus of the postmodern discourse on identity: a post-identity order. The self remains unified and coherent with a structure of rules externally imposed and referred to as a 'game'.

What Bauman's notion of self is about is the formulation, by invention, of the universality of identity without reference to the everyday lives of people. The categories of self, tourist etc. are presented as a form of postmodern pastiche, but there is no poststructuralist critique of the essential identity, and no reference to individual people's lives within the postmodern condition; no appeal to the experience of people; the diversity of their lives or their struggles to achieve an identity that they want or desire. The self is stripped of any meaningful past, because it is an invention. Invented histories; invented biographies; invented affinities. For example, let us take the simple question: what does it mean to be a woman? To be a woman is a project in itself that involves a personal and political struggle. The male to female transsexual has to fight to be a woman, which can be both threatening as well as exciting. To lose this fight is to be plunged into a world of non-identity. Our identity is forged, as a practical accomplishment within a context, or a history. The understanding of the individual self, as a self, is inextricably bound up with our understanding of the collectivities we have to combat as agents. In a world of nationalism, ethnic cleansing, religious fundamentalism, racial violence and crises of gender identity, what is the point of Bauman's feeble attempt to invent a set of strategic essentialisms which have little, if any, relationship to the experience of individuals' lives?

What is the nature of self and self-identity in the postmodern condition? Above all, what life strategies do individuals employ to make their passage in the world? How do individuals' selves navigate a life in fragments?

What makes being a self such a complex activity in the postmodern condition is that the context is open to a number of valid interpretations, and in the absence of an agreed moral code to guide the self in the choice of right and good, this can generate feelings of insecurity. So the construction of an imaginary world for the self becomes a much more difficult activity; and having to cope with unforeseen consequences is a skill which the self must continually exercise. Living is now a highly skilled activity, and our key human skill is to direct the course of the fragments that constitute human existence in an effort to feel comfortable and secure. Individuals as dynamic agents attempt to secure or formulate *all* forms of solidarity, including those of class, community, race and gender. This is because, for individuals, class, race and gender have lost all influence on life events and life chances. In the postmodern condition, individuals have no independent identity other than that which they create for themselves; this is a world in which class, race and gender are immaterial. In the postmodern world you are what you appear.

In contrast to Bauman's view the self in the postmodern condition is a series of activities that are conscious of their own existence. The self must define itself; the self must define and maintain its parameters and at the same time contribute to the construction of a context in which it feels both physically and ontologically secure; the self must select and construct motives and intentions, a worldview, a moral code, notions of right and wrong, true and false; the self needs to develop modes of reflexivity, which may take place outside of time and space. The self exists within a context, but must maintain some degree of independence from that context in order to maintain itself as an independent self.

Most definitions of the self assume that it is a physical entity or make use of geographical reasoning, assuming that the self is to be found within distinct geographical regions of the brain. As John Macmurry comments: 'As agent, therefore, the Self is the body' (1957: 91).

Thinking about its own existence, thinking about its own intentions, and thinking about accumulating resources to satisfy those intentions – these are the basic reflexive issues for any self. The physicality, if any, of the self is minimal. In this sense, the self may have a form like a virus; the physicality of the entity is of little, if any, significance: what we are primarily interested in is its activity. Something with minimal physicality can send messages to the body and manipulate DNA. If the self does have any organic element to it, this is better understood as a form of scaffold, to be disposed of at the earliest opportunity. The self also has the skill of bodily manipulation, but in addition also has consciousness, and above all else knowledge of its own existence as something independent of its context. Finally, the self has knowledge of its own finitude. It is an element of the universalising logic of modernity that the self should be conceived of as an organic entity. In the postmodern condition, no such objective basis can be assigned to the self: it is the product of its own subjective construction.

The self must maintain its own parameters, which are self-defined. The self resists all efforts to universalise it by outside agencies. Without such parameters the self is engulfed by the context: such a person has no thoughts of their own, they simply follow the values, attitudes and beliefs of a group, without question. Parameters of selfhood are maintained by the appropriation of resources; at the most basic level the self needs to maintain a body. Without a body, the self as we know it cannot fulfil all its goals and intentions. The self must also maintain communicative resources and ascetic resources. These are necessary for accessing pleasure and avoiding anything unpleasurable for the self. For this reason an understanding of the postmodern self must make use of the concept of **performativity**, because the self is searching for the best possible input/output equation. This does not have to be on rational grounds (as in public choice theory, for example) but on the basis of any criteria which the individual self considers reasonable or acceptable. Goffman (1959) was the first to discuss the use of such resources. In addition, the self must main-tain its own security; this is not simply a question of physical security but also what Giddens (1990) terms 'ontological security'. Most philosophies would argue that ontological security is maintained by positioning the self within a moral code. Most postmodernists argue that morally 'anything goes'.

The postmodern self is concerned with doing things: with or *activity*, or performativity. Social action is about making a difference in the world. All social action will make to some extent change the context, so we would expect that social action will always meet some form of resistance. Social action can be brought about only if the self has sufficient power to overcome the resistance to change, or to the direction of change. This means that all social action will involve the use of power, and the self's ability to accumulate resources will enable it to make a greater difference in the world. We must also keep in mind that social actions have both intended and unintended consequences. For this reason, the self needs to develop an almost infinite number of modes of reflexivity. Reflexivity can allow the self to gain maximum outcome from a social action, with-out having to make use of all the resources available to it. For most individuals there will be a reflexive element in action: the individual will decide if a given action will have the desired result. This involves the self recreating an imaginary world, which is the context where the projected action will take place. In this world, the self can contemplate an infinite number of possible choices of action and possible consequences of moving from the here now to the there then. All effective social action is then both active and reflexive, because action for the self means choice, choice of direction and choice of resources. It is up to you. The choice is yours.

Bauman: the critique of life in the postmodern condition

In his books that have been published since the turn of the century Bauman has been highly critical of the circumstance of life in the post-modern condition.

The Individualised Society (2001b) is a collection of papers and lectures which outlines the human consequences of a process of articulation which has seen society move away from the 'warm circle' of community, where people lived happily together by agreeing, sharing and respecting what they shared, to a situation of individualisation. For Bauman there has been a *'decolonization* of the public sphere'. There has been a devaluation of order and the public sector institutions no longer provide security. An individualised society is a society in which all messes that a person finds himself or herself in are assumed to be of the individual person's own making. The ways in which society operates are assumed to be of no consequence to an individual's destiny. Blame has been turned away from public institutions and towards the self, and particularly the inadequacies of self. This change exposes people to endemic insecurity both in terms of position and action; public issues have become privatised and deregulated.

For Bauman we are living in an atmosphere of **ambient fear**, charac-terised by uncertainty, unpredictability and instability, in which there is 'unqualified priority awarded to the irrationality and moral blindness of market competition', unbounded freedom given to capital and finance, destruction of safety nets which were once formally provided by the state and informally by the family, friends and the community. People are becoming subjected to polarisation, hesitation and lack of control. We are also uncertain about the political agency that we can draw upon to chal-lenge this unnerving experience. Bauman's argument is that: *'specifically postmodern forms of violence arise from the privatization, deregulation and decentralization of identity problems'* (2001b: 92). We have a fear of strangers that gives raise to a politics of exclusion that has a tribal element to it, or as Bauman expresses it 'the balkanisation of human coexistence' (2001b: 96).

The same themes are developed in *Community: Seeking Safety in an Insecure World* (2001a) where Bauman builds upon his critique of com-munitarianism in *Postmodernity and its Discontents* (1997) and *Work, Consumerism and the New Poor* (1998b).

Communitarianism is a modernist approach, claims Bauman, which demands:

> the power of enforcement. The power to make sure that people would act in a certain way rather than in other ways, to taper the range of their options, to manipulate the probabilities; to make them do what they otherwise would probably not do, (if they would, why all this fuss), to make them less than they would otherwise be. (Bauman, 1997: 191)

Bauman has now supplemented this view by arguing that 'community' has no foundation other than shared agreement. The 'warm circle' of community that we find in communitarian discourse is built upon two 'collapsed together and confused' (2001a: 72) notions of community. First, that people are individuals who should resolve their own problems, and secondly that community should be built upon 'fraternal sharing'. 'Community' has then an ethical foundation. The 'community' of communitarian discourse cannot survive self-conscious critique, contemplation or scrutiny. When subjected to such evaluation we see 'community' for what it is: 'numb – or dead' (Bauman, 2001a: 11).

Sociologically, Blair, Clinton and others have attempted to bring together 'freedom' and 'security' by rebuilding the idea of 'the community' within a postmodern world. In the postmodern condition fragmented culture allows individuals to select their own identities. However, the Blair government in the UK does not want to allow people to choose an identity that does not include work. Bauman makes reference to Chancellor of the Exchequer Gordon Brown's suggestion that the unemployed should be provided with mobile phones so that they can be kept in touch with the job market. Communitarianism sacrifices freedom for greater security.

Bauman (1998b) argued that we should see the work ethic as something that generates a 'moral economy' filled with 'concentrated and unchallenged discrimination'. In its place we should have an 'ethics of workmanship' which recognises the value of unpaid work, currently classed as nonwork. In addition, we should consider 'decoupling income entitlement from income-earning capacity' (Bauman, 1998b: 97). This is an interesting choice of words, but it cannot hide the stale, old message: let's bring back the 'warm circle' of community. Bauman is saying the same as Marx did in the nineteenth century: 'From each according to his abilities, to each according to his needs.' Not only has socialism been rejected fully and comprehensively by almost everybody (including Bauman in a range of publications), but this highlights a flaw in both Bauman's analysis and socialism. When we take responsibility for the Other, we run the risk of imposing our will on the Other and this can lead to cruelty. Bauman fails to take into account the ability of people to take responsibility for their own lives and their own actions and at the same time undermines the assumptions of his own work since *Postmodern Ethics* (1993).

In conclusion Bauman's discussion of self and identity is an attempt to invent a set of strategic essentialisms, which have little if any relationship to the experience of individual people's lives. Bauman's discussion of self takes place within a problematical *habitat* that on closer examination turns out to be the modernist social, by another name, not a world of postmodern diverse counter-publics.

Deleuze and Guattari

thought thinks only by means of difference, around this point of ungrounding. (Deleuze, 1997: 276)

To me this is full-blown postmodernism, but is it possible for Deleuze and Guattari to construct a social theory that can deliver?

Gilles Deleuze and Felix Guattari have made what many people consider to be a significant contribution to postmodern thought. Any summary of the work of any writer involves the selection and prioritising of some concepts and ideas and the neglect of others. In the work of Deleuze and Guattari such a summary is not possible, as it goes against the spirit of their work. For Deleuze and Guattari writing should take the form of a rhizome. Think of the structure of writing, and the structure of thought, as a strawberry plant: no one part of the plant is superior to any other part. If we stamp on one section another will spring up. So the reader must view the summary that follows as a journey through the work of Deleuze and Guattari. I have done as they suggest the reader should do; the places where I stop are like my favourite tracks on a CD, and I just want to play them again.

The texts are very difficult to follow, and can almost defy exegesis. Wonderful-sounding phrases such as 'body without organs' is said to be 'the body without an image' (Deleuze and Guattari, 1983: 8) and 'nothing but bands of intensity, potentials, thresholds, and gradients' (1983: 19). Here I attempt to identify what I consider to be the modernist assumptions upon which their key contribution to postmodern thought is built. In other words this is exegesis with an edge. Deleuze and Guattari discuss a number of highly inventive concepts, which in the first instance appear to direct analysis into areas previously disregarded by modernist thinkers: desiring-machines; the body without organs; the nomadic subject.

Deleuze and Guattari derive a number of concepts from the physical sciences in order to understand the human condition, most notably the notion of 'the singularity', which is used to describe a 'blackhole'. They also build their analysis upon a modernist notion of structure, usually a variation of Saussure's structuralism. They argue that a minimal structure should be seen as two heterogeneous series of terms that are set in relation by, and converge in, a paradoxical element.

This notion of structure is given a postmodern gloss by Deleuze and Guattari, who redefine structure in the form of a 'game'. This suggests that the structure of society is a human creation, whereas in their work it is not, yet at the same time the game is rule governed and involves the exercise of constraint in a clearly modernist fashion.

Deleuze and Guattari suggest that modernist thought takes the form of a hierarchy, in which some ways of thinking are seen to be superior to other ways of thinking. They ask us to consider the notion of the 'tree of knowledge'. Freud, for example, looks for roots in his analysis, rather than developing his thought in the form of a 'rhizome'. In contrast to hierarchical ways of thinking, Deleuze and Guattari draw upon the Nietzschean concept of 'the will to power': people whose ways of thinking are accepted as superior are simply making use of their ability to dominate others. Deleuze and Guattari criticise such discourses and institutions that repress desire and proliferate fascist subjectivities. The discourses and institutions of modernity impose a definition of normality from the perspective of the powerful. Deleuze first introduced the rhizome concept in his study of Leopold von Sacher-Masoch:

> A popular joke tells of the meeting between a sadist and a masochist; the masochist says: 'Hurt me.' The sadist replies: 'No.' This is a particularly stupid joke, not only because it is unrealistic but because it foolishly claims competence to pass judgement on the world of perversions. (Deleuze, 1989: 40)

What is philosophy?

In *What Is Philosophy?* (1994) Deleuze claims that the question 'What is philosophy?' should be poised only late in life. Philosophy is not about contemplation, reflection or communication. The answer is that philosophy is about 'creating' concepts. Concepts are not to be seen as gifts which we can purify and polish; we have to create them in a form that makes them more convincing than rival concepts.

Philosophy has three elements for Deleuze:

o **immanence** – a pre-philosophical plane that must be explained;
o **insistence** – the conceptual persona that must be invented and brought to life;
o **consistency** – the philosophical concepts that need to be created.

The first principle of philosophy is that universals in themselves explain nothing. The universal statement itself must be explained. To do this we need exceptional concepts, as it is through our concepts that we find knowledge.

One of the main themes running through the text is about the conceptual persona. Concepts need a conceptual persona and the notion of 'friend' is one such persona. In other words, we distrust rival concepts. As Deleuze explains: 'Concepts are not waiting for us ready-made, like heavenly bodies. There is no heaven for concepts. They must be invented, fabricated or rather created and would be nothing without their creator's signature' (Deleuze, 1994: 6).

It is for this reason that concepts are often signed with the author's name, such as 'Descartes' cogito'. In addition, concepts are not like a jigsaw puzzle: their edges do not neatly fit together. The concept is more like the throw of a dice in terms of the new possibilities that the concept launches. Concepts form a skeletal frame across a chosen plane, informing us what it means to think and how to make use of thought. The plane of immanence, which plays a key role in the thought of Deleuze and Guattari, is being constantly woven 'like a gigantic shuttle' (Deleuze, 1994: 38) and has a 'fractal' nature with movements caught and 'folded' in the others. Immanence is radically empirical in character. Empiricism is only concerned with events and people and is an important strategy for formulating concepts. The various elements of the plane, such as thought and nature, are 'diagrammatic features' (which are 'directions' or 'intuitions') whereas concepts are 'intensive features' – which are 'absolute dimensions' or 'intentions'.

The plane of immanence is surrounded by illusions, which take the form of ready-made paths of dominant opinions for us to follow. The reason why these paths appear so attractive is because they appeal to our intolerance of people who deviate from the norm. The illusions form a thick fog around the plane that prevents us from fully constructing our nomadic journey between the singularities. Such illusions include:

o   illusion of transcendence – in which immanence is made immanent to something other than itself;
o   illusion of universals – when concepts are confused with the plane. Universals do not explain anything: we must explain the existence of the universal itself;
o   illusion of the eternal – when we simply forget that concepts need to be created;
o   illusion of discursiveness – when propositions are confused with concepts.

What is a concept?

Whilst looking at the nature of the concept as a philosophical reality, Deleuze explains that there are no 'simple' concepts. Every concept is a multiplicity. All concepts are made up of a number of components. All concepts have a history; a 'becoming' that involves their relationship with concepts situated on the same plane. It is by reference to the plane that we can articulate support and coordinate the problems that the concept is concerned with:

o   Every concept relates to other concepts, their history, and becoming and present connections.
o   Concepts have a 'consistency', they make components internally consistent.
o   A concept is in part an accumulation of its components.
o   A concept is incorporeal. It is both absolute and relative: relative in relation to its own components, the plane on which it is situated and in terms of the problems it addresses; and absolute in the way it 'traces the contour of its components' (Deleuze, 1994: 17).

Deleuze uses the notion of 'construction' to unite the relative and the absolute dimensions of the concept.

What are conceptual personae?

Conceptual personae are not reducible to 'psychological types': 'The role of conceptual personae is to show thought's territories, its absolute deterritorializations and reterritorializations' (Deleuze, 1994: 69).

Deleuze outlines the features of conceptual personae:

o **pathic features**, associated with the idiot, madman and schizo-phrenic, people who want to think for themselves, people who discover in thought the inability to think;
o **relational features** – such as the friend who has a relationship only through the thing loved;
o **dynamic features** – which insert themselves into existing moving energetic networks;
o **juridical features** – lays claim to what is right;
o **existential features** – inventing new ways of living or possibilities of life.

The conceptual persona and the plane of immanence presuppose each other:

> Conceptual personae constitute points of view according to which planes of immanence are distinguished from one another . . . and constitute the condition under which each plane finds itself filled with concepts of the same group. (Deleuze, 1994: 75)

Deleuze makes clear that the concepts are not deduced from the plane. The conceptual personae are needed to construct concepts on the plane, just as the plane itself needs to be laid open and constructed itself. There are countless planes; each has an alterable curve, and the planes group together or separate themselves according to points of view composed with the use of a chosen conceptual persona.

Libidinal flows

Deleuze and Guattari attempt to decode libidinal flows created by the institutions of capitalism. They do this by attempting a 'schizoanalytic' destruction of the ego and the superego and putting forward the notion of a dynamic unconscious. They refer to this as a process of becoming. This 'becoming' leads to the emergence of new types of decentred subjects, the schizo and the nomad, who are free from fixed and unified identities, modernist/Freudian subjectivities and their bodies.

Nietzsche

According to Ronald Bogue (1989), Deleuze's book *Nietzsche and Philosophy* (1983) contains many of the central themes that Deleuze develops in later works. For Deleuze, Nietzsche is an intellectually consistent thinker, whose major goals were to

o overturn Platonism;
o develop a philosophy of becoming based on a physics of force;

o replace Hegel's 'negation of negation' with a philosophy of affirmation;

o complete Kant's project for critical philosophy by directing it against the traditional principles of Western rationality.

Nietzsche has two key concepts that Deleuze draws upon: the 'will to power' and the 'eternal return'.

Meaning

For Deleuze meaning is indifferent to questions of truth or falsehood, existence or non-existence; it has no fixed and stable objects or subjects, and is devoid of irreversible relations of implication, including relations of cause or effect, before and after, bigger and smaller. In other words, meaning both precedes and is indifferent to:

o designation – the relation of the proposition to a state of things;
o manifestation – the relation of the proposition to a state of things;
o signification – the relation of words to general concepts, and of syntactic links to the implications and consequent assertions of concepts.

Meaning is then a simulacrum, a paradoxical, contradictory entity that defies common sense. In this respect Deleuze discusses the work of Lewis Carroll, whose *Alice in Wonderland* and *Alice through the Looking-glass* are normally classed as nonsense works: they are not devoid of meaning, he argues: the message in these texts embraces both logical and illogical meanings.

Deleuze calls the *loguendum* – the ground or condition upon which language rests. The *loguendum* is the contradictory simulacrum within language.

Anti-Oedipus

In their *Anti-Oedipus* (1983) Deleuze and Guattari challenge a range of psychological theories. For Deleuze and Guattari, the fundamental problem with psychoanalysis is its conception of desire. They argue that desire is social rather than familial. The Oedipal family structure is one of the primary modes of restricting desire in capitalist societies, and psychoanalysis helps to enforce that restriction. The Oedipus complex ensures that human desire is concentrated in the nuclear family. In contrast to psychoanalysis's view, desire should not be treated as a 'lack'. Desire is a form of production. It is an unbound, free-floating energy, similar to what Freud terms the libido and what Nietzsche terms the will to power. In other words, desire is unconscious. The best guide to desire is the schizophrenic id rather than neurotic ego. What this means is that their notion of desiring-production is derived from the experiences of psychotics. This allows them to reveal the genuine questions of unconscious desire which all people face, but which psychotics confront in a particularly direct manner. Psychotics often experience various parts of their bodies as separate entities, and sometimes as invading, persecuting machines. Schizophrenics enter catatonic states in which they seem to inhabit a body that has no organs. Finally, some schizophrenics have shifting, multiple personalities. These three psychotic experiences form the basis of the fundamental components of desiring-production:

o desiring-machines
o the body without organs
o the nomadic subject

Deleuze and Guattari present a universal history of desiring-production which focuses on the relationship between the *socius* – the natural divine presupposition of production:

o the body of the earth of primitive societies
o the body of the despot of barbaric societies
o the body of capital of capitalistic societies

and its related network of desiring-machines. In relation to this they discuss:

o primitive societies and the exchangist model of structural anthropology
o despotic societies and theories of the state
o capitalist societies and Marxist economics.

The three machines therefore are roughly described as pre-state, state and post-state machines.

They subsume Marx and Freud within a Nietzschean framework and attempt to libidinalise Marx. This notion of libidinalised production subverts the traditional Marxian distinction between production, distribution and consumption. The coupling of desire and production also problematises the Marxist distinction between use value and exchange value. Deleuze and Guattari assume a libidinal nature of groups and a social nature of the unconscious. Capitalism is identified as a force for concomitant deterritorialisation and reterritorialisation. The state is a machine of anti-production: it controls and limits production.

The singularity

Singularities are a set of singular points (ideal events) which are not based upon the generality or universality of a concept. They are pre-individual, non-personal and a-conceptual. They are the points that characterise a mathematical curve, a physical state of affairs a psychological and moral person.

To reverse Platonism, claims Deleuze, we must remove 'essences' and substitute events in their place as jets of singularities. The distribution of singularities form fields of problem. And the paradox is the locus of the question.

> Singularities are turning points of inflection; bottlenecks, knots, foyers, and centers; points of fusion, condensation, and boiling; points of tears and joy, sickness and health, hope and anxiety, 'sensitive' points. Such singularities, however, should not be confused either with the personality of the one expressing herself in discourse, or with the individuality of a state of affairs designated by a proposition, or even with the generality or universality of a concept signified by a figure or a curve. (Deleuze, 1990: 52)

Singularities are beyond direct human experience: they are intuitive and abstract events that control the formation or generation of individuals as persons, a process that Deleuze refers to as 'becoming'. Singularities belong to a sphere of operation that is impersonal. They manifest on the surface of the unconscious in the form of a 'nomadic distribution' that is not fixed.

The singularities run parallel with a series that is very varied in its content, but organised into a system that is neither stable nor unstable but described as 'metastable'. This series has the ability and the energy to bring about events. In addition, singularities automatically unify into a series. This unifying process is always mobile and in conflict with any preconceived notions. The series contains a paradoxical element which lies across the series and which echoes to all corresponding singularities in the form of a chance ordering which underpins their composition as a series. Singularities are potentials, and the individual is descended from the plane of singularities. So a singularity is an unstable resource that individuals draw upon in a process of becoming. Individual people actualise singularities, in other words, they draw something from the singularity that they use to make a life for themselves. This allows various points to converge that can be followed by a person as a way of living their life. In this way, 'singularities are actualised both in a world and in the individuals which are parts of the world' (Deleuze, 1990: 110). Singularities allow us to make sense of the world if they are placed within a 'community of organs', that is, if we can superimpose some of the organisation upon the way they are distributed. We know about the existence and distribution of singularities before we know their nature.

Nomads

The nomad is said to have neither a past nor future: it has only becomings. Nomads have no history, they have only geography. Deleuze describes the notion of 'becoming' in the following terms:

> To write is to become, but has nothing to do with becoming a writer. That is to become something else . . . The becomings contained in writing when it is not

wedded to established order-words, but itself traces lines of flight are quite different . . . There is a woman-becoming in writing. (Deleuze and Parnet, 1987: 43)

Power and becoming

In Deleuze's view all power formations have a need for a form of knowledge to make the execution of that power effective. He gives the example of the Greek city and Euclidean geometry. 'It was not because the geometricians had power but because Euclidean geometry constituted the knowledge, or the abstract machine, that the city needed for its organisation of power, space and time' (Deleuze and Guattari, 1988).

The argument here is that all states have an image, or an axiomatic system, of how the individual should behave and think in every situation and circumstance. This self-evident system of thought is what Deleuze terms the 'abstract machine'. Today it is the human sciences that have taken on this role of providing the abstract machine for the modern apparatuses of power.

One of the central themes in Deleuze is the relationship between power and desire.

Desire

In his discussion of the process of becoming, Deleuze describes two types of 'plane'.

The plane of organisation   This plane is concerned with the formation of subjects and attempts to crush desire by use of forces like the law. This plane is said to be made up of *molar lines with segments*; both individuals and groups are made up of 'lines'. This molar line includes such things as the family, the school, the factory and retirement. It is one of 'rigid segmentarity' in which individuals are moulded to behave and think in appropriate ways. Deleuze gives us the examples of people in the family telling others: 'Now you're not a baby any more', and at school 'You're not at home now'. Segments are devices of power in that they fix a code of behaviour within a defined territory. In the last analysis, the state 'overcodes' all the segments. This overcoding 'ensures the homogenisation of different segments' (1988: 129). This is achieved by the use of 'the abstract machine' that imposes the normal/usual ways of thinking and behaving from the point of view of the state.

The plane of consistence/the plane of immanence   In contrast to the molar line with segments, the plane of consistence is concerned with *molecular fluxes with thresholds or quanta*. These are lines of segmentarity that are molecular or supple. These lines are concerned detours and modification; this is a line of becoming. On the plane of organisation, the segments depend upon 'binary machines': you are one case or its logical alternative, for example you are one class or another; one sex or the other;

one race or the other. These classifications appear to be dichotomic but operate diachronically. If you are not a man or a woman then you are a transvestite. To move along this plane one must first construct it: the plane does not pre-exist desire. As we move along this plane that we have constructed we become a **body without organs**. By this term Deleuze means a body without organisation – one who fulfils their desires by attempting to liberate themselves from the plane of organisation. Desire exists only when it is assembled or machined. The plane of consistence is concerned with movement, and it deals with 'hecceities' rather than subjects. Hecceities are degrees of power. The plane of consistence is described as:

> successions of catatonic states and periods of extreme haste, of suspensions and shootings, coexistences of variable speeds, blocks of becoming, leaps across voids, displacements of a centre of gravity on an abstract line, conjunction of lines on a plane of immanence, a 'stationary process' at dizzying speed which sets free particles and affects. (Deleuze and Parnet, 1987: 95)

Every person or group can construct a plane of immanence on which to lead his or her life.

Territorialisation/deterritorialisation

The issue of territorialisation is about the problem of 'holding together heterogeneous elements (Deleuze and Guattari, 1988: 323). Not to follow the line of organisation is referred to as 'deterritorialisation'. In this process 'knots of arboresence' – by which Deleuze and Guattari mean thinking hierarchy – become 'resumptions and upsurges in a rhizome' (1988: 134). Territory for Deleuze is an 'assemblage', it is an environment experienced in harmony, with a distance between people marked by 'indexes' which form the basis of 'territorialising expressions' and 'territorialised functions'. The basis of territory is aggressiveness. However, territory regulates the coexistence of individuals of the same species by keeping them separated. The effect of territory is to allow different people to coexist by specialising in different activities.

The direction of the process of 'territorialisation' is referred to by Deleuze as a 'refrain' – which is an aggregate of expressions and territorial motifs. The refrain acts upon whatever surrounds it and forms an organised mass. As Deleuze and Guattari explain, within a territory: 'Every consciousness pursues its own death, every love-passion its own end, attracted by a blackhole, and all the blackholes resonate together' (1988: 133).

This is the operation of the line of organisation and it is about killing desire by preventing 'the absolute deterritorialisation of the cogito' (Deleuze and Guattari, 1988: 133). It is within deterritorialisation that we construct the field of immanence or the plane of consistency – a very different assemblage from the line of organisation. The assemblage that makes up the field of immanence is constructed piece by piece: a person 'takes and makes what she or he can, according to taste' (1988: 157). This is the 'body without organs', the 'connection of desires, conjunction of flows, continuum of intensities' (1988: 161). The body without organs may not be easy to compose and there is no guarantee that it will be understood.

The person is made up of bundles of lines, such as:

o   lines of flight
o   lines of drift
o   customary lines

Some of these lines are imported from the outside, some emerge by chance, and some are invented. The lines have singularities, segments and quanta and they are not easily differentiated, notably because the lines themselves are an invention of cartography.

Becoming

In *What Children Say* (1998), Deleuze explains that children never stop talking about what they are doing or trying to do. Children do this by means of dynamic trajectories and by drawing mental maps of those trajectories. Such maps are essential to our psychic activity. They form lines, such as the line of immanence, which are constantly referred to in Deleuze's work.

For Deleuze, there is no fixed conception of 'being'; instead he looks at the self as an imminent or emerging 'becoming' which has no established elements that define or constrain our identity. The emergent becoming is built upon a practical ontology. Becoming is 'molecular' in nature and is described in terms of emitting particles which enter into proximity with particles of the thing which the self wishes to become: woman, child, animal, dog, vegetable, minor, imperceptible, etc. Becoming is a tension between modes of desire plotting a vector of transformation between molar coordinates. Becoming is then directional; 'becoming' allows the self to emerge into anything it chooses, a process in which the body is involved in leaving its normal habitat. This process is not simply a matter of imitation or metamorphosis as imitation involves respect for the boundaries that constrain the self. All forms of becoming are said to be 'minoritarian' in nature, in that they involve movement away from the 'standard man' that is firmly rooted on the plane of organisation. This movement can be taken to the point where identity in any conventional sense is destroyed. Immanence is immanent only to itself. This is what Deleuze and Guattari refer to as 'becoming-imperceptible' which sweeps away the majority.

The self has three elements in Deleuze's work:

o   a foundation – which is described as a synthesis of habit;
o   a past – which is a synthesis of memory;
o   a spiritual repetition that allows the self to make a distinction with others.

In the case of becoming-dog, a person does not literally become a dog in the way that Kafka's character Gregor Samsa becomes an insect. Rather, when a person is involved in becoming-dog this means becoming a body without organs, escaping Oedipality and leading a life which is entirely immanent in nature.

Becoming is the process of individuation, free from organisation. 'Becoming produces nothing other than itself' (Deleuze and Guattari, 1988: 238).

o   It is involutionary
o   It is creative
o   It is not imitating
o   It is not identifying
o   It is not regressing–progressing
o   It is not corresponding
o   It is not producing
o   It is not a filiation

Becoming is about the process of desire: it means liberating the body from the line of organisation. If we take the example of 'becoming-woman', the line of organisation imposes a universal woman upon some bodies. Young women will be told, 'Stop behaving like that; you are not a little girl any more', 'You're not a tomboy', etc. This is what Deleuze refers to as aborescence, which is the submission of a person to the line of organisation, the installation of a semiotic and subjectification on to the body. Psychoanalysis is one technique used for achieving this imposition, and hence for repressing desire. The body without organs is what is left when you take away all organisation and aborescence, allowing becoming to happen.

Aborescence is submission to molar segmentation, which is rigid but can guarantee certainty and security: 'The more rigid the segmentarity, the more reassuring it is for us. That is what fear is, and how it makes us retreat into the first line' (Deleuze and Guattari, 1988: 227–8). The human being is often seen to be a segmentary animal, and is segmented in a binary fashion: male–female, adult–child, etc.

Becoming-animal

Becoming-animal is absolute deterritorialisation (Deleuze, 1975: 13). It is the schizo escape from the Oedipus complex. However, for Deleuze, in the case of Gregor Samsa this ends in failure as he attempts to re-Oedipalise himself, as the transformation is incomplete. Becoming-animal was explored by Kafka in a number of stories, including 'The Metamorphosis', in which Samsa becomes-insect, which involves the deterritorialisation of his family relationships and his bureaucratic and commercial relationships from his working life. Other Kafka stories are: 'Investigations of a Dog'; 'Report to the Academy' and 'Josephine the Singer'.

When faced with a simulacrum, animals, children and the ignorant, who do not possess the antidote of reason and knowledge, lose the distinction between truth and illusion. The animal could never have a real thought because it would simultaneously forget what it was on the verge of thinking. To become-animal is to make use of a machine of expression that expresses itself first and conceptualises later. This is pure content which is not separate from its expression.

Modernist assumptions

Deleuze and Guattari, as we have seen, draw upon terms from the physical sciences to describe the human condition, most notably their notion of 'the singularity', a term which is used to describe a 'blackhole'. They build their analysis upon a modernist notion of structure, which they often redefine in terms of a 'game'.

Structure The convergence of the corporeal and the incorporeal forms the basic structure of meaning.

According to Deleuze: 'Structure is in fact a machine for the production of incorporeal sense (*skindapsos*)' (1990: 71). Within any structure there are two series, one signifying and the other signified. The signifying is characterised by 'an excess' and the signifying by a 'lack'. This is seen as a relationship of 'eternal disequilibrium' and 'perpetual displacement'. The signified series is known and arranges produced totalities. The signifying series arranges produced totalities (Deleuze, 1990: 48).

Totalising ways of thinking can be based on either

o the 'error of reformism or technology', which is about imposing partial arrangements of social relations according to the rhythm of technical achievements; or
o the error of totalitarianism, which attempts to constitute a totalisation of the signifiable and known, according to the rhythm of the social totality existing at a given moment.

'The technocrat is the natural friend of the dictator' (Deleuze, 1990: 49).
The minimal conditions for a structure are presented as:

o Two heterogeneous series exist: one signifying, the other signified.
o Each series exists only in terms of its relationship with the other.
o The series is made up of the attachment of singular points known as *singularities*.

- o The two heterogeneous series converge towards a paradoxical element which is their 'differentiation' – this is the principle of the emission of singularities.
- o The singularity appears at the same time as an excess and as an 'empty box' – in other words as part of both of the two heterogeneous series.
- o The singularity has the function of articulating the two series to each other.
- o The distribution of singularities corresponds to each series from fields of problems.

The problem for Deleuze and Guattari is that difference cannot be thought in itself, it is inaccessible to representative thought. Difference can only become thinkable when it is tamed, in other words when it has representation forced upon it. Deleuze outlines four 'iron collars' of representation, which were first put into place by Plato, 'who rigorously established the distinction between essence and appearance, between the model and the copy. The purpose of this is the subjection of difference' (Deleuze, 1997: 264).

The 'iron collars' are:

- o identity in the concept
- o opposition in the predicate
- o analogy in judgement
- o resemblance in perception

Difference not rooted in one of these is believed to be unbounded, unco-ordinated and inorganic. Such difference, it is suggested, cannot be thought and cannot exist. As such, these unthought differences are said to be 'non-being'. Deleuze describes the assimilation of difference into 'non-being' as 'unjust' (1997: 268). The role of philosophy, for Deleuze, is to invent techniques to explore such differential relations and singular points in which 'essences in the form of centres of envelopment around singularities' (1997: 264). This sounds wonderful, but it is not possible for Deleuze and Guattari to proceed in this fashion: they fall back on good old modernist 'representation' in order to present meaning to their readers. Most notably, this occurs when they make use of the analogy of 'game' to present a resemblance in our perception of the similarity of 'structure' to 'game'.

Game   The notion of structure is given a postmodern gloss by Deleuze and Guattari, who redefine it in the form of a 'game'. This suggests that the structure is a human creation, whereas clearly in their work it is not, yet at the same time the game is rule governed and involves the exercise of constraint in a modernist fashion.

In Deleuze and Parnet's *Dialogues* (1987), the games with which we are associated are said to contain a number of principles:

o   It is necessary that a set of rules pre-exists the playing of the game – a categorical value.
o   These rules determine hypotheses which divide and apportion chance: hypotheses of loss or gain.
o   Hypotheses organise the playing of the game (i.e. how many throws).
o   The hypotheses outline the consequences of throws, i.e. 'victory' or 'defeat'.

As Deleuze and Parnet explain: 'The characteristics of normal games are therefore pre-existing categorical rules, the distributing hypotheses, the fixed and numerically distinct distribution, and the ensuing results' (1987: 59).

In contrast to this, Deleuze outlines a 'pure' game, which has the following characteristics: there are no pre-existing rules; each move invents its own rules. 'Far from dividing and apportioning chance in a really distinct number of throws, all throws affirm chance and endlessly ramify it with each throw' (Deleuze and Parnet, 1987: 58):

> Each throw is itself a series, but *in a time much smaller than the minimum* of continuous, thinkable time; and, to this serial minimum, a distribution of singularities corresponds. Each throw emits singular points – the points on the dice, for example. But the set of throws is included in the aleatory point, a unique cast which is endlessly displaced throughout all series, *in a time greeted than the maximum* of continuous thinkable time. (Deleuze and Parnet, 1987: 59)

The game 'is the reality of thought itself and the unconscious of pure thought'. 'Each thought emits a distribution of singularities in one long thought, causing all the forms or figures of the nomadic distribution to correspond to its own displacement' (1987: 60).

Deleuze and Guattari, like many postmodern thinkers, claimed to present an analysis which was built upon an 'anything goes' triumphalism. However, in the end they take a look over the brink of their own postmodern plateau and then pull back from the full implications of their analysis. The postmodern condition is a world without 'the social'; it is a world without 'the self'. Deleuze and Guattari, despite their own theories, look for roots rather than assemble rhizomes; they describe a self constituted by lines of singularities, together with some elements such as libido, from the Freudian conception of self. In other words, the self is constituted out of 'grand narrative' conceptions: it is an assemblage constructed outside of the individual human being, independently of the human's own agency. Moreover, this self inhabits a world constituted of concepts drawn from the language of the physical sciences. As suggested above, Deleuze describes singularities as beyond direct human experience, as intuitive and abstract events which control the formation or generation of individuals as persons, a process that he refers to as 'becoming'. Singularities belong to a sphere of operation that is impersonal. The emission of singularities is on the surface of the unconscious in the form of a 'nomadic distribution', which is not fixed.

What is the 'postmodernism' of Deleuze and Guattari? A modern self in a modern world, described by two modern thinkers.

Jean Baudrillard (1929–present)

In a series of essays, *The Transparency of Evil: Essays on Extreme Phenomena* (1993), Baudrillard attempts to describe a situation that he refers to as 'after the orgy'. This is the situation that now exists in the areas of sexuality, economics, politics, etc., after the struggles for liberation of modernity. We need to rethink what we understand by 'value'. Baudrillard explains that we have moved through a number of stages, from

o   a **natural** stage (use value)
o   a **commodity** stage (exchange value)
o   a **structural** phase (sign value)
o   to a **fractal** stage (or **viral** or **radiant** stage) of value.

In this last stage Baudrillard explains, 'there is no point of reference at all, and value radiates in all directions . . . without reference to anything what so ever, by virtue of pure contiguity' (Baudrillard, 1993: 5).

A sociology of cultural products

The work of Baudrillard is an attempt to make intelligible the significance of the proliferation of communication via the mass media. He argues that a new cultural form has emerged which traditional theories such as those of Durkheim, Weber and Marx cannot make sense of. **Simulations** – objects or discourses that have no firm origin and no foundation – now dominate culture. Baudrillard is a former Marxist who became a postmodernist; he turned his back on the Marxist theory of culture and ideology because of its inadequacy in dealing with issues of culture and value. For Baudrillard, objects are not given value because of 'use value', but because we desire them.

Starting with *The System of Objects* (1968) and his other early works, from a neo-Marxist position, and drawing upon both Freud and Saussure's structuralism, Baudrillard argues that classification within our social order is now based upon consumption. Objects have 'meaning' for a consumer, and advertising codes products into a system of signs. This is a network of floating signifiers that invite desire. At this stage in his career, Baudrillard argued:

let us not be fooled: objects are categories of objects which quite tyrannically induce categories of persons. They undertake the policing of social meanings, and the significations they engender are controlled, their proliferation, simultaneously arbitrary and coherent, to materialise itself effectively under the sign of affluence. (Baudrillard, 1968: 16–17)

In order to become an object of consumption, the object must become a sign; that is, in some way it must become external to a relation that it now only signifies, a sign arbitrarily and non-coherently to this concrete relation, yet obtaining its coherence, and consequently its meaning, from an abstract and systematic relation to all other object-signs. It is this way that it becomes 'personalised' and enters the series. In the pre-industrial world signs were symbolic, they had 'referents' which related directly to the real meaning of objects. In the twentieth century, signs were separated from their referents, and became more like signals, in the same way that traffic lights have a relation to the traffic.

We no longer have signs which represent the true meaning of the object. In their place are **simulacra**, with no referent or ground in any 'reality' except their own – a **hyperreality**, a world of self-referential signs: for example the television newscast that creates the news so that it can narrate it. There is no representational subject, and no categories such as 'truth' and 'fiction'. Simulations are immune from rational critique. If we take the case of advertising, in the 1950s adverts were straightforward; the message was: 'Buy this, it is nice'. The situation today is rather different. We conceive the meaning of a product through advertising. Consensus on the meaning is based upon nothing but faith. An arbitrary sign induces people to be receptive, it mobilises our consciousness, and reconstitutes itself as a collective meaning. Advertising ratifies its own meaning.

Implosion

According to Baudrillard the mass media is opposed to mediation. It is concerned with one-way communication – there is no exchange. This simple emission/reception of information can be viewed as the forced silence of the masses. The 'stupor' that the masses appear to be in is said by Baudrillard to make the masses radically uncertain about their own desires. Media images are no longer differentiated from 'reality' or 'human nature', but this is not because of some simple manipulation in a Marxian sense: the masses have an almost infinite abundance of entertainment and other forms of useless information. They have a greater and greater desire for spectacle, and it is because of this demand that films become ever more expensive to produce, have better and better special effects, the promotion and hype are more intense and the merchandising includes all possible commodities. We have a televisually created politics of disillusion and disaffection. The end result is a series of implosions: class conflict between labour and capital; politics and entertainment; high culture and low culture. All such divisions collapse in on themselves to form a political void, ending often in the 'sudden crystallisation of latent violence' (Baudrillard, 1993: 76), which manifest as irrational episodes.

Spectators turn themselves into actors, inventing their own spectacle for the gaze of the media. Baudrillard discusses examples such as violence at the Heysel Stadium, the Real Madrid–Naples European Cup Final and Margaret Thatcher's conflict with the miners.

There is then no 'law' of value at the **fractal** stage. There are no criteria for judging 'good' and 'evil', 'beautiful' and 'ugly', because these are freed from points of reference. 'Things', 'signs' and 'actions' can follow their own trajectory and start an endless process of self-reproduction. As Baudrillard explains: 'This is where the order (or rather, disorder) or metastasis begins . . . the rule of propagation through mere contiguity' (Baudrillard, 1993: 7). Metaphor disappears in a general tendency towards transsexuality:

o   Economics becomes transeconomics.
o   Aesthetics becomes transaesthetics.
o   Sex becomes transsexuality.

The essential point here is that there is a confusion of categories. There are no agreed or acceptable criteria for judgement in areas as diverse as aesthetic judgement and pleasure. If we take the example of art, Baudrillard argues that all present day art is a set of rituals without reference to any objective aesthetic judgement. We 'read' works of art, film, etc., according to ever more contradictory criteria. This is the situation of metastasis: 'a fundamental break in the secret code of aesthetics' (Baudrillard, 1993: 17). We are released from the need to decide between beautiful and ugly, real and unreal, transcendence and immanence. We are condemned to indifference, claims Baudrillard. All such disappearing forms attempt to reproduce themselves by means of simulation.

Transsexuality

Baudrillard does not discuss the 'transsexual' (in the anatomical sense). Rather he views 'transvestism' as 'playing with the computability of the signs . . . the lack of differentiation' not just in terms of sex (Baudrillard, 1993: 20). In any area of activity, transsexuality is underpinned ingenuity, in terms of the reinvention and rereading as well as simply playing with categories which were once seen as fixed, but which are now seen as irrelevant to our life. Sexual liberation, like all revolutions, is seen by Baudrillard as one stage that we went through on the road to transsexuality and has now become a 'transsexual myth' because it depends upon redundant fixed categories of sex and sexuality. However, it is not just sexual culture, but also political culture and the economy that are affected by transvestism. Such transvestism becomes the central element in our search for difference and the basis of our behaviour. After the orgy we are now left looking for an identity. As Baudrillard illustrates, we all seek a *look*: not simply a need to be seen but an image. We 'play at difference without believing in it' (Baudrillard, 1993: 24).

In the process of transsexuality we become 'transpoliticals':

> politically indifferent and undifferentiated beings [who have] embraced, digested and rejected the most contradictory ideologies and were left wearing only [our] masks: we had become, in our own heads and perhaps unbeknown to ourselves – transvestites of the political realm. (Baudrillard, 1993: 25)

Transeconomics

Our society, claims Baudrillard, is founded on proliferation, on growth that cannot be measured against any clear goals: where growth is uncontrollable and the causes of growth disappear. In contrast to Marxian accounts, the motor of such change is not the economic base: 'but rather the destructuring of value, the destabilisation of real markets and economies and the victory of an economy unencumbered by ideologies, by social science, by history – an economy freed from "Economics" and given over to pure speculation; a virtual economy emancipated from real economies' (Baudrillard, 1993: 34).

In Baudrillard's analysis speculation is totally detached from production and the creation of surplus value in a Marxian sense. Speculation has its own revolving motion irrespective of the amount of labour power that went into its production.

What we have is a situation of great uncertainty or total unpredictability, about the reality of objects. We attempt to escape from this uncertainty by depending more on information and communication systems. However, with the collapse of codes in the political, sexual and genetic spheres, and the constant exposure on all sides to images and information, this merely exacerbates the uncertainty.

The end of history

Baudrillard attempts to describe the turn that history is now taking. We are moving not towards the end of history but towards historical reversal and elimination. This is why Baudrillard suggested that the year 2000 would never occur, because we are on a reverse trajectory. We look as though we are approaching the end, only to veer off at the last moment in the opposite direction.

Gianni Vattimo (1936–present)

Gianni Vattimo is a professor of philosophy at the University of Turin. He argues that many of the issues that postmodernists are concerned with were first raised by Nietzsche and Heidegger. Vattimo attempts to outline a philosophical basis for making sense of our human existence at the end of modernity. For Vattimo modernity is concerned with stable beings within strong structures, and the prefix 'post' means to take leave of modernity. Modernity is seen as an era of history opposed to ancient ways of thinking. It is dominated by the idea of 'progressive enlightenment', in that the history of Western thought is one of recoveries, rebirths and returns, in other words, progressive development. Gianni Vattimo attempts to show that the work of Nietzsche and Heidegger – notably Heidegger's critique of humanism and Nietzsche's view of 'accomplished nihilism' – seriously question the heritage of modern European thought.

Referring to 'accomplished nihilism', Nietzsche argues that 'man rolls from the centre toward X', in other words that there is nothing left of Being and that nihilism is the only hope for the person. Nietzsche sums up this process in his notion of the death of God. God is allowed to die because knowledge no longer needs to have absolute causes, the world is becoming ever less real and we no longer need to believe in an immortal soul. A number of social theories have attempted to stand in the way of the accomplishment of nihilism, notably phenomenology and Marxism.

Nietzsche and Heidegger challenge the foundations of 'progressive enlightenment', yet neither bases his philosophy on another, truer foundation. It is the absence of true foundations to their thought that make Nietzsche and Heidegger philosophers of postmodernity, claims Vattimo. Both Nietzsche and Heidegger are also relevant to recent debates about postmodernity because they provide rigour and credibility to often incoherent postmodern theories.

> . . . the post-modern not only as something new in relation to the modern, but also as a dissolution of the category new – in other words, as an experience of 'the end of history' – rather than as the appearance of a different stage of history itself. (Vattimo, 1988: 4)

Vattimo does not treat postmodernity as 'the end of history' in any catastrophic sense, but as the end of 'historicity'. We cannot see history as an objective process within which we are located. History has become a problem for theory, not simply fact gathering. The idea of the 'end of history' dissolves the idea of 'history as progress' that has underpinned Western thought. History then loses its unity. There is not one *history*, but many *histories*. History was written from the 'point of view of the victors', and used to legitimise their power. We now have an awareness of the 'rhetorical mechanisms' contained within historical accounts, and this gives us the resources to reject any narrative and reconstruct the past in any way we wish. In addition, because of the global spread of the mass media there are more centres giving out information about events, which can be used to construct our histories.

Likewise, for Vattimo, the 'truth' becomes an interpretative matter, similar to an aesthetic or rhetorical experience. Truth becomes a fable. However, he claims, this is not to say that 'truth' is reduced to 'subjective' emotions and feelings. It is to say that 'truth' is not simply the recognition and reinforcement of 'common sense': 'On the contrary, it is a first step towards recognizing the link between truth on the one hand and what may on the other hand be called the monument, the social contract, or the very "substantiality" (in the Hegelian sense of the objective spirit) of historical transmission' (Vattimo, 1988: 12).

Using the aesthetic experience as a model to experience truth is to say that truth is more than common sense. Our 'discourses' do not simply reproduce what already exists, but form 'more intensely concentrated nuclei of meaning' (1988: 13) that are capable of criticising what is said to exist.

Nietzsche and Heidegger allow us to pass from a critical and negative description of the postmodern condition to the postmodern condition as the destruction of ontology, as a positive possibility and opportunity.

Nietzsche is described by Vattimo as the first radically non-humanistic thinker, who argued that the absence of any transcendental foundation has brought about a crisis of humanism. In contrast to the Frankfurt School, and others who argue that the crisis of humanism and the dehumanism that comes with it were brought about by the spread of technology and rationalisation, Vattimo argues that:

> the subject that supposedly has to be defended from technological dehumanism is itself the very root of this dehumanization, since the kind of subjectivity which is defined as the object is a pure function of the world of objectivity, and inevitably tends to become itself an object of manipulation. (1988: 46)

Vattimo casts doubt on the stable structures of Being, which provided certainty for the major contributions to Western thought in the nineteenth century. Both Nietzsche and Heidegger saw Being as an *event*.

For Vattimo there is a relationship between Being and truth that is at the core of the argument about the nature of the postmodern condition. Truth is not a 'metaphysically stable structure but an event' (1988: 76). Truth is an 'opening' of the world, which is future oriented – a form of anticipation. However, a view of progress has a tendency to dissolve our vision of Being. The individual is viewed as *Dasein* – Being in the world – as a hermeneutic totality. This means that *Dasein* is 'always already familiar with a totality of meanings, that is, with a context of references' (Vattimo, 1988: 115).

Dasein has a threefold existential structure:

o   *Befindlichkeit* – state of mind;
o   *Verstehen–Auslegung* – understanding–interpreting;
o   *Rede* – discourse.

This hermeneutic constitution of *Dasein* is nihilistic in nature. First, because such a structure of *Dasein* brings about a situation in which the human person recognises that they have no foundation. Secondly, we recognise that every foundation is already given within a specific epoch of Being, but that epoch is not founded by Being.

When constructing the essence of reality by the use of *Verwindung* (our critical overcoming), history no longer appears to be linear, it appears as a form of distortion. The foundations of thought, history, metaphysics, morality and art are seen as a set of 'false constructs'. So-called 'metaphysical truths' are said by Vattimo to be no more than the subjective values and opinions of individuals or groups imposed upon us. *Verwindung* is a form of emancipation and by the use of it 'the real world has become a fiction' (Vattimo, 1988: 169).

Nihilism is the destiny of Being itself.

Critiques of postmodernism

One of the most well-publicised critiques of postmodernism is that of Sokal and Bricmont. In *Intellectual Impostures* (2000) they attempt to undermine all the big names of postmodern writing: Luce Irigaray, Bruno Latour, Jean-François Lyotard, Jean Baudrillard and Deleuze and Guattari. However, instead of engaging with the ideas, Sokal and Bricmont choose to reproduce long quotes from postmodern writers and attach some insult, such as 'meaningless from a scientific point of view', 'stupefyingly boring', and of course 'the emperor has no clothes'. The reader is left to read the quotes with no guidance as to why Sokal and Bricmont come to the conclusions that they do. When postmodernists write about science, they reject the assumptions and ways of reasoning that are commonly shared by scientists; it is this that Sokal and Bricmont seem to find so objectionable.

In 1996 Sokal submitted a paper called 'Transgressing the boundaries: towards a transformative hermeneutics of quantum gravity' to the American journal *Social Text*. It was a carefully crafted parody of postmodern writing: from the start, Sokal intended the paper to be nonsense. As Richard Dawkins's review of Sokal and Bricmont explains:

> Sokal's paper must have seemed a gift to the editors because this was a *physicist* saying all the right-on things they wanted to hear, attacking the 'post-Enlightenment hegemony' and such uncool notions as the existence of the real world. They didn't know that Sokal had also crammed his paper with egregious scientific howlers, of a kind that any referee with an undergraduate degree in physics would instantly have detected. It was sent to no such referee. The editors, Andrew Ross and others, were satisfied that its ideology conformed to their own, and were perhaps flattered by references to their own works. This ignominious piece of editing rightly earned them the 1996 Ig Nobel Prize for literature. (Dawkins, 1998: 141–3)

Jürgen Habermas argues that for the postmodern observer: 'The premises of the Enlightenment are dead; only their consequences continue on' (1987: 3). With Arnold Gehlen as his target, Habermas describes postmodernism as 'neoconservative' and 'leave-taking from modernity' (ibid.). Taking Nietzsche as their starting point, postmodernists believe they have moved beyond the Enlightenment tradition of reason which modernity makes use of to understand itself. However, claims Habermas: 'postmodern thought merely claims a transcendent status, while it remains in fact dependent on presuppositions of modern self-understanding that were brought to light by Hegel' (Habermas, 1987: 4–5).

Postmodernism is then counter-Enlightenment rather than post-Enlightenment. What Habermas is doing here is challenging postmodern theories by outlining in advance a set of rationalistic assumptions that he uses to evaluate theorising. He is refusing to look critically at his own assumptions for testing the validity of theorising, even when it is those very Enlightenment assumptions that are the focus for postmodern approaches.

If postmodernism is inspirational, in the way that Habermas suggests, it is so because nothing is left outside or beyond critique, even the very benchmarks that we use to judge the effectiveness of our critiques.

In his introduction to Habermas's *The Philosophical Discourse of Modernity* (1987) Thomas McCarthy argues that Habermas's aim was to attempt to reconstruct an 'abstract core' of moral institutions, a moral principle against which all competing normative claims could be fairly and impartially adjudicated. McCarthy argues that the rejection of moral universalism by postmodernists had undervalued the key Enlightenment concepts of fairness, tolerance and respect for the individual. Habermas was attempting to reinforce the value of the common good by identifying its 'structural aspects'.

In contrast to this approach, Stanley Fish, who has taken on board many of the arguments and assumptions of postmodernists, challenges the Enlightenment conception of reason that Habermas makes use of. *'Toleration is exercised in an inverse proportion to there being anything at stake'* (Fish, 1994: 217, italics added).

From the publication of *There's No Such Thing as Free Speech* (1994) a common theme in the work of Stanley Fish has been a critique or deconstruction of some of the key assumptions that underpin liberal thought. In particular Fish makes objection to the notion of *reason* and other liberal procedural mechanisms that are used to enclose biased positions in a non-biased structure. It is reason that stands in opposition to all forms of dogma, because reason is independent. Real world issues become reduced to problems of moral algebra, claims Fish. The only people who reject reason stand for ideological intransigence. These are the people who fight religious wars; who have theological disputes; and who will not subject their thinking to the cool logic of reason. What reason provides is a 'market place of ideas' where no ideology is preferred to any other, where all points of view are heard and assessed without prejudice. As Fish explains: 'if you propose to examine and assess assumptions, what will you examine and assess them *with*? And the answer is that you will examine and assess them with forms of thought that themselves rest on underlying assumptions' (Fish, 1994: 18).

In contrast to the liberal view, Fish argues that reason is not a neutral category that regulates conflicting ideological positions without regard to their content. On the contrary, Fish argues, whenever reason is successfully invoked it is to present the arguments of our opponents as unreasonable. Reason is then a political entity derived from our personal and institutional history. Moreover, our opponents may not see our arguments as reasoned, but as forms of politically motivated irrationality: 'At that moment the appeal to Reason will have run its course and produced the kind of partisan impasse from which Reason supposedly offers us an escape' (Fish, 1994: 18).

However, I have to say that I accept Habermas's critique of postmodernism, but whereas he sees something fundamentally wrong with the postmodern approaches, because they fall short of his own unquestioned Enlightenment assumptions, I would blame the cowardice of the authors. Lyotard, for example, seems to look at the consequences of his own argument – that there is no adequate theory of society and no adequate theory of the person – and retreat into modernist conceptions of the 'social'.

A number of more ideological critiques of postmodernism are developed in the volume, *Market Killing: What the Free Market Does and What Social Scientists Can Do About It* (2000), edited by Greg Philo and David Miller. The central aim of Philo and Miller's book is to demonstrate that since the emergence of Thatcherism/Reaganism in the late 1970s, much social science has 'wandered up a series of dead ends which made it socially irrelevant as a discipline and incapable of commenting critically on the society within which it existed' (Philo and Miller, 2000: 2). Above all else, they argue, there is a need for social scientists to reposition themselves on a firm positivist footing, to become engaged in independent empirical research, which can identify key social problems and possibilities for change. The main thrust of their argument is 'back to modernity' and their main target is postmodernism.

The book starts with an essay by Greg Philo and Davis Miller, followed by essays from Noam Chomsky, Derek Bouse, Angela McRobbie, John Corner, Chris Hammett, Andrew Gamble, Philip Schlesinger, Barbara Epstein, James Curran, Danny Schecter and Hilary Wainwright.

Philo and Miller mourn the demise of the concept of ideology in academic work, a theme taken up by John Corner. They state that the social relations of production and the tendency for capitalists to accumulate capital exist today as they did when Marx was writing. Moreover, changes that have taken place, such as the development of global corporations 'based in powerful nation states which defend their interests', were fully anticipated by Marx, 'a process which Marx referred to as the internationalisation of capital' (Philo and Miller, 2000: 23). Philo and Miller's introduction is full of Marxism-sounding sentences such as 'So in place of a collective commitment to the use and value of what is produced, there is division and competition' (2000: 7). Marxian-sounding questions are also posed: 'How does change in the production/exchange of commodities affect the growth of new attitudes, motivations and behaviour and how are these "market values" contested or rejected?' (2000: 10). Most Marxist purists would no doubt be dismayed by Philo and Miller's references to 'elites' rather than the ruling class or, better still, the bourgeoisie: these latter terms never get a mention in the text.

There are several problems with Greg Philo and David Miller's approach. The first is their emphasis on ideology: 'We have described above the social relationships of power and interest which structure our society as it is. The purpose of social ideologies is to justify and legitimise those relationships' (2000: 26). I would have expected that they would give their reader some indication of how to identify and empirically measure ideology. Instead of this difficult empirical task that they identify, they choose to bring together quotes and statistics from newspapers, television news and official statistics. Drawing 'evidence' from the capitalist media, the capitalist state and capitalists themselves such as Park Human Resources Limited is flawed in itself, but more importantly, Philo and Miller get nowhere near the difficult task of identifying and measuring what they claim ideology is capable of.

Marxists have a very simplistic notion of 'representation' contained within the concept of ideology. In the Marxian analysis, working-class people have their ideas and worldview manipulated. The bourgeoisie are said to be capable of taking any object or idea and give it a new representation or meaning in the minds of the working class. This new representation is supportive of capitalism, justifies the position of the bourgeoisie and legitimises the exploitation of the working class in their own minds.

I would like to see Greg Philo and David Miller demonstrate the *real* existence of an ideology and demonstrate empirically how it *really* works. As it currently stands, their argument is that we should trust their notion of ideology because they have seen it on the telly or read it in the papers! The respect that the authors have for journalists needs some justification. 'It is interesting that television journalists could pose the issue of political power and the use of information so acutely, just as media studies was moving away from the analysis of ideology and propaganda' (Philo and Miller, 2000: 31). This last point is surprising given the authors' comment that 'Acquisition and material desire are thus officially sanctioned and parts of television (notably the news) took on a public relations function for these key values of the 1980s' (2000: 8). For some reason this reminded me of a televised 'debate' shortly after the publication of *Bad News* in 1976 in which Labour MP Michael Meacher and Greg Philo were discussing bias in the media. I can recall vividly Kelvin McKenzie, who was later to go on to become editor of the *Sun*, waving a copy of the *British Journal of Sociology* at Greg Philo and demanding that he justify the simple content analysis. Greg was unwilling or unable to do so; this was a low point for the social sciences.

The rest of their opening chapter outlines a weak 'critique' of post-modernism and truth, which is very well rehearsed. Philo and Miller's argument rarely gets above the level of name-calling: postmodernists are responsible for television violence, the Ridings School, Black Monday, Pulp Fiction, the Smurfs, Michael Barrymore, the state of the NHS, school bullying, BSE, AIDS . . .

At first sight the papers by Noam Chomsky and Hilary Rose are a little out of place in this volume. However, Rose wants to 'restore natural science to its proper place' (2000: 123), which for her involves a critique of new developments in biology, a critique of Steve Hawkin as a 'new ager' and a repetition of the tired critique of postmodernism that we read in the introduction, that postmodern positions suffer when their own arguments are pointed against them. However, Rose ends her paper by praising the 'achievement' of 'conflicting cultural currents and plural epistemologies' (2000: 123). What these two papers do is to cast doubt upon the assumption in Philo and Miller's introduction that doing empirical research is unproblematic in nature.

Both Derek Bouse and Chris Hamnett are critical of the difficult language that postmodern writers often use. Hamnett is also critical of the ways in which postmodernists have looked at conceptions of 'truth' and 'science' as 'a product of localised beliefs', by reference to perceptions of the Holocaust. There are problems for scientists when dealing with the Holocaust. The 'scientists' who carried out experiments on involuntary inmates were 'real' scientists, the experiments were conducted using strict experimental designs and their findings are high in validity and reliability. However, most doctors will not make use of this scientific data, because this truth is 'relativised into a language game' or 'final vocabulary' that is part of a 'cultural context' they find abhorrent.

Angela McRobbie distances herself from the introduction, and in her thought-provoking paper discusses the issues and problems facing a new generation of feminists who have moved away from the concerns of the women's movement in the 1970s and 1980s, such as the politically unanchored TV blonde.

The collection ends with a paper by Hilary Wainwright, 'Political frustrations in the post-modern fog', which starts in the same vein as the Philo and Miller introduction: 'The belief underlying this essay is that much of what came to be described as "post-modernism" clouded and distorted the political choices that we faced in the 1970s and 1980s' (2000: 240). However, as she continues the argument becomes less and less hostile to the postmodern contribution:

> We share with post-modernists, for instance, a commitment to scrutinise and deconstruct the cultural consensus; to challenge simplistic uses of universal concepts such as 'citizenship' and 'human rights' to hide differences and inequalities; to subvert modernist optimism in technological 'progress' and reveal values embedded in shaping our cultural and social life rather than simply reflecting a reality 'out there'. (Philo and Miller, 2000: 243)

Wainwright's conclusion, although grudging and guarded, is that the tools we need as social scientists and researchers are to be found within the postmodern discourse.

However, James Curran's excellent contribution gives a well-balanced and well-informed critical account of current media theory and research. The book is worth looking at for his contribution alone.

What Greg Philo and David Miller seem unwilling to come to terms with is the simple point that many people embrace postmodern positions because of the total and complete intellectual collapse of Marxism as the basis of an explanatory framework for anything. Marxists are incapable of theorising about capitalism, 'base' has collapsed into 'superstructure', value is now related to fad, fashion and desire, capitalists can generate surplus value without the need for labour power, capitalists exploit other capitalists . . . and so it continues.

Activity

What do you understand by the terms modernity and post-modernity?

What do you consider to be the differences between modernity and postmodernity?

Complete the boxes with your own definitions.

Definition of modernity | Definition of postmodernity

Differences between modernity and postmodernity

Modernity	Postmodernity
1 In the modern world 'grand narratives' are needed as a foundation for 'truth'.	1 In the postmodern condition 'grand narratives' are seen as oppressive and irrelevant.
2 There is 'truth'.	2 There is no truth.
3	3
4	4

In conclusion: living in the postmodern condition

If we had to speculate as to what life is like for an individual living in the postmodern world, what could we say? Below are some possible outcomes of how life is experienced by individuals in the postmodern world:

Lyotard

If we accept what Lyotard has to say then people should demonstrate 'incredulity' towards grand narratives and be engaged in a 'war' on 'totality', through a re-examination of the Enlightenment. People should feel that the social bond is dissolving. They should speak to each other by the use of 'micrologics' as they make language for their own ends, and reject universalist discourses.

Deleuze and Guattari

The self has a sense of uncertainty that emerges with the process of becoming. The postmodern self is aware of the internalised discipline and constraint derived from the 'will to power', used in modern society for the construction of the modern person in accordance with the 'line of organisation'. The postmodern self is both aware of and can choose to become a detached subject – a schizo, nomad or 'body without organs'. This Deleuze and Guattari refer to as *becoming reactive*, in which people draw upon the resources of the singularity.

All problems that people have are based upon a foundation in 'virtual structures', not 'actual structures' – we make problems become more actual by making ourselves believe this or our process of individuation.

Baudrillard

For Baudrillard the postmodern self has a confusion of categories. What were once fixed categories such as 'value' can no longer be measured against clear and objective goals. Postmodern *society* is founded upon proliferation. What we have is great uncertainty. The postmodern self attempts to escape from this by having a greater degree of dependency on information and communication systems. However, with the collapse of codes in the political, sexual and genetic spheres, and the constant exposure on all sides to images and information, this merely exacerbates feelings of uncertainty.

Vattimo

For Vattimo we are unstable beings with no strong structures. We have lost our faith in 'progressive enlightenment'; we have no justification for truth claims. The postmodern self should express this destruction of ontology as 'possibilities' and 'opportunities'. The postmodern self should become an 'accomplished nihilist' – there should be nothing left of 'being'. The world should be experienced as becoming less 'real', and as made up of 'rhetorical mechanisms'. The postmodern self should be continually rewriting its past, creating an account of the own biography which it feels most comfortable with. This ontological insecurity should allow the postmodern self to dissolve, decentre or otherwise deconstruct any problem.

Rorty

If we accept what Rorty has to say, then people should experience a need for continual self-creation and a need to continually reflect on core beliefs. Given Rorty's view that the self is created by vocabulary – a set of words to defend actions and belief and to organise our individual lives – people should spend a great deal of time reflecting on whether they have chosen the wrong vocabulary.

In summary, people should experience:

o epistemological uncertainty
o ontological plurality

However, social theory has since its beginning attempted to make sense of the world, in an effort to generate feelings of certainty in a rapidly changing world. Many postmodernists have, I believe, underestimated the capability of *early modernist* writers such as Durkheim or Parsons to deal with issues of uncertainty and the relationship between agency and structure in a changing world.

References

Archer, M.S. (1988a) 'Structuration versus morphogenesis', in S.N. Eisenstadt and H.J. Helle (eds), *Macro-Sociological Theory: Perspectives on Sociological Theory*, Vol. 1. Sage: London.

Archer, M.S. (1988b) *Culture and Agency.* Cambridge University Press: Cambridge.

Archer, M.S. (1995) *Realist Social Theory: The Morphogenetic Approach.* Cambridge University Press: Cambridge.

Ashley, D. (1997) *History without a Subject.* Westview Press: Boulder, CO.

Ayer, A. (1957) *The Problem of Knowledge.* Penguin: London.

Baudrillard, J. (1968) *The System of Objects*, trans. J. Benedict. Verso: London.

Baudrillard, J. (1990) *Fatal Strategies*, trans. P. Beitchman and W.G.J. Niesluchowski. Semiotext(e) and Pluto: New York and London.

Baudrillard, J. (1993) *The Transparency of Evil: Essays on Extreme Phenomena* (1983), trans. J. Benedict. Verso: London.

Bauman, Z. (1972) *Between Class and Elite: The Evolution of the British Labour Movement. A Sociological Study.* Manchester University Press: Manchester.

Bauman, Z. (1973) *Culture as Praxis.* Routledge: London.

Bauman, Z. (1976a) *Socialism: The Active Utopia.* George Allen & Unwin: London.

Bauman, Z. (1976b) *Towards a Critical Sociology: An Essay on Commonsense and Emancipation.* Routledge: London.

Bauman, Z. (1978) *Hermeneutics and Social Science: Approaches to Understanding.* Hutchinson: London.

Bauman, Z. (1989) *Modernity and the Holocaust.* Polity: Cambridge.

Bauman, Z. (1991) *Modernity and Ambivalence.* Polity: Cambridge.

Bauman, Z. (1992) *Intimations of Postmodernity.* Routledge: London.

Bauman, Z. (1993) *Postmodern Ethics.* Blackwell: Oxford.

Bauman, Z. (1994) *Alone Again: Ethics After Certainty.* Demos: London.

Bauman, Z. (1995) *Life in Fragments: Essays in Postmodern Morality.* Blackwell: Oxford.

Bauman, Z. (1996) 'From pilgrim to tourist – or a short history of identity', in S. Hall and P. Du Gay (eds), *Questions of Cultural Identity.* Sage: London. pp. 18–36.

Bauman, Z. (1997) *Postmodernity and its Discontents*. Polity: Cambridge.

Bauman, Z. (1998a) *Globalization: The Human Consequences*. Polity: Cambridge.

Bauman, Z. (1998b) *Work, Consumerism and the New Poor*. Open University Press: Buckingham.

Bauman, Z. (2001a) *Community: Seeking Safety in an Insecure World*. Polity: Cambridge.

Bauman, Z. (2001b) *The Individualised Society*. Polity: Cambridge.

Benjamin, A. (ed.) (1989) *The Lyotard Reader*. Blackwell: Oxford.

Bogue, R. (1989) *Deleuze and Guattari*. Routledge: London.

Craib, I. (1992) *Anthony Giddens*. Routledge: London.

Dawkins, R. (1998) 'Postmodernism disrobed', *Nature*, 394: 141–3.

Deleuze, G. (1975) *Kafka: Towards a Minor Literature*. University of Minnesota Press: Minneapolis.

Deleuze, G. (1983) *Nietzsche and Philosophy* (1963), trans. H. Tomlinson. Columbia University Press: New York.

Deleuze, G. (1989) *Masochism*. Zone Books: New York.

Deleuze, G. (1990) *The Logic of Sense*. Columbia University Press: New York.

Deleuze, G. (1994) *What is Philosophy?*, trans. H. Tomlinson and G. Burchell. Columbia University Press: New York.

Deleuze, G. (1997) *Difference and Repetition*, trans. P. Patton. The Athlone Press: London.

Deleuze, G. (1998) *Essays Critical and Clinical*, trans. D.W. Smith and M.A. Greco. Columbia University Press: New York.

Deleuze, G. and Guattari, F. (1983) *Anti-Oedipus: Capitalism and Schizophrenia*. University of Minnesota Press: Minneapolis.

Deleuze, G. and Guattari, F. (1988) *A Thousand Plateaus: Capitalism and Schizophrenia*. The Athlone Press: London.

Deleuze, G. and Parnet, C. (1987) *Dialogues*. Columbia University Press: New York.

Durkheim, E. and Mauss, M. (1963) *Primitive Classification*, trans. R. Needham. Cohen & West: London.

Fish, S. (1994) *There's No Such Thing as Free Speech*. Oxford University Press: New York.

Giddens, A. (1984) *The Constitution of Society*. Polity: Cambridge.

Giddens, A. (1990) *The Consequences of Modernity*. Polity: Cambridge.

Giddens, A. (1992) *Modernity and Self Identity*. Polity: Cambridge.

Giddens, A. (1993) *The Transformation of Intimacy*. Polity: Cambridge.

Giddens, A. (1995) *Beyond Left and Right*. Polity: Cambridge.

Goffman, E. (1959) *The Presentation of Self in Everyday Life*. Penguin: Harmondsworth.

Habermas, J. (1987) *The Philosophical Discourse of Modernity*. Polity: Cambridge.

Habermas, J. (1989) *The New Conservatism*. Polity: Cambridge.

Kilminster, R. and Varcoe, I. (1998) 'Three appreciations of Zygmunt Bauman', *Theory, Culture & Society*, 15(1): 23–9.

Layder, D. (1995) 'Giddens' structuration theory', in *Understanding Social Theory*. Sage: London.

Lyotard, J.-F. (1984a) 'Philosophy and painting in the age of experimentation', *Camera Obscura*, 12: 111–23, trans. M. Minich Brewer and D. Brewer.

Lyotard, J.-F. (1984b) *The Postmodern Condition: A Report on Knowledge*, trans. G. Bennington and B. Massumi. Manchester University Press: Manchester.

Lyotard, J.-F. (1988) *The Différend: Phrases in Dispute*, trans. G. van den Abbeele. Manchester University Press: Manchester.

Lyotard, J.-F. (1992) *The Postmodern Explained to Children*. trans. D. Barry. University of Minneapolis Press: Minneapolis.

Macmurray, J. (1957) *Self as Agent*. Faber & Faber: London.

Morawski, S. (1998) 'Bauman's ways of seeing the world', *Theory, Culture & Society*, 15(1): 29–38.

Nietzsche, F. (1967) *The Will to Power*, trans. W. Kaufmann. Random House: New York.

Nietzsche, F. (1968) *The Antichrist* (1888), trans. W. Kaufmann, in *The Portable Nietzsche*, ed. Walter Kaufmann. Viking Press: New York.

Nietzsche, F. (1997) *Beyond Good and Evil: Prelude to a Philosophy of the Future* (1886), trans. H. Zimmern. Dover Publications: Mineola, NY.

Nietzsche, F. (1999) *Thus Spake Zarathustra* (1888), trans. T. Common. Dover Publications: Mineola, NY.

Philo, G. and Miller, D. (eds) (2000) *Market Killing: What the Free Market Does and What Social Scientists Can Do About It*. Longman: Harlow.

Rorty, R. (1989) *Contingency, Irony, and Solidarity*. Cambridge University Press: Cambridge.

Sokal, A. (1996) 'Transgressing the boundaries: towards a transformative hermeneutics of quantum gravity', *Social Text*, spring/summer, 46/47: 217–52.

Sokal, A. and Briemont, J. (2000) *Intellectual Impostures*. Profile Books: London.

Thompson, D. (1989) 'The theory of structuration', in D. Held and J. Thompson, *Social Theory of Modern Societies: Anthony Giddens and His Critics*. Cambridge University Press: Cambridge.

Vattimo, G. (1988) *The End of Modernity: Nihilism and Hermeneutics in Post-modern Culture*, trans. J.R. Snyder. Polity: Cambridge.

Wagner, P. (1994) *A Sociology of Modernity: Liberty and Discipline*. Routledge: London.

Wheale, N. (1995) *The Postmodern Arts*. Routledge: London.

Index